Waccamaw Legacy

CONTEMPORARY AMERICAN INDIAN STUDIES
J. Anthony Paredes, *Series Editor*

WACCAMAW LEGACY
Contemporary Indians Fight for Survival

Patricia Barker Lerch

THE UNIVERSITY OF ALABAMA PRESS
Tuscaloosa

Copyright © 2004
The University of Alabama Press
Tuscaloosa, Alabama 35487-0380
All rights reserved
Manufactured in the United States of America

Typeface: Bembo

∞
The paper on which this book is printed meets the minimum requirements of American National Standard for Information Science–Permanence of Paper for Printed Library Materials, ANSI Z39.48-1984.

Library of Congress Cataloging-in-Publication Data

Lerch, Patricia Jane Barker, 1947–
    Waccamaw legacy : contemporary Indians fight for survival / Patricia Barker Lerch.
       p. cm. — (Contemporary American Indian studies)
    Includes bibliographical references and index.
    ISBN 0-8173-1417-2 (cloth : alk. paper) — ISBN 0-8173-5124-8 (pbk. : alk. paper)
  1. Waccamaw Indians—Ethnic identity. 2. Waccamaw Indians—Tribal citizenship. 3. Waccamaw Indians—Legal status, laws, etc. 4. Federally recognized Indian tribes—Southern States. 5. Indian termination policy—Southern States. 6. United States—Race relations. 7. United States—Politics and government. I. Title. II. Series.
    E99.W114L47 2004
    305.897′0757—dc22

2004009057

Contents

List of Figures and Table   vii

Preface   ix

1. The Eastern Siouans: "We Was Always Indians"   1
2. Society along the Borderlands   17
3. "From the Time of the Indians until 1920"   31
4. Tribal Names as Survival Strategies: Croatan and Cherokee   48
5. The Wide Awake Indians   64
6. "I Was an Indian, I Was Outstanding"   78
7. The Waccamaw Bill and the Era of Termination   95
8. The Powwow Paradox   117
9. Waccamaw Siouan Indians   143

References   147

Index   165

Figures and Table

FIGURES

3.1. Corps of "trumpeters" heralds the Pageant of the Lower Cape Fear, 1921   33

3.2. Scene from pageant showing Indians seated to extreme right   35

7.1. View of front of Wide Awake Indian School described in Jennings Report of 1949   100

7.2. Chief R. T. Freeman with students in front of Wide Awake Indian School, 1949   100

7.3. Old home of wood construction in Waccamaw community, early 1990s   112

7.4. Tobacco farming near Waccamaw community, early 1990s   113

8.1. Chief Pricilla Freeman Jacobs delivers welcome address, 1992   126

8.2. Waccamaw Indian School in 1992; view of administrative offices   127

8.3. Waccamaw Indian School in 1992; view of classroom wing   127

8.4. Parade car carrying Little Miss Waccamaw Siouan Princess 1992–1993   128

8.5. Color guard begins the Grand Entry   129

8.6. Grand Entry   130

8.7. The 1999 powwow grounds   134

8.8. Dance circle on eve of powwow   135

8.9. Dancers enter the circle   140

8.10. Drummers and singers at 1992 Waccamaw powwow   141

TABLE

Table 8.1. 1999 Powwow dancer registration by tribe and gender   133

Preface

When someone asks an Indian a question like "What tribe do you belong to?" the answer makes a statement about the past and a relationship with other people. The answer also centers on self-identity and group affiliation. For the answer to be acceptable, both parties must share a common understanding of the past and present (Barth 1998; Clifton 1989). Our sense of self and identity, then, is always relational; "we draw on models of identity provided by the cultures we inhabit" (Eakin 1999:46). A "working consensus" forged in relation to others is reached (Braroe 1975). Most people are surprised that Indians survive in the southeastern United States at all and very few know how hard they have struggled to preserve their Indian identity. Creating a working consensus with others has often been a long and difficult process.

Part of the working consensus on Indian identity throughout the United States includes policies of the federal government like the Bureau of Indian Affairs Federal Acknowledgment Process of 1978. I first learned of this policy in 1981 at a meeting attended by representatives of the state-recognized Waccamaw Siouan Indians of North Carolina. Their similarity to the Lumbee Indians, described by Karen Blu (1980) in *The Lumbee Problem,* made an initial impression on me. Their story of struggle, of forging a working consensus, intrigued me.

Two questions came up in our conversations about federal acknowledgment. The first, readily answered by the Indians, was "What tribe do you belong to?" They answered they were Waccamaw Siouan. Checking the standard references on Indians of the Southeast, I noted the location and brief historical summaries provided on the Waccamaw. The second question, "Who qualifies as an Indian of federal status?" was answered in relation to what non-Indians, particularly the federal government, have to say on the matter. For example, George Roth, a staff anthropologist with the Branch of Acknowledgment and Research of the Bureau of Indian Affairs, says,

"Federally recognized status means that the federal government recognizes a 'government to government' relationship with the United States and the existence of a trust responsibility for the tribe. This recognition gives such tribes a unique legal status within the United States as partially sovereign entities" (Roth 1992:184). As Roth explains, "this definition is derived from case law that forms the basis of the unique legal status of federally recognized tribes in the United States. As such, it reflects non-Indian concepts about the nature of 'tribes,' although it is influenced by ethnological considerations as well" (Roth 1992:184).

Before the 1978 Federal Acknowledgment Process, it was common for Congress to establish the federal status of tribes. For example, in 1950, the Waccamaw Siouan asked Congress to pass the "Waccamaw Bill," making them wards of the government and giving them federal tribal status. When they asked for this status in 1950, they wanted to be included in the group of tribes over which the "federal government had accepted or asserted a fairly broad jurisdiction" and "a fairly broad responsibility for services and protection, within the context of the policies of the times" (Roth 2001). At that time, the federal government imposed two conditions on federal recognition. First, it had to determine whether the tribe existed as a "distinct political community," that is, whether it was a "community that governed itself and was socially and politically separate and distinct from non-Indians." Second, it had to see whether the "federal government had taken an action which acknowledged that it had both a political relationship with the specific tribe and a responsibility for it." In this case, qualifying "actions" included "treaties, laws, presidential orders, and other acts that specifically affected the tribe in question" (Roth 2001:50). In 1950, the Waccamaw Siouan tribe was one of many American Indian tribes that had never been recognized by the federal government. Such tribes had "come under colonial control before the United States became independent and had never established a relationship with the federal government by treaty or otherwise" (Roth 2001:50). So unless the federal government took some special action in their favor, it did not assume jurisdiction or responsibility for them. In the eyes of the federal government, such "unrecognized" Indians were citizens of the United States, with all the rights of any other citizens.

The federal government recognized tribes or groups of people. The people claiming membership in the tribe had to qualify as Indian by some acceptable federal standard. Over time, scholars have recognized three essential dimensions of Indian identity in that federal standard. These are blood and descent, relations to the land, and a sense of community. Within these, individuals must negotiate their identity in "interaction with another person or group" (Fogelson 1998:41). Critics of federal policy argue that too much stress is placed on "blood" and not enough on other factors like community and social participation in Indian life (Blu 2001). Qualities like self-identification and tribal membership must be added to blood quantum for a broader understanding of Indian identity (Snipp 1997:678–680). Billy L. Cypress (2001:225), a Seminole Indian, sees the emphasis on blood as "a necessary evil." Some balance between culture, society, and blood is essential (Hudson 1976:478–501; Paredes 1995:343). Few would deny that all three of these factors are part of any definition of Indianness, yet how and when they come into play may be dependent on historical factors and power relations (Churchill 2004). Among Cherokee, the mixed-blood and full-blood divisions within the tribe have translated into differences of opinion on issues like allotment and adherence to traditional behavior, language, and assimilation for most of the twentieth century (Finger 1991; Gulick 1960; Kupferer 1968; Neely 1991; Thomas 1961). In 1950 when the Waccamaw Bill was considered by Congress, Levine (1972:11) observed, "Real 'Indianness' . . . [was] not necessarily measured on racial lines." It was widely known that the weight given "blood" in determining tribal membership varied from tribe to tribe.

Sometimes questions about a tribal name and tribal origin have disguised a probe into racial history and racial purity defined according to the white racial categories of the time. There are many remnant Indian groups in the East and Southeast whose ancestors have mixed with whites, Hispanics, and African Americans. Some of these groups faced an uphill battle in their struggle for recognition as Indian in part because whites preferred to define them as anomalous, as mixed bloods or "tri-racial isolates," regardless of how they defined themselves (Beale 1957; Berry 1945, 1963, 1978; Dane and Griessman 1972; Frazier 1966; Gilbert 1945, 1946a, 1946b, 1948; Griessman 1972; Thompson 1972). In recent research, scholars recognize the increasing number of American Indians with mixed heritage, and concepts like "multi heritage" and "mixed ancestry" occur as often as "mixed blood" in discussions of these populations (Krouse 1999:73; Mihesuah 1998:196; Snipp 1997:678).

Colonialism is a key experience for American Indians (Thornton 1998: 4). As foreign ideas and lifestyle were imposed on American Indians, dominating concepts of race redefined American Indians in relation to European Americans and African Americans. Nineteenth-century racial concepts put American Indians above African Americans but below European Americans in their evolutionary schemes. Concepts like "primitive" and "savage" described American Indians in opposition to the "civilized" European Americans. European Americans "searched for the primitive" in American Indians and defined themselves as civilized and modern by comparison (Biolsi 1997:135).

American Indians have experienced racism differently than African Americans. When white people placed American Indians in "colored status," American Indians resisted and fought against these categories. American Indians and African Americans viewed the Civil Rights Movement differently. African Americans sought social inclusion and equal rights whereas American Indians struggled to prevent social inclusion on any other terms besides their own. They preferred to separate themselves and articulate with the dominant society rather than assimilate (Levine 1972:12, 28–29; Lurie 1972:300–302; Thornton 1998). In rejecting white peoples' attempt to lump Indians into the same social category as African Americans, American Indians in the East and Southeast avoided close identification with African American institutions and actions. This distancing behavior was a necessary step in maintaining articulation with the dominant society (Lerch 1988; Lurie 1972). In the contemporary Indian scene, as Lurie described it, Indians faced a choice between "economic marginality as Indian communities and prosperity through individual assimilation." To succeed and survive, Indians chose to articulate with the dominant society, forming successful "interactive relationships" Lurie (1971:419). Basic to that successful articulation was self-definition as Indian as a starting point in forming those interactive relationships.

Federal recognition did not solve all Indian problems, but without it people like the Waccamaw Siouan had to struggle locally for recognition as Indians. Walter L. Williams (1979) brought attention to these struggles in his book *Southeastern Indians since the Removal Era*. White attitudes, ideas, and statements about Indians formed a central place in reconstructing these histories because "the way of life of these Indian remnants (often in ways that the people themselves did not recognize) was to a great extent determined by the non-Indian majority" (Williams 1979:xv). Williams wrote, "*The major problem for all southern Indians of the last century and a third has been to define their ethnic status as a third group within a bi-racial society.*" Until the twentieth century, the history of these groups was determined more by local situations and interactions than by federal Indian policy. Living in the South brought Indian groups into contact with large numbers of African Americans. By the nineteenth century, a rigid biracial system with a castelike character defined social relations with "tragic effect" for American Indians (Williams 1979:23). The Indians' struggle for recognition is a persistent theme in their history as whites lumped them into the same social race category as "coloreds" (Williams 1979:194).[1] Whites resisted any attempt by American Indians to break out of this castelike system, fearing the biracial society would not survive such a change. Throughout the South and Southeast, American Indians chose isolation and social distance from African Americans in order to survive (Williams 1979:198).

Many of these same themes appeared in J. Anthony Paredes's (1992) recent work entitled *Indians of the Southeastern United States in the Late Twentieth Century*. In most cases, the Indians had to struggle against assimilation in order to survive into the twentieth century. After reviewing the recent history of these groups, Paredes (1995) proposed an interpretive framework that takes a comprehensive look at "the interplay of political, economic, and social forces" currently determining the contemporary variation found among Southeastern Indians. Central to their survival is "modernism" and specific structures that have molded, shaped, reinforced, reinterpreted, and strengthened Indian institutions and identity. Despite the common belief that Southeastern Indians have become extinct, a view aided by the "ethnographic present fallacy" and the equation of timeless and unchanging cultures with "real Indians," scholars are calling for an inclusion of Southeastern Indians in the historical narratives of the South (Paredes 1995; Perdue 1998). Historians and anthropologists have documented their resilience (chronologically: Swanton 1946; Sturtevant 1954; Gulick 1960; Fogelson 1961; Kupferer 1968; Evans 1971; Roundtree 1979, 1990, 1992; Blu 1980; Perdue 1985; Kidwell 1986; Porter 1986; Merrell 1989; Finger 1991; Neely 1991; Gregory 1992; Kersey 1992; Peterson 1992; Taukchiray and Kasakoff 1992; Sider 1993). The twentieth century brought many adjustments to modern life that strengthened Indian society. Pan-Indianism and the powwow infused new energy into many Southeastern tribes (Paredes 1995:345; Williams 1979:206).

The question of federal recognition remains essentially a legal issue. But the struggle for recognition starts locally as Indians take a stand and assert their identity. The Waccamaw Siouan story has been preserved in the written word and the oral traditions handed down through the generations. As I read these documents and heard these stories, it seemed to me that the Waccamaw Siouan had been engaged in a long conversation or dialogue with non-Indians about their identity. These dialogues did not all take place in face-to-face interactions, although they sometimes did. The Waccamaw Siouan, whether present or not, have been shaped and molded by these dia-

---

1. Social race is used following Wagley (1975:174) to describe categories of people that are "socially, not biologically, defined."

logues. The standard historical summaries and ethnographic accounts of Indians became part of the conversation because these were used as voices of authority, consulted for guidance, and depended upon for answers. This book begins with the Waccamaw Siouan assertion of Indianness and tribal identity in 1950. Their struggle for recognition raises questions about Indian identity and how it relates to the opinion and authority of non-Indians. Who were the Waccamaw? Who were the Siouan Indians? How and why did the modern Waccamaw come to refer to themselves as Croatan, Cherokee, Wide Awake Indians, and finally Waccamaw Siouan? A "working consensus" had to be forged based on the strongly held belief the Waccamaw had in their own heritage as Indians. Thus, this book is not a point-by-point case for federal recognition as it is defined by the 1978 federal acknowledgment guidelines. It is a look into the dialogue about Waccamaw Siouan Indians stimulated by their struggle to preserve and forge their Indian identity. Who are the Siouan Indians and the Waccamaw Indians? Where did they come from? What do we know of them before 1950? This is the subject of this book. The Waccamaw used different names for themselves throughout their struggle for recognition. When historical overviews or ethnological summaries describe Indians as having become extinct or assimilated, they overlook the strength of Indian identity in the region. Likewise if we ignore the historical and cultural contexts of tribal names and of name changing as it occurred for groups like the Waccamaw Siouan, then we are in danger of representing them as just another people whose story is not part of the standard history and cultural summaries of the region.

I want to thank the Waccamaw Siouan for including me in their conversations about Indian identity. They raised questions that made me aware of how answers are shaped and molded in different historical and cultural contexts. Tribal chief Pricilla Freeman Jacobs has always made me feel welcome. I am grateful to a kindly older generation of leaders who have talked with me over the years. The staff at the tribal office works hard every year to present the powwow. They alerted me very early to the importance of this annual event. I want to thank them all. I apologize for any errors of interpretation that I may have made and take full responsibility for them ahead of time.

A special thanks goes to my husband, Alfred, and my children—Jessica and Al—for patience and understanding during the long periods of writing that took me to libraries and archives and away from them.

Waccamaw Legacy

I

The Eastern Siouans

"We Was Always Indians"

We was always Indians. Like Mary [a girl friend] was asked one time. Man come through and ask her something or "nother" about what she was. Said she was Indian. What tribe? [he asked.] She says, "I don't know what tribe, but I know one thing, I'm Indian." One of my girl friends. [She laughs.] So we always called the Indians, even so we didn't know what tribe . . . I guess the old folks did.
—August 1983

We, the Council of Wide Awake Indians, Waccamaw Tribe of the Siouan Nation, submit the attached information as evidences to support our plea for recognition and acceptance as Wards of the Government of the United States.
—Freeman et al. 1949

Forty years ago the old woman quoted in the epigraph above was in her thirties and her father, mother, and cousins and kin backed an effort to become a federally recognized tribe of the United States. On February 6, 1950, a Californian named Norris Poulson described the Waccamaw as "a lost tribe of Indians" with a tragic story. The congressmen listening to him asked, Who were the Siouan Indians? Where did they come from? Who were/are the "Waccamaw tribe"? In this chapter, I trace the meaning of "Waccamaw" and "Siouan," relating these words to the language, culture, and history of peoples of the Southeast. Anthropologists, historians, archaeologists, and linguists play important roles in defining and giving meaning to these terms.

In 1950 as the Waccamaw Bill was before Congress, the standard ethnological and linguistic references identified Siouan as an important language spoken by American Indians. An early authoritative work on the subject entitled *The Siouan Tribes of the East* by anthropologist James Mooney established Siouan as one of several major language stocks in the East (Mooney 1894:6–8). Later, anthropologist John R. Swanton expanded Mooney's work into a comprehensive study, which he published in 1946 as *The Indians of the Southeastern United States.* In addition to the Siouan stock, Algonquian, Iroquoian, Muskhogean, Tunican, and Caddoan were also present in the Southeast (Swanton 1946:10).

Linguists use word lists to determine to which group a tribe belongs. Sadly, for most of the so-called Siouan tribes, such vocabularies were never collected (Mooney 1894:6). Yet Mooney (1894:9) was convinced that the western Dakota or Siouan language stock originated in the East. This explained the presence of Siouan speakers like the Catawba, Woccon, and Tutelo in the Carolinas (Gatschet 1900, cited in Swanton 1923:33; Gallatin cited in Hudson 1970:6). Mooney classified all the other Siouan tribes on the basis of their association with the Catawba. Later, Frank G. Speck (1935:203), an expert on the Catawba, agreed that Siouan speakers once inhabited more of eastern Virginia and Carolina before being driven out into the piedmont. Speck (1935:201), who studied the last remaining speakers of Catawba, lamented, "the hope entertained since 1893 among students of native history and institutions, that the confusion of tribal names mentioned in the early narratives of the Carolinas would sooner or later be cleared up has not as yet been realized." Meticulous research with the last two people speaking Catawba did not promise to improve the picture either. While Speck agreed with Mooney's early classification of the Tutelo, Woccon, and Catawba as Siouan, he hesitated about the inclusion of twenty-two "other" tribes, determined to be Siouan only through the inference of their political relations with the Catawba. Before their decline, there may have been 24,000 speakers of Siouan in the southeastern United States, making Siouan the third-largest language grouping in the region (Swanton 1946:12). Yet, there was much to learn about the elusive Siouan. A hiatus in knowledge remained (Hudson 1970:6, 1976).

The 24,000 Siouan speakers represented a wide array of tribes. Some of these were known only from their tribal names mentioned briefly by Europeans. Nevertheless, Mooney's Siouan classification extended to many tribes in the central Carolinas. He included the Catawba, Tutelo, Woccon, Monacan, Saponi, Occaneechi, Sara, Keyauwee, Eno, Waxhaw, Sugaree, Peedee, Sewee, Santee, Wateree, Congaree, Mahoc, Nuntaneuck, Mohetan, Meipontsky, Shoccoree, Adshusheer, Sissipahaw, Cape Fear, Warrennuncock, Waccamaw, Winyaw, Hooks, and Backhooks.[1] Linguistic classification remained uncertain yet scholars continue to regard most of these tribes as Siouan.

The Siouan tribes lived within the Southeastern Culture Area, where they shared certain basic features that distinguished them from their neigh-

---

1. Tribal names appear in various forms and spellings in original sources. I am following Mooney's spellings whenever appropriate.

bors (Driver 1969:17). Swanton's generation of anthropologists defined "culture areas" primarily by listing traits believed typical of the people within these areas. At least by 1950, this was a common anthropological approach and influenced the understanding of the word *Siouan*. Some of the widespread aboriginal cultural patterns were intensive cultivation, the building of earthen mounds in the center of towns, social and political stratification, elaborate art forms, and a complex ideology. Other common traits were "the use of fish poisons; distinctive, though diverse, methods of processing acorns; the 'black drink'; a rectangular, gabled house, thatched and with walls of mud wattle or other earth covering; the practice of going barefoot most of the time" (Spencer and Jennings 1977:411). Other features usually found were "houselike storage structures; gourd ladles; hewing, eating, drinking, or licking of tobacco; the litter for nobility; carved wooden stools with legs; the blowgun with unpoisoned dart" (Spencer and Jennings 1977:410). Charles Hudson's (1976) *The Southeastern Indians* listed matrilineal descent, gender stratification, concepts of purity and pollution, orderliness, community-wide rituals, and a social ethic of harmony as some additional common patterns throughout the region after contact. These broad patterns most likely characterized the late prehistoric cultures of the region. Studies of the Cherokee by James Mooney revealed details of a complex belief system probably typical of the region (Hudson 1985:xiv–xvii). Sun worship or the belief in a sun deity was associated with temple fires that symbolized the earthly representation of the Sun. The Cherokee characterized fire and water as opposites, with fire representing the order of the Upper World and water standing for the disorder of the Under World. Each year annual renewal rites known as "going to water" prepared the Cherokee for a new year, purifying them of the sins of the past as they faced daily life in This World. The Green Corn ceremony, emphasizing the importance of corn in the diet of the region, celebrated the harvest and the renewal of the society. Rituals of purification and cleansing prepared individuals for the next year. Another important pattern was the ball game, an early form of lacrosse. These patterns were widely shared during the late prehistoric time and likely characterized many of the cultures of the region. Contact altered the later societies following significant declines in aboriginal population as a result of disease (Crosby 1972; Dobyns 1983).

The Waccamaw and the Eastern Siouans begin to have a story of their own in the literature when Europeans write about their interactions with specific Southeastern tribes. The story of the Eastern Siouans, to use James Mooney's (1894) description, is preserved in the colonial records of European interests in trade, peace, or war with the Indians. We turn now to the colonial relations that involved the Waccamaw and other Eastern Siouans during the sixteenth, seventeenth, and eighteenth centuries. Some of this history is well known, but presenting it from a "Waccamaw-centric" perspective shifts attention to the modern Waccamaw Siouan story.

The Waccamaw formed a large tribe whose territory ranged from Winyah Bay along the Waccamaw River up toward the Cape Fear River and beyond to the Neuse River in the piedmont. They may have been known to Europeans under three different names: Waccamaw, Cape Fear Indians, and Woccon. Douglas Rights (1957:39) suspected there was a link between the Woccon and the Waccamaw. Wondering how the Woccon, a large and important tribe, could escape mention in the colonial record, he proposed that they were a part of the tribe known as the Waccamaw. John R. Swanton of the Bureau of American Ethnology agreed with this theory (Swanton 1946:100). Thus, the Waccamaw name was used primarily in South Carolina and the Woccon name in northern North Carolina. Both tribes may have been glossed over as the Cape Fear Indians, a label the early European explorers of the Cape Fear region attached to the indigenous peoples they encountered there. The Cape Fear Indians were very likely the Waccamaw-Woccon Indians (Swanton 1946:75).

The Spanish left a clue to the identity of the Indians living in the Cape Fear region in 1513 (Lee 1965:9–10). The entire Cape Fear region, which includes the coastal plain of the southeastern United States lying north and south of the mouth of the Cape Fear River, received the enchanting name "Chicora," as one of the provinces of "Pascua de Flores" (Florida), when Ponce de Leon claimed the eastern United States from Florida to the north for Spain. In 1521, the Spanish subdivided Chicora, naming one part "Guacaya," which may be Spanish for Waccamaw (Milling 1969:205; Swanton 1946:203). The Waccamaw Indians lived near the southern end of the Cape Fear region, on "St. John the Baptist" River, identified later as either the Pee Dee or the Waccamaw River, at Winyah Bay (Milling 1969:204; Quattlebaum 1956:11–12; South 1972:32; Trinkley and Hogue 1979:3). The Waccamaw River reaches up into the Cape Fear region, touching Lake Waccamaw. If these Guacaya were the same people as the Waccamaw, then this is their earliest recorded encounter with Europeans. However, the indigenous peoples of the region were simply referred to as the Cape Fear Indians in subsequent encounters.

In 1524, Giovanni de Verrazzano, an Italian explorer for the French crown, sailed along the "continental coast west of Cape Fear, near the place where today's boundary line between the Carolinas reaches the sea" (Wroth 1970:79). Verrazzano does not name the Indians along the Cape Fear, but it is a strong possibility that they were Waccamaw. The natives watched Verrazzano's vessel, the *Dalphine,* approach the shore, then turned and fled into the interior. Only after Verrazzano and his men made "various signs" to reassure them did they return. He says, "some of them came up, showing great delight at seeing us and marveling at our clothes, appearance, and our whiteness; they showed us by various signs where we could most easily secure the boat, and offered us some food" (Wroth 1970:134). Verrazzano left a description of their general appearance, commenting on their nakedness, feathered garlands, dark color "like Ethiopians," and "thick black hair." Time prevented him from learning the "details of the life and customs," although he noted similarities with other Indians he had come upon along the coast (Wroth 1970:134).

Their environment was filled with "an abundance of animals, stags, deer, hares; and also of lakes and pools of running water with various types of birds, perfect for all the delights and pleasures of the hunt" (Wroth 1970:135). Moving along the coast, which "veered east," Verrazzano saw "great fires because of the numerous inhabitants" (Wroth 1970:135). Needing water, Verrazzano anchored offshore and sent twenty-five men to locate a new supply. The natives appeared friendly: "We saw many people on the beach making various friendly signs, and beckoning us ashore" (Wroth 1970:135). One of the sailors who swam toward shore with some "trinkets" for the natives nearly drowned in the rough surf. Much to Verrazzano's surprise, the natives rescued him and proceeded to examine him on shore before letting him return to his ship. Continuing north, along the coast, Verrazzano never again found natives as open and congenial as those along the Cape Fear coastline. Perhaps those tribes located farther north had met Europeans prior to Verrazzano's visit, since he reported that they fled in terror when they sighted the *Dalphine* (Wroth 1970:136).

Europeans did not disturb the Indians living along the Cape Fear coast again until the 1660s, but when they did they gave them the name "Cape Fear Indians." On March 24, 1663, King Charles of England granted eight Lords Proprietors rights to "Carolina" (Lee 1965:27–28). But a few years earlier, plans to settle the area had already gotten under way in the Massachusetts Bay Colony, where William Hilton received a commission to explore the area (Lee 1965:31). On October 4, 1662, he entered the "stream called Charles River . . . which is now known as Cape Fear" and proceeded upriver (Lee 1965:31). Hilton explored the Northeast Branch, where the land and resources impressed him. He arranged a purchase of the area from the one hundred or so natives (Lee 1965:32).

Hilton's good impression of the region motivated the "Adventurers about the Cape Fayre" to settle the area in February 1663. After a short stay, they left in April 1663, abandoning their livestock and posting a warning notice at the point of the Cape Fear River that made no mention of the

Cape Fear Indians (Lee 1965:33). Either the Indians actually posed no real barrier to settlement or the colonists felt confident that they could engage the Cape Fear Indians in friendly relations through trade. If the second were true, then the future settlers expected to share the area with the Cape Fear Indians.

Soon another settlement attempt took place. Arousing interest from wealthy Barbadian planters, Hilton was sent back to the area in 1663 (Lee 1965:36). On this mission, Hilton was to determine the best place for a colony and move forward with the purchase of some one thousand square miles from the Cape Fear Indians. Hilton's second voyage left him even more convinced that the Lower Cape Fear was ideal for an English settlement.

The Cape Fear Indians helped Hilton and his men find food and supplies during their expedition. Indians acted as guides and supplied his ship with "fresh fish, large mullets, young bass, shads, and several other sorts of very good, well-tasted fish" (Salley 1911:45). Hostile encounters happened rarely, but they reveal something of Hilton's perception of native economic and political organization. As he and his men explored the river, they came upon four Indians in a canoe, who approached them offering acorns for sale. After completing the sale, the Indians appeared to leave the area. But, Hilton reports, "one of them followed us on the shoar some two or three miles, till he came to the top of a high bank facing on the river." Hilton's men rowed their small boat just below this ridge to find that as they passed beneath, "the said Indian shot an arrow at us, which missed one of our men very narrowly, and struck the edge of the boat, which broke in pieces" (Salley 1911:49). Hilton's men went to shore and pursued the culprit but lost his trail. They picked it up again when they heard "some sing further in the woods, which we thought had been as a challenge to us to come and fight them." They had started toward the singers when shots from their boat called them back. Evidently, the nervous crew fired at an Indian "creeping on the bank." This strange encounter ends with the arrival of two Indians, crying "Bonny, Bonny." Apparently, they came to trade their arrows for beads (Salley 1911:50). Hilton showed them the arrow that narrowly missed his crewman. They expressed their sorrow over the incident, making it clear they knew nothing about it. After this, Hilton and his men called the place "Mount-Skerry" (Salley 1911:50). Hilton later got his revenge when he came upon the "guilty" Indian's hut, which he went to and pulled down and "brake his pots, platters, and spoons, tore his deerskins and mats in pieces, and took away a basket of akorns" (Salley 1911:50).

The Cape Fear Indians practiced a mixed economy, dependent upon horticulture and foraging. The deerskins in the Indian's hut give evidence of hunting and the acorns of gathering. They planted corn in "several plats of ground cleared by the Indians after their weak manner, compassed round with great timber-trees; which they are no ways able to fall, and so keep the sun from their cornfields very much" (Salley 1911:50). Despite Hilton's low opinion of their gardens, he grants that "nevertheless we saw as large cornstalks or bigger, than we have seen any where else."

The hostile incident also gives us a look at the blossoming relationship between the Cape Fear Indians and the English explorers. Several times, Hilton records, Indians attempted to catch the attention of his ship by shouting "Bonny, Bonny." This greeting is often linked with trade and other peaceful social interactions. Hilton himself interpreted "Bonny, Bonny" as "great signes of friendship." Again, in an unexpected encounter with some Cape Fear Indians, the hostile incident described earlier became the basis of an apology offered to Hilton. Why would seemingly unrelated Indians apologize for the behavior of this one misbehaving Indian? It seems obvious that they hoped to engage Hilton in trade. In any event, Hilton was persuaded by their persistent gestures of friendship, and he went ashore, where he met "several Indians, to the number of near forty lusty men [who] came to us, all in a great sweat, [to tell] . . . us Bonny" (Salley 1911:51). Then, Hilton continues, "the chief man of them" made a "large speech, and threw beads into our boat, which is a signe of great love and friendship." Furthermore, Hilton interpreted the chief's behavior as an apology for the "affront which we had received, [as] it caused him to cry." To underscore their disgust at this hostile act, the chief made it clear that "he and his men were come to make peace with us," and if they ever caught the offender, then they would "tye his arms, and cut off his head." As a further gesture of their goodwill, and perhaps also as a way to strengthen their link to Hilton, they presented two tall young Indian women to the English. Hilton believed the women to be the "king's daughters, or persons of some great account amongst them." The women appeared quite willing to go into the boat with Hilton and his men. Hilton reciprocated this friendly gesture by presenting the "king a hatchet and several beads, also beads to the young women and to the chief men, and to the rest of the men, as far as our beads would go" (Salley 1911:51). After this exchange, the Indians left Hilton promising "in four days to come aboard our ship." Hilton named this place "Mount-Bonny," because as he notes, "we had there concluded a firm peace." Apparently, this chief and his people lived two or three leagues farther downriver, where Hilton encountered them again (Salley 1911:51).

Land was purchased from the Cape Fear Indians at the close of Hilton's voyage. On December 1, 1663, Hilton "made purchase of the river and land of Cape-Fair, of Wattcoosa, and such Indians as appeared to us to be the chief of those parts" (Salley 1911:52). At that last meeting, Wattcoosa and his people apparently gave Hilton a supply of fresh fish for their journey home or perhaps as a last feast to celebrate their new relationship.

Hilton makes few comments about large villages, so perhaps the native population had declined since Verrazzano's visit in 1524. In that year, Verrazzano described numerous fires lighting the coast as he sailed by. Hilton, however, only saw the "hut" of the hostile Indian who shot at him and a couple of plantations (the Necos Indian plantation and "Sachems P" or Sachem's plantation). From Hilton's account it appears that there may have been one hundred warriors (total population four hundred) in the area. Unfortunately, he never discusses the size of the various "plantations." Tribal organization may have consisted of local towns, each presided over by a local chief. Hilton thought he bought the entire region from "Wattcoosa and other Chiefs," but just what the extent of their authority was is difficult to determine from Hilton's description (Lee 1965:74).

The Cape Fear Indians faced a new future in 1664 when Clarendon colony, with people from Barbados, was set up (Lee 1965:16). The colony was near the Indian town called "Necos plantation," located on "Indian River" or Town Creek. A friendly trade soon began between the Indians and settlers. By 1666, the settlement stretched sixty miles along the "Charles River" (Cape Fear River). The main settlement, called Charles Town, was located on the west bank of the river at or near the mouth of what is now Old Town Creek (Lee 1965:17). The new colony established a lucrative trade with the local Indians, "who came from great distances to exchange their furs and skins for coveted English goods" (Lee 1965:17). Among those who came, most certainly, were the Siouan tribes of the Cape Fear, Woccon, and Waccamaw. Soon, the colonists fell into conflicts over land allotments, which caused many to leave (Lee 1965:17). Those remaining saw an Indian uprising in which many of their cattle were killed or driven off. According to stories of this colony collected by John Lawson in 1701 (Lawson et al. 1967), "the irregular Practices of some of that colony [Clarendon] against the Indians" included sending Indian children away, "(as I have been told) under Pretense of instructing them in Learning the Principles of the Christian Religion" (Lawson, cited by Lee 1965:50). The Indian children were very likely enslaved, turning the Cape Fear Indians permanently against the colony. By 1667, this new colony was completely deserted. A lingering dislike for Europeans led the Cape Fear Indians to take their revenge on shipwreck victims, and this earned them a reputation as being "the most barbarous of any in the province" (Lee 1965:75).

Thirty years later, in 1695, the Cape Fear Indians found themselves plagued by Indian enemies, some of whom were in alliance with the colonial government in Charleston. To protect themselves, the Cape Fear Indians voluntarily became tribute Indians and agreed to stop killing shipwreck victims (Lee 1965:76). Living up to their agreement, the Cape Fear Indians rescued fifty-two passengers from a New England vessel along their seacoast (Milling 1969:220). These friendly relations continued until the eighteenth century.

The name "Woccon" first appears in 1701, being used by surveyor John Lawson, who traveled into their territory. The Woccon lived at Yupwauremau and Tooptatmeer, on the lower Neuse River. While there, Lawson recorded 150 words of the Woccon language. Twentieth-century linguists later used this word list to identify the Woccon as Siouan speakers. The Woccon did not leave their villages until after the Tuscarora War (1711–1712). Defeated in the Tuscarora War, the Woccon split into two groups, one fleeing north with the Tuscarora and the other heading south toward the Catawba (Swanton 1946:90). Since the Woccon are believed to be part of the Waccamaw tribe and part of the Indian population long known as the Cape Fear Indians, they probably found refuge in the south with them. If so, upon their arrival in the southern end of the Cape Fear region, they found the Waccamaw taking sides with the English against their old allies, the Tuscarora.

Although the reference in 1521 to the "Guacaya" province of Chicora appears to describe the Waccamaw, the tribal name "Waccamaw" occurs for the first time in 1670. The English find the Waccamaw living along the Waccamaw and Lower Pee Dee Rivers near the Pedee and Winyaw Indians (Swanton 1946:203). Their name is used a second time in 1711, when they are mired in the Tuscarora War as allies to the English. In the first expedition against the Tuscarora, the neighbors of the Waccamaw, such as the Watterees, Peedees, Wineaws, Hoopengs, and Warepares,[2] were part of Captain Bull's company in Barnwell's army (Barnwell 1908:31). By the end of January 1712, as Barnwell headed north toward the Neuse River, he came upon the "Wattomas" (probably Waccamaw) and Saxapahaw. The Saxapahaw were unhappy because the Tuscarora had recently chased them from their settlements (Barnwell 1908:32). Barnwell (1908:33) may have gotten both the Saxapahaw and the "Wattomas" to join his force. This supposition is based on a reference to the injured men in Captain Bull's company, who included "1 Saxaphaw & 4 Wattaw wound." The first expedition ended in a brief truce in April 1712.

By August 1712, the truce broke and Barnwell was called upon to help mount another expedition against the Tuscarora. In advising the South Carolina House of Assembly on how to gain the cooperation of the Indian allies, he said that the help of the "Wachamaw and Cape Fear Indians"

---

2. The various spellings reflect common usage of the times.

should be secured by whatever means necessary, including offering them guns, ammunition, and payment for scalps (Barnwell 1909:43). The defeat of the Tuscarora benefited the Cape Fear Indians and the Waccamaw, because the Tuscarora often attacked their settlements. Perhaps the Tuscarora, like Barnwell, recognized that the Cape Fear Indians and the Waccamaw were closely associated—even the same people. (After the Tuscarora War ended, the Woccon joined the Waccamaw and Cape Fear Indians, too.) However, the English continued to refer to them as if they were separate, but closely allied, peoples. Perhaps this was because the Waccamaw lived mostly within South Carolina and the Cape Fear Indians mostly in North Carolina. However, the boundary between the two colonies was uncertain and extended right up to the western side of the Cape Fear River.

Each colony gained from trading with the Indians living within its territory. The abuses by unregulated traders and the insatiable slave trade that stimulated intertribal raiding contributed to the outbreak of hostilities in the Tuscarora War (Oakley 1996). Both governments vowed to avoid problems involving trade and Indian slavery after the Tuscarora War. To that effect, they passed laws to license traders and set up a commission or board to review and handle most matters concerning Indian affairs.[3] Since the boundary between the two Carolinas was uncertain, some traders took advantage of the confusion. When North Carolina issued a license to Landgrave Thomas Smith, he subsequently used this license to challenge the authority of Charleston. Smith refused to secure a license from South Carolina, claiming that the Cape Fear and other northern tribes were beyond their jurisdiction in South Carolina. He attempted to establish a trading fort on a tract of land granted him by North Carolina. His chosen site was either on the east bank of the Cape Fear at its mouth or on Smith or Cape Island (Lee 1965:78). The Smith case led the South Carolina governor to request that the Cape Fear Indians be brought officially under his government. He also requested that the boundary be properly surveyed. The Lords Proprietors never settled the issue, leaving both the Cape Fear Indians and the boundary in limbo (Lee 1965:78–79).

Following the Tuscarora War, North Carolina needed time to recover and let the boundary line dispute and any hopes of increasing the number of settlers go for a while (Lee 1965:79). However, South Carolina moved ahead with its own plans. Between 1713 and 1715, settlers were encouraged to go

---

3. The General Assembly of South Carolina appointed a board of nine commissioners to regulate the Indian trade by 1707 (McDowell 1992a:viii). By 1723, a single commissioner instead of several oversaw Indian trade (Salley 1936:3).

to the western banks of the Cape Fear River. This brought the disputed boundary and problems with the Indian trade back into the picture. Of course, Indians already inhabited lands to the west of the Cape Fear River. Living near the 610 recorded Waccamaw in 1715 were the Winyaw on the western side of the Pee Dee River, near its mouth, the Pedee on the middle course of the Pee Dee River, on the eastern bank, and the hostile "Sarraws" or Cherraws (Cheraw) farther up the Pee Dee River (Mooney 1894:76–77). Two hundred or so Cape Fear Indians lived farther north toward the Cape Fear River (Milling 1969:222).

The movement of settlers into the territory of the Waccamaw probably convinced both the Waccamaw and Cape Fear Indians to join in the Yamassee War of 1715 with the Cheraw and other Indians. The Yamassee War erupted because of intertribal hostilities caused by the trade in Indian slaves promoted by the English since 1699. Most Indians believed that the English census of the Indian population of 1715 was motivated by a desire to know how many Indian slaves could yet be obtained (Swanton 1946:77–78). The Yamassee War united the Apalachee, Catawba, Apalachicola, Creek, and Cherokee against the English. Many of the smaller Siouan tribes got involved, too. English victories over the Yamassee and Catawba eventually convinced the others to stop fighting. In the end, many tribes moved south, away from the English: the Yamassee, Apalachee, Apalachicola, and Lower Creek moved toward Florida and inland to the Chattahoochee River.

The Yamassee War demonstrates the extent to which the Waccamaw and Cape Fear Indians acted as allies. An incident involving Colonel Maurice Moore of North Carolina records the cooperation and joint fate of these two groups. Moore marched through the Cape Fear River region with an army of Tuscarora-Coree Indians coming to aid South Carolina. Word came to him that he was about to be attacked by the Cape Fear and Waccamaw Indians. He succeeded in surprising them by marching into their towns, seizing their ammunition, and taking eighty captives. Moore's attack on the Cape Fear and Waccamaw is described in the *Boston Newsletter* (1715):

We are inform'd from North-Carolina, That Col. Moore who went from thence to South-Carolina with Forces to their Assistance against the Indian Enemy, coming to an English Plantation, where he expected to meet English, he found about 70 Indians, whom he mistrusted to have killed the Planter and his Family, upon which he Tortur'd Two of the Indians in order to make em confess, but they would not, the Third fearing the same Punisshment, confessed that they had Murdered the Planter and his Family, upon which Col. Moor[e] kill'd and took Prisoners all the rest, The Prisoners he sent in Vessels by Water to Charlstoun.

Moore's raid on the Waccamaw and Cape Fear allies hit the Cape Fear Indians hard. As a smaller branch of the Waccamaw tribe, they suffered great losses. In 1715, they numbered two hundred men, women, and children; shortly after the war and Moore's fatal attack, their numbers drastically fell. Eighty people were taken captive and sent to South Carolina. Those remaining in the Cape Fear region faced the possibility of hostile attacks from their old native enemies. Some of the Cape Fear sought refuge in the white settlements of South Carolina to avoid the worst of these attacks (Lee 1965:82). Evidently, this move did not completely alter their ability to act as a sovereign nation, seeking aid from the South Carolinians when they needed it.

The South Carolinians may have been surprised by the involvement of the "Northward Indians" (Waccamaw, Winyaw, Pedee, and Cape Fear) in the Yamassee uprising, because they had worked hard to establish close trading ties at the Winyah Bay factory. Pressured and threatened by the Sarraws (Cheraw) to join the Yamassee uprising, the Northward Indians thought they might gain access to the lucrative Virginia trade and vast riches from plunder (Saunders and Clark 1886:2:251). Guns and ammunition came through the Sarraws to the Waccamaw (McDowell 1992a:235–242). By the summer of 1716, the Waccamaw, Pedee, Winyas (Winyaw), and Waiwee made peace with Charleston and began a new trading relationship.

The Waccamaw and their neighbors continued to be of significant size and strength—enough to warrant a special trading factory (McDowell 1992a:132). To keep them satisfied and to secure their own borders, the South Carolinians offered the Indians a better deal than the Virginians (Saunders and Clark 1886:2:252). To start with, in 1716 Charleston opened its trade relations with the Waccamaw by appointing a special agent, William Watis (Waites), Sr., as factor at Winyaw (Wineau) (McDowell 1992a:74). The factory was located at the "old Casekey's House on Black River at Wineau," because it reached a substantial population of Indians (McDowell 1992a:74). Freelance traders were now forbidden to trade with the Waccamaw Indians. Strict rules governed the Waccamaw trade. The factor could sell arms, ammunition, liquor, goods, and wares in return for skins, furs, and slaves but could not "buy any free Indian for a slave nor to make a slave of any Indian that ought to be free" (McDowell 1992a:95). Nor could he extend credit to Indian hunters beyond the value of one skin. Factors had to behave in a friendly and peaceable manner toward the Indians and prevent others from abusing them. They were expected to engage in "reciprocal present giving with the Indians" and to "send all trade goods and unsold merchandise back down to Charles Town" (McDowell 1992a:95). Such terms applied only to the Indian allies of the colony such as the "Wawees, Wakamaws, Pedeas, and Schovonas."

The Waccamaw and their neighbors desired the normal European goods of arms, ammunition, liquor, and cloth, but clearly they also desperately wanted corn. Their white neighbors, aware of their need for corn, feared that they would raid their fields (McDowell 1992a:105). Corn was sold to the Indians to keep them from bothering the settlers (McDowell 1992a:106). The request for "corn, blankets, shirts, knives, buttons, beads, tools, and other things for building a house" indicates the extent to which the Waccamaw Indians and their neighbors had accepted the use of European manufactured goods and the degree to which they depended on non-Indians for corn, a crop that their ancestors had grown for subsistence (McDowell 1992a:109).

Trading factories had to be located near the Indian population in order to be successful. Distance from Charleston, easy access to a path or river way, and security all had to be considered. When the Wineau (Winyaw) factory was first put at the "old Casekey's House" along the Black River, it seemed an ideal location for trading with the Waccamaw and their neighbors. The commissioners of Indian Affairs decided this on July 13, 1716, but later, on the recommendation of William Waites, agreed to move it to Saukey, described on July 16, 1716, as being better located to reach all the tribes. However, Waites changed his mind on September 21, 1716, after working with the Indians for only two months. The commissioners reported that he wanted to move the factory to Uauenee or Great Bluff, which Waites described to them as "safe and convenient" (McDowell 1992a:111). Waites argued that Uauenee was a good place to trade with the Northward Indians, especially the Waccamaw, and in a better position to get news to the settlements, too. The Waccamaw offered protection, as "being contiguous to the Wackamaws lies doubly fortified against any foreign attempt" (McDowell 1992a:134).

The tribes along the northern frontier in 1717 remained hostile, demanding guns and ammunition for the trading factory at Uauenee. Problems persisted along the northern frontier and the Santee River, involving the Cherokee, Cheraw, Waccamaw, and various other tribes. The commissioners must have hoped that by engaging the Waccamaw in trade they would secure their friendship and prevent further trouble along the northern frontier. The Waccamaw shifted their demands away from corn to guns and ammunition. William Waites informed the commissioners of this change on December 10, 1716, writing, "all the Indians want to buy is ammunition"

(McDowell 1992a:137). In response, the commissioners urged Waites to be cautious, because complaints had reached them about the Waccamaw from "the inhabitants of Wineau," who reported that "the Wakamaws continue to destroy and prey on their cattle." Consequently, the commissioners ordered Waites to forbid this. Difficulties with the Cheraw eventually forced the movement of the factory back closer to the settlements (McDowell 1992a:144). Trade continued at Black River in 1717 and 1718 at a place where the Waccamaw, the Catawba, and others could be served (McDowell 1992a:258). However, the Cheraw were specifically cut off from the trade until they agreed to the English terms (McDowell 1992a:175–176).

William Waites informed the commissioners of his ill health in early December 1716. To assist him, they appointed a Mr. Hughes but encouraged Waites to stay at his post for as long as he could, fearing that Hughes was too inexperienced to be left completely on his own (McDowell 1992a:144). Hughes, however, must have taken over as factor by January 1717, when William Waites retires from the scene.

The trouble with the Cheraw continued into August 1717. The factor, Mr. Hughes, feared them and convinced the commissioners of their danger. The commissioners noted his fear, saying, "the dread you have of the Charraws hath occasioned your removal from our trading house, at YourEnee, and interrupted the commerce you had with the Indians there" (McDowell 1992a:202). They suggested that Hughes try to come down to Charleston, bringing two or three chief men of the "Wackamaw" and "not forgetting such of them as have been most zealous of our interest" (McDowell 1992a:202).

The Waccamaw chiefs' visit to Charleston in the fall of 1717 gave them the opportunity to express their opinion as to the best location for the trading factory. Differences of opinions hint at the relative locations of the tribes in reference to the factory. The "Indian kings," named Johnny and Cary, both Waw-we captains, as well as several of the chief men of the "Wackamaws and Wineaus" and one "Peadea Indian," appeared before the commissioners. Since they or their tribes had paid their "submissions to the government," they were given the right to express their opinions concerning matters of the trade. The "Wackamaws and Wineaus" wanted the trading house back at Black River, describing it as a safer place. The Black River location was the original one approved by the commissioners on July 10, 1716, when it was described as being located at the "old Casekey's House on Black River at Wineau" (McDowell 1992a:74). The "Peadea" man said his people preferred "Your-henee" but that they would come down to Black River. Until now, the records of the commissioners made it difficult to distinguish between the original location at Black River and Uauenee or

"Your-henee," but from this Peadea man's statement (and in the opinion of archaeologists Trinkley and Hogue [1979:4–5]), the Uauenee site was north of the Black River on the west side of the Lower Pee Dee River. Finally, Johnny, described as "King of the Wineaus," said that he and part of his people now living on the Santee River wanted to return to their old habitation during the fall. They complained of many hardships they had experienced living "with the White people; for as much as they were forced to pay Mr. Weekley two dres't deer skins per man for the land upon which they planted upon; neither could Capt. Gaillard, the Santee trader, furnish them with goods so well as Mr. Hughes, the Wineau Trader, had done" (McDowell 1992a:207–209). The commissioners listened and then ordered "provisions be given to the Catabaw, Wineau, Wakamaw, and other Indians now in Charles Town."

The Waccamaw had to stay in their territory to secure the frontier, as the Cheraw continued to disturb and disrupt peaceful relations in the region (McDowell 1992a:207–209). On January 30, 1718, the factor wrote to the commissioners, saying, "the Charraw Indians have often insulted our said factor, and still persist in their villainy, and grow more dangers, as appears per the enclosed" (McDowell 1992a:253–254). A month later the Cheraw were reported as not so "turbulent (at present) as they have been; but not withstanding the inhabitants are under apprehension of their mischievous designs, and desire to have them removed" (McDowell 1992a:257). Again, moving the factory's location to a safer place was considered. On March 7, 1718, the trading factor answered questions about this possibility. There were dangers in moving closer to the Cheraw (McDowell 1992a:258). Part of the danger came from the fact that the Waccamaw had "removed to the south of Black River, which makes the neighborhood at Wineau uneasie on account of the Charraws, who, notwithstanding their message to the Governor for a peace, have since made friendship with the Wackamaws, with a design (as they infer) to engage them in a war against us; and have threatened the white people of a combination to that purpose" (McDowell 1992a:264). The return of the Waccamaw was vital to the security of the region. So, to entice them back, the trading factory was moved once more in order to be closer and more convenient to the Waccamaw (McDowell 1992a:275).

In the end, the Waccamaw could not be persuaded to return to their settlements and a short war broke out in 1720 between the English and the "Vocamas (a nation on Winea River; not above 100 men)." Sixty Waccamaw were taken prisoner or killed. The causalities were low in this war, with just one "Winea Indian killed" (Milling 1969:226–227; Swanton 1946:207). In the years just after the Vocamas War, the Waccamaw and their neighbors to the north of the Winyaw settlements faced even greater challenges.

In summary, colonial efforts in the seventeenth and eighteenth centuries focused almost entirely on subduing, trading with, enslaving, and even removing the Waccamaw and their neighbors. All eventually became an obstacle to the expansion of the colonial society. The Indians reacted to this pressure, responding to force with force, to diplomacy and trade with peaceful agreements, to the Indian wars and slave trade by participating in the lucrative sale of captures, and to the pressure to remove them with both acquiescence and resistance as their size and strength allowed. The colonial record is confusing and incomplete when it comes to the ultimate question of their final disposition. Yet we do get an idea of how they accommodated to these pressures as they wandered the borderlands of the colonial society.

2
Society along the Borderlands

The eighteenth century brought enormous changes to the Siouan peoples and their neighbors. The Yamassee War of 1715 transformed many independent societies into "Settlement Indians," living dependent within the boundaries of or along the edges of colonial settlements (Wood 1989:48). The colonial economy grew increasingly dependent on enslaved African labor, forever altering the ratio between whites, African slaves, and Indians. Resettlement and realignment of tribes toward the "Catawba Nation," as revealed through a study of Indian maps (Waselkov 1989), shows just how far the changes penetrated Indian life. The Catawba Nation, itself a conglomeration of tribes and languages, symbolized the reorganized "New World" of the Indian, according to historian James Merrell (1989). In this chapter, I look at the society along the borderlands where the Waccamaw, Cape Fear Indians, and others found themselves in the eighteenth century. These borderlands encompassed the sparsely settled regions outside Charleston, South Carolina, north and northeast toward the border with North Carolina and the Cape Fear River region. The Siouan Indians lived in the borderland society, where they were harassed by Algonquian and Iroquoian enemies, cheated by traders making deals to buy their lands, and encouraged to join the colonial militia where they became indispensable to the colonial defense system.

The Yamassee War of 1715 changed the Indians' world forever. The small coastal tribes, allied with the English, numbering perhaps eight hundred at the start of the war, suffered the heaviest loss and experienced the greatest disruptions. The Wimbee, Combahee, Kussah, and Ashepoo, for example, fought the war in their home territory, south of Edisto Island and the Port Royal area. At the end of the war, they became heavily dependent on the English, who thereafter referred to them as "Indians residing within the Settlement." Their numbers continued to drop so that by 1730 there were only five hundred or so left. After 1743, most of their names were never recorded again in the colonial record. Scattered about the settlements, they lived in small family groups. Waccamaw and Cape Fear Indians lived just beyond the borders of the English settlements, where they fared a little better than their coastal neighbors.

At the start of the Yamassee War, the Waccamaw were the largest of the smaller Siouan nations living in the frontier north of Charleston. According to an Indian census taken in 1715, there were 57 Seawees (Sewee), 106 Weneaws (Winyaw), 125 Santees and Congarees, 206 Cape Fears, 510 Sarows (Cheraw), 610 Waccomassus (Waccamaw), and 1,470 Catapaws (Catawba) (Milling 1969:222, n. 57). After the Yamassee War, the frontier proved to be a dangerous place for the European settlers, as well as the Waccamaw, Cape Fear, Cheraw, and other small tribes.

Before 1730, the southern colony of Carolina was "a squat triangle of settlement the base of which was the coast between Winyah Bay and Port Royal Sound, its apex the great bend of the Santee fifty miles inland, its white population ten thousand, its slaves twice that number" (Meriwether 1974:3). Many changes occurred in the white settlements during this period. In 1719, the South Carolinians overthrew the rule of the Lords Proprietors, whose political power was transferred to the crown. Under a more liberal government and the protection of the British crown, the colony was set to expand. German and Scotch-Irish immigrants flooded in, pushing the colony's boundaries northward and pressuring the Indians. The rice plantations located within the boundaries of the colony drew upon the labor of thousands of African slaves. As the slave population expanded to meet this demand, the white population shrank to one-third of the total of thirty thousand by 1729 (Meriwether 1974:6). Colonists feared both an internal rebellion of their slaves and the external threat of hostile Indians.

The Crown centralized all functions of the colonial government in Charleston, and the General Assembly met there each fall. The journals of the government meetings provide an extensive record of Indian affairs. From these journals, we can see that attention turned toward the frontier and the "middle country," where settlement, trade, and military activity shifted away from the coast toward the "pine belts, between the tidewater and the sand hills" (Meriwether 1974:10). Between the settlements and the middle country, in the tidewater region, there remained small pockets of Indians, like the "Cape Fairs," "Ittewans, Cussoes, Winyas, St. Helenas and others." They survived along the margins of the settlements, ranging freely but subject to punishment by the local justices of the peace if they misbehaved.

In 1720, the middle country lay beyond the line of coastal settlements where military forts and garrisons guarded the northern perimeter. In fact, the middle country was not entirely settled until the 1760s. Cattle kept at "cowpens," staffed by rough frontiersmen, were scattered throughout the region. For many years, this region was the gateway to the lucrative Indian trade with its major trading paths and rivers leading to the Catawba, Cherokee, Creek, Chickasaw, and Choctaw. Beyond the borders of the middle country were other small tribes such as the "Uchees on the Savannah below Ft. Moore, a few Creeks about the Palachuccolas, the Waccamaws beyond the Santee, and the Peedees on the river of that name" (Meriwether 1974:12). Living farther north in North Carolina, the Tuscarora raided the southern tribes, making them miserable.

English settlers moved in from the south and down from the northern colonies of Pennsylvania, Virginia, and North Carolina. Tension increased when the northern Indians like the Seneca, Tuscarora, and Shawnee, allied with the Cherokee, came to raid and carry away captives from the smaller, weaker tribes. While the settlers could move closer to Charleston or call upon the colonial militia, the Waccamaw and Cape Fear, like the smaller tribes, faced difficult choices. On the one hand, they could move closer to the large Catawba Nation and get some protection from sheer numbers. On the other hand, they could move down toward the settlements to live as "Friendly Tribes" near and/or among the colonists. Or they could stay where they were and try to somehow survive the attacks of the northern enemies. For some, the "exodus toward Catawbas" was a powerful draw (Merrell 1989:102).

Pressure from the expanding settlements and increasing raids by the northern Iroquois enemies pushed many of the smaller tribes toward the Catawba Nation. The Waccamaw (and their neighbors the Eno, Pedee, Saxapahaw, Winyaw, Sugaree, Shuteree, and Cheraw) had a great deal in common with the Catawba. They probably spoke a Siouan language, easing intertribal cooperation, and they shared a broad Southeastern cultural pattern and heritage with the Catawba (Merrell 1989:102). They were already accustomed to meeting to discuss strategy and planning with the Catawba, since they fought on the same side in the Yamassee War. For example, after the war ended, delegations of Waccamaw, Cape Fear, Keyauwee, Pedee, and Winyaw met together in Charleston where the terms of peace were worked out. Another delegation, with Catawba, Waxhaw, Cheraw, Pedee, Saxapahaw, Sugaree, Shuteree, Keyauwee, and Eno traveled all the way to Williamsburg to arrange peace terms (Merrell 1989:102–103). Such previous contacts made moving toward the Catawba Nation an easier choice for many of the tribes (Merrell 1989:103).

The Catawba Nation was still remote from the settlements and enjoyed a lucrative trade with the English. Their towns were located ninety miles north of the Congarees and stood in between the middle country and the biting attacks of their fierce Iroquois enemies in New York and their Cherokee foes in the mountains (Meriwether 1974:13). Their policy was to aid runaway Indian slaves and shelter their allies (Merrell 1989:105–106). It proved wiser to be a Catawba ally than enemy and subject to their fierce raids (Merrell 1989:106).

Two powerful forces trapped the Waccamaw, Cape Fear, Wateree, Pedee, and Cheraw. On the one hand, the Catawba offered their allies shelter, protection, and relief from raids, although this alliance would cost the Waccamaw their independence later when the colonists pressured them to subordinate themselves to Catawba authority. On the other hand, the colonists offered protection in their settlements where the Friendly Tribes might live along the borderlands, wandering nomadically as they sought a place to live. The Cape Fear also paid a heavy price for their choice of seeking protection near the settlement if, as many did, they worked for wages in the Rangers, as slave catchers, or as hired porters for the settlers. Some tribes refused to join the Catawba, while others split up into smaller groups under the pressure. The Waccamaw, Wateree, Pedee, and Cheraw apparently split into small groups, with some going up to Catawba "in the 1710s and 1720s, some in the 1730s, and some not at all" (Merrell 1989:106). By the mid-1740s, traders like James Adair noticed the considerable linguistic diversity in the Catawba Nation (Merrell 1989:110).

The Cape Fear found some protection living near the settlements. Like other tribes who made this choice, however, the colonists now described them as Settlement Indians or "Parched-Corn Indians." The sight of "Friendly Indians" wandering in small family groups along the margins of the settlements became familiar to the colonists. For example, in 1723, the "Ittawach [Etiwans]" were seen living "scattered up and down" the settlements, suggesting a fate that many of the small tribes probably suffered (Merrell 1989:107). Others developed close ties to local planters like James Coachman, who gave refuge to some Pedee Indians. The colonists knew them as "Coachman's Indians." Coachman aided them by writing letters on their behalf and generally defending them, while they served him by working as slave catchers and traders (Merrell 1989:107). The Commons House of Assembly approved this arrangement, reimbursing a Captain John Bee ten pounds, "it being cash given to the Pedee Indians who went down to Pon Pon with Capt. James Coachman in pursuit of rebellious Negroes" (Easterby et al. 1951–1953:1952:182). The Notchee Indians got help from Coachman, too. In 1739, he bought land for "use of the Notchee Indians" (Easterby et al. 1951–1953:1952:105). Although the Cape Fear Indians lived near the Pedee Indians in 1749, it is unclear whether they too were "Coachman's Indians" (Merrell 1989:319). The Cape Fear Indians moved often to avoid their enemies.

The Cape Fear Indians were near the settlements in 1723. Ironically, they had to petition to live on "public land" that undoubtedly used to belong to their ancestors. The Journal of the Council and the Journal of the Commons House of Assembly report that "the Cape Fear being driven away by the northward Indians are now about the Winyaw Settlement, where they are straightened for land to plant." From this entry, we learn that the Cape Fear Indians still hoped to settle in the area of Winyah Bay, where they might be able to stay long enough to plant their crops. The record then tells us that the Cape Fear moved closer to their old allies the Waccamaw and their neighbors the Winyaw. Since they did not get the land they ask for, they may have decided to return to their homes in the Cape Fear region. However, going home proved very difficult. Local tradition in North Carolina tells the story of the "Battle of Sugar Loaf," in which the Cape Fear Indians were hit hard by a local planter and chased out of the region. The story goes that "King Roger Moore," developer of Orton plantation and Brunswick Town, gathered a small army of men from among his slaves and attacked the Cape Fear Indians. Sugar Loaf was a high ridge located just about opposite the colonial settlement known as Brunswick Town, along the Cape Fear River. Moore sought revenge for an attack on Orton plantation that he apparently blamed on the Cape Fear Indians. If it was Cape Fear Indians, then they must have attacked Moore's plantation out of desperation, looking for supplies. The Battle of Sugar Loaf, locals believed, drove the Cape Fear Indians south once again (Ashe 1908:1:213; Sprunt 1992:16–18).

The Battle of Sugar Loaf, which took place in 1725, forced the Cape Fear Indians to move back toward Winyah Bay, where both the Waccamaw and the Winyaw Indians lived. Unfortunately, their move south did not end their troubles. They could not have known that the Seneca were already raiding the Waccamaw, capturing and enslaving them just about the same time that King Roger Moore was defeating them at the Battle of Sugar Loaf (Mereness 1961:138; Merrell 1989:98). In November 1726, the Commons House of Assembly heard a report that "the Kings of the Cape Fears and Winyaws were come to town to desire protection from the Government," and a letter from Landgrave Thomas Smith was read in the house giving an account of the Tuscarora who "crept up in the night to the fort of our Friendly Indians" (Salley 1946:14–15). Smith had been a trader licensed by North Carolina to trade with the Cape Fear Indians just after the Tuscarora War (1711–1712) (see Chapter 1). The Charleston government told the "Kings of the Cape Fears and Winyaws" the best thing to do was to go "to the Southern part of the province" where the northern Indians would be less likely to attack them. Retreating into the settlements could not keep the Susquehannah, Seneca, and Tuscarora away forever. The Cape Fear Indians moved closer to their old allies, the Waccamaw, at Winyah Bay to find that the Waccamaw had moved closer to the Cheraw and the Catawba to avoid the very same sorts of problems. They then prepared to go further south, assisted by the government. Orders came down in January 1726 or 1727 "for taking up necessary Perriaugers for transporting the Cape Fear Indians from Mr. Nicholl's Plantation to the southward parts where they are going to settle" (Salley 1946:58).

The Waccamaw found a safe harbor near the Catawba Nation. The Nation was actually just a cluster of towns: Nassau (Nauvasa or "Catawba Town"), Newstee, Sugaree, Shuteree, Weyapee, and Weyaline (Weyanne or "King's Town") (Merrell 1989:109). A rare deerskin map, drawn between 1721 and 1725, offers us a chance to see the Indian world from the perspective of the Indian cartographer who prepared the map (Waselkov 1989:293). Rather than exact geographic positions, the Catawba Deerskin Map depicts "social distance (based for example on degree of kin relatedness between groups)" and "political distance (the degree of cooperation between groups, or the extent of control over groups)" (Waselkov 1989:300–302).

The Catawba Deerskin Map describes the locations of and relationships between a set of core Catawba towns and ten others representing mostly Siouan tribes that lived nearby. The Waccamaw town is among the latter group of peripheral towns. There are seven peripheral towns of predominately Siouan speakers. Among them are the Cheraw, Wateree, and Waccamaw (Waselkov 1989:323–324). Waselkov interprets the Indian cartographer's circles to represent social groups, arguing that the circle has been a basic symbolic form in the Southeast since prehistoric times. Foreign social groups like those formed by the English are depicted using squares or rectangles. The lines draw the important trading paths, radiating out from the Catawba core towns to the periphery and beyond to the English. Strategically located, the Catawba reveal themselves as important in this network of Siouan and non-Siouan peoples.

The Catawba Nation was a loose confederacy of towns. For example, the Waccamaw town of several hundred people operated independently, having its own headmen and fields. Despite this independence, the Waccamaw found a way to cooperate with the Catawba Nation in their common language and shared cultural experiences. After the Yamassee War, the Waccamaw apparently recognized the need to work with the mostly Siouan tribes gathered near the Catawba to preserve and protect themselves. When trader James Adair visited the Catawba towns in 1743, he heard more than twenty-three languages spoken there and listed the Eno, Cheraw, Congaree, Natchez, Yamassee, Wateree, and Coosah as residents. Merrell (1989:110) thinks that the list could be lengthened to include the Waccamaw, Saponi, Pedee, Santee, Saxapahaw, Keyauwee, and others.

The Waccamaw town was located at the periphery of the Nation near their old neighbors like the Wateree, Pedee, and Cheraw. The Waccamaw town leaders directed war parties, organized hunting grounds, and supervised planting of spring fields. Small parties of Waccamaw hunters circulated between the periphery of the Nation and the Winyaw area in Craven County, where they had villages a decade earlier. In November 1725, an unfortunate African American man was shot and killed by a jittery "Andrew Collins, at the time when the people of Winyaw were under arms from some apprehensions they had of the Waccamaw Indians designing mischief against them" (Salley 1945:22). The Upper House Journal of South Carolina reported in 1727 that the Waccamaw lived near the Nation (Merrell 1989:111). In 1728 and 1733, the Waccamaw were reported to be in the Low County (Merrell 1989:319). They moved often enough to leave some confusion about their eventual location as late as 1755 (Merrell 1989:319). The Waccamaw continued to act independently of the Catawba even though they chose to live near them.

The Waccamaw participated in a new political organization centered on the "eractasswa," the Catawba chief or king. The Waccamaw "wise old men" offered their support to the Catawba eractasswa and war captains arose when the deliberations of the other political leaders failed to ensure peace. The presence of the Waccamaw town on the periphery of the Catawba Nation provided security to the core Catawba towns in the 1730s and 1740s. Even so, on October 6, 1737, the Seneca attacked the Catawba with such ferocity that the Waccamaw and other small tribes could do little to protect them. The Catawba, weakened and nervous, sought permission from Charleston to move to the now deserted town of their former enemies the Waxhaw, located much closer to the settlements. However, this idea was not popular in Charleston since the government needed the Catawba right where they were in order to protect settlements from direct attacks by northern Indians (Easterby et al. 1951-1953:1951:335). In return for the Catawba agreeing to remain in their old settlements, the Charleston government agreed to try to arrange a peace with the Seneca. Clearly, the Catawba needed to keep the smaller tribes living near them as allies for their own protection, too.

The Waccamaw "wise old men" offered political support to the Catawba eractasswa, but they could not guarantee that their warriors would listen to the eractasswa's counsel. Indeed, the eractasswa had trouble controlling the tribes at the periphery of the Nation. Perhaps distracted by the relentless attacks from the northern Indians, the eractasswa was helpless in preventing the Waccamaw warriors and those of other small tribes living on the Nation's periphery from conflicting with the settlers who were moving into former Indian lands. Trouble was liable to break out at any time, as when an overseer at Black River near Georgetown shot a Pedee man named "Corn-White Johnny" in 1732. King Harry, Captain Bill, George, Dancing Johnny, and some of his relatives appeared in Charleston to give an account of what they knew of his death (Gregg 1967:8).

Old neighbors of the Waccamaw like the Cheraw and Pedee saw their former hunting grounds and fields surveyed and divided up between 1735 and 1736 (Mcriwether 1974:90). For example, John Thompson, Jr., lived near Prince Frederick Church on the lower Black River, where he had a thousand acres surveyed on a point between Jeffrey's Creek and the Pee Dee River. Thompson used to trade with the Cheraw Indians when they lived on the east bank of the river at the shoals. The colonists now referred to the whole area as "the Cheraws."

Another part of the old Cheraw and Pedee territory soon attracted the eye of the settlers. The Welch Tract of 173,840 acres, "lying 70 miles north of Queensboro and 20 miles beyond the North Carolina line as later surveyed" and described as very fertile land, good for growing "hemp, flax, wheat and barley," opened for settlement next (Meriwether 1974:91). Despite "selling" portions of the land to traders like Thompson, neither the Cheraw nor the Pedee recognized the settlers' rights to all the land and its resources. So they continued to return to their old homeland, causing complaints about "Cheraw and Pedee Indians who by running among their settlements under the pretense of hunting, caused the settlers great uneasiness." The former trader to the Cheraw, John Thompson, Jr., was called before the lieutenant governor and council in 1739 to answer to charges that he was encouraging Cheraw discontent. He denied responsibility for "any misunderstanding between the Welch and Indians or Virginians etc" (Meriwether 1974:93). Thompson profited from his former relationship with the Cheraw, who he claimed sold him "all the lands of these Indians on the river including about forty old fields." The government paid him for his efforts with both money and land. For a long time the Welch Tract had an unsavory reputation of being "plagued by horse thieves" (Meriwether 1974:95). "Outlaws and fugitives from the colonies of Virginia and North Carolina," most of whom were "Mullatoes or of a mixed blood," people complained, lived there untaxed and free of quit rents. These "pests and nuisances" refused to obey the laws. Some Welch settlers wanted them driven out but as they "were part of the band of robbers sought by the Virginia government" many had sympathy from their neighbors (Meriwether 1974:95). This untamed region remained outside of governmental control throughout the 1740s. The old allies of the Waccamaw, the Cheraw and Pedee Indians, as well as outlaws and mixed bloods, all found some refuge in "the Cheraws," as the settlers called the area.

Another neighbor to the Waccamaw, the Wateree Indians, appear in trouble with the colonial government on February 25, 1737, when the Journal of the Commons House of Assembly recorded "murders at Pine Tree Creek" and "insults on the frontiers of Craven County" (Easterby et al. 1951–1953:1951:482). Craven County, one of three proprietary counties laid out in 1682, stretched just to the north of Berkeley County to Winyah Bay, the former home of the Wateree and Waccamaw. Since the Wateree town was located on the periphery of the Catawba Nation, the angry South Carolina government sent a strong message to the Catawba "king" to act against the guilty parties. The "Charraws" and the Wateree were both cited for disrupting the lives of the settlers. Problems with white settlers were to be handled by the white government of the colony, not by the Indians themselves. To ensure a peaceful and safe border between the settlements and the Nation, a six-man patrol of Rangers was organized. The governor also warned the Catawba that the efforts it was making on the Catawba's behalf to pursue peace with the Seneca could be withdrawn if they refused to cooperate on these matters.

The Wateree Indians were angry about the approach of settlers onto their lands along the Wateree River. Thomas Brown, an Indian trader of the Congarees, purchased land around Wateree Neck from the Wateree Indians in 1736. These lands between the Santee and Wateree Rivers were inhabited and possessed by the Wateree Indians when he bought them. The government refused to recognize his claim but the damage was done because settlers were moving into the Wateree Indian homelands. The government received a "petition" from people of the "frontier of Craven County" that set forth "many instances of the late flagrant and insolent behavior of the Wateree Indians" (Easterby et al. 1951–1953:1951:477). In 1740, the Wateree Indians sent word to the government of their dissatisfaction through Colonel Fox, who described the "uneasiness of the Wateree Indians, who claim the land in and about Wateree Township, and insist upon satisfaction" (Easterby et al. 1951–1953:1951:410). Cox recommended that the chief men be brought to Charleston and offered gifts. The Wateree Indians visited Charleston in 1742, where it was required that they be supplied with provisions and fed during their stay (Easterby et al. 1951–1953:1953:315, 343). The custom of welcoming the Indian leaders to Charleston continued even after the small tribes moved up to the Catawba Nation. Catawba and Cheraw Indian chiefs came to Charleston in 1739, where they "expect[ed] on their arrival to meet with the usual reception and entertainment" (Easterby et al. 1951–1953:1951:716). Clearly, despite having moved nearer to the Catawba Nation, the Waccamaw, Wateree, and Cheraw leaders continued to speak for their people independently of the Catawba king.

While the Waccamaw, Wateree, and Cheraw were coping with encroaching settlers of the "middle country," the Cape Fear Indians were drifting back and forth along the outskirts of the settlements looking for a secure place to settle themselves. Temporary retreats into the settlements were broken up with forays back toward the Black River and possibly to the Cape Fear River region. By the 1730s we find two conflicting accounts of the whereabouts of the Cape Fear Indians. Hugh Meredith, a visitor to the Lower Cape Fear, gives the first in the autumn of 1730:

> There is not an Indian to be seen in this place the Senekas (who have always lived in amity with the English) with their tributaries the Susquahannah and Tuscarora Indians having almost destroyed those called Cape Fear Indians, and the small remains of them abide among the thickest of the South Carolina inhabitants, not daring to appear near the out settlements, for the very name of a Seneka is terrible to them, as indeed it is to most of these southern Indians.

It appears that in 1734 neither the Cape Fear Indians nor the Waccamaw were completely gone from the area. The following is an account given by an unknown traveler making a trip to South Carolina and part of North Carolina in 1734 (Sprunt 1992:43). In his description of Lake Waccamaw he says:

> There is an old Indian field to be seen, which shows it was formerly inhabited by them, but I believe not within these fifty years, for there is scarce one of the Cape Fear Indians, or the Waccamaws, that can give any account of it.

There is the distinct possibility that one or both of these groups remained in the vicinity of Lake Waccamaw in 1734. Unfortunately, the unidentified traveler does not tell us whether he talked to Waccamaw and Cape Fear Indians he met in the vicinity of Lake Waccamaw or back down closer to Winyah Bay and the settlements. Yet, they appear to have maintained "their separate existence within the English settlements . . . [and were] last noticed in 1751 as one of the small friendly tribes with whom the South Carolina government desired to be at peace with the Iroquois" (Mooney 1894:67).

What is remarkable about this is that the Cape Fear Indians continued to be a recognizable group—their enemies and their friends knew who they were and where they were located. When the government took an Indian tribe under its protection, it often remained free to travel within the settlements and beyond. Sometimes, however, the whites objected to this wandering. In May 1749, as reported in the Journal of the Council, the Cape Fear Indians received provisions, ammunition, and powder from the government, which recognized that "the Indians commonly called the Cape Fear Indians are abused and drove from their hunting ground by some White People living in those Quarters, and whereas the said Indians are under the protection of this Government, these are therefore strictly to charge and require all Persons whomsoever not to disturb or molest the said Indians or any other, but as they are a peaceable and inoffensive People under the Protection of this Government to allow them freely and without Molestation or interruption to hunt as Heretofore" (Milling 1969:226). Since the white settlers wanted to inhabit the lands of the Cape Fear and of other Siouans, they pushed them to their limits, isolating them with several Pedee Indians in what later became the parishes of St. Stephen and St. John.

After 1751, the Cape Fear Indians had several options before them. First, they could relocate somewhere less populated than the white settlements in Craven County. Their white neighbors certainly were in favor of this inasmuch as the settlers' encroachments were "driving them out of their hunting grounds." The fact that they had "hunting grounds" in 1751 indicates that they were still a recognizable entity. They also had recognized leaders in "King Johnny" and "Prince." King Johnny and Prince evidently represented two different peoples, one the Pedee and the other the Cape Fear. Conflict between these two "leaders" erupted when South Carolina Governor Lyttleton gave "Prince" a "commission of Captain General and Commander-in-Chief of the two tribes, which superseded Johnny" (Ramsay 1959:292). King Johnny protested Prince's promotion to leader by Lyttleton, coming to blows over it: "Some shots were exchanged but not mischief done." Friendly relations between the Pedee and the Cape Fear ended after this incident.

Second, they could make their claim to land as individuals, as many people already were doing. A deed for Abraham Freeman, dated December 14, 1750, shows that 150 acres of land in Craven County and the Welch Tract were reserved for him. These lands lay on the southwest side of the Pee Dee River, "between Hurricane and Flat Creeks: bounding on all sides upon vacant lands" (Meriwether 1974:112). Abraham Freeman's descendants are listed as Indian in the 1910 and 1920 federal censuses of Bladen and Columbus Counties, North Carolina, where they form the heart of the contemporary Waccamaw Siouan tribe. When and how did Indians learn the importance of land ownership by deed?

The Cape Fear Indians, including the Waccamaw, adapted to the colonial frontier. Europeans offered guns, ammunition, clothing, tools, and ideas to the Indians. Private property was not an indigenous concept but neither was the use of guns. Traders likely taught the Indians about property, its value and its worth as a saleable item. As the above examples of the Cheraw and Wateree land sales to traders show, the Indians sold land but never completely abandoned their own concepts of land. Deeded lands, especially lands near those of other tribal members, may have become a strategy to preserve the Indian community for future generations. Claiming land as individuals like the settlers allowed the Indians to secure a legal foothold in their old homelands.

After 1751, the Cape Fear Indians became a Friendly Tribe or Settlement Indians in the eyes of the colonists. The Waccamaw may have had the same status, but the English do not list their name in records of this kind of Indian. These Friendly Indians could earn money as Rangers in the militia. Governor Glenn recommended that the "Troop of Rangers" include the captain, the lieutenant, fifteen men, and "five Indians from the settlements" (McDowell 1992a:42–43). The Indian Rangers were paid less than the white Rangers, but like them, the security of the settlements was in their hands. The Rangers protected an area described as "the Congrees or Saludy to 96,[1] betwixt the Congrees and the Catawbas" (McDowell 1992a:42). They patrolled the area, "punishing or capturing hostile Indians, especially the Northward Indians." The Rangers knew that the Cherokee, then English allies, and other Friendly Indians had permission to pass through the area. The participation of Friendly Indians in the Rangers was necessary to the defense of the expanding settlements and Indian trade. In May 1751, in case of war with the Cherokee, the militia reported the need for a "regiment of 650 whites and officers, 100 Catawba, 60 lower Chickasaws, and 40 neighboring Indians" (Olsberg 1974:447).

Settlement Indians were treated the same as the larger autonomous tribes like the Catawba and Cherokee in peace negotiations. At the Albany Conference of 1751, William Bull tried to arrange a peace with the Six Nations of Iroquois Indians (Northern Indians), the Catawba, and "the Friendly small nations in the settlements," who are not mentioned by name. Bull pointed out to the Six Nations that "the bright chain" that held the En-

---

1. The designation "96" marked a point along the trading path that estimated the number of miles it took to reach Keowee, the nearest Cherokee town (Meriwether 1974:118).

glish and the Six Nations together also included the other Indian allies of the English. If such a friendly chain of Indians could be forged, one that linked the Northward Indians to the Southward Indians and all the other small Friendly Indians living within or near the settlements, then the colonists would live in a more secure environment (Gregg 1967:13; McDowell 1992a:106). As part of the peace agreement, captives had to be returned, including those taken from the Settlement Indians (McDowell 1992a:99).

Between 1751 and 1753, the Friendly Indians lost many people in raids on them by the Northward Indians. Even the Cherokee who were English allies in 1751 joined in these raids with the Indian allies of the French. With Cherokee assistance, the French Indian allies attacked the Catawba and then went "through our very settlements to attack and destroy those our friends and allies wherever they found them" (McDowell 1992b:158). Governor Glenn of South Carolina described the Friendly Indians as helpless victims, "a quiet and inoffensive people who are at war with no nation whatever" (McDowell 1992b:190). He protected and controlled the Friendly Indians in order to secure the frontier. For example, Glenn did not encourage an alliance between the Cherokee and Friendly Indians that he did not approve ahead of time (McDowell 1992b:191).

The Cape Fear Indians, like other Settlement Indians, were trapped in a web of dependence on the English colonists by 1751. Fear of raids kept them nearby since they were "greatly harassed and driven by the enemies from one place to another, insomuch that they cannot plant, or even go hunting to procure a subsistence" (Olsberg 1974:510–511). Recognizing this, the colonists gave each tribe "a bushel of corn per month" for six months, to prevent them from starving or stealing food from the settlers who moved daily onto former Indian lands. William Bull received compensation for supplying corn to the "Pedees and Cape Fears, two tribes of neighboring Indians" in January 1752 (Lipscomb and Olsberg 1977:49). This support kept the Friendly Indians in the settlements, where they could be useful to the colonists.

Raids by the Northern Indians continued in 1752 and 1753, despite Governor Glenn's peace efforts. The Savannah were accused of capturing Friendly Indians described as "a people who make war with nobody" (McDowell 1992c:443). Yet despite this peaceful image, Friendly or Settlement Indians were encouraged to hunt down guilty Northern Indians who committed murder and took captives. And when the Catawba needed reinforcements and allies, they asked Governor Glenn to let the "great many Pedee living in the settlements" come to "live like brothers" with them. Taking an interesting line of argument, the Catawba king argued that the Pedee would be safer living with them now that the Northern Indians were at peace (McDowell 1992b:367). However, in case war broke out again, the Catawba needed help in order to face the powerful Cherokee Nation living to their north (Saunders and Clark 1887:5:32). By this time, the small tribes of Friendly Indians, some of whom lived in the peripheral towns of the Catawba Nation in 1726, offered more relief than the Indians of North Carolina. There were probably only a handful of "Tuskeruro Indians 100 men and 201 women and children in all 301" in Bertie County, leaving few potential Indian allies for the Catawba or anyone else. This sharp decline in the North Carolina Indian population began years before with the diseases, slave trade, and colonial wars that ravaged the area (Oakley 1996:76–79). The Tuscarora War (1711–1712) alone accounted for some seven hundred Indian deaths. The slave trade in Indian war captives fueled the intertribal wars and drove the emerging capitalist economy of the settlements. By 1750, the Tuscarora, once a large nation with many warriors, was the lone survivor to be counted in the census of the Indian population living in North Carolina. Much reduced in size, the Tuscarora no longer posed any threat to the colonists nor offered hope to the beleaguered Catawba who were searching for Indian allies.

Once there were many coastal and piedmont tribes from the Siouan, Algonquian, and Iroquoian language families; by 1750, most had been uprooted, relocated, or hidden from view of the census takers. Settlement Indians adapted to colonial ways in dress, habit, and adoption of English surnames. Generations later their descendants lived from the old borderland areas ranging from Charleston, South Carolina, to Wilmington, North Carolina, in rural, swampy regions. Hidden from view as "people of color," their isolation allowed them to survive the Indian Removal of 1830 and persist in Indian communities that would emerge again in the late nineteenth century.

3
"From the Time of the Indians until 1920"

In Wilmington, North Carolina, the story of the Siouans and other coastal tribes was retold in the great Pageant of the Lower Cape Fear. Indian history was condensed into a single episode, entitled "Springtime Gathering of the Indians, 1663." The date of 1663 defines European contact and settlement as the salient moment of Indian history. As the pageant unfolds, time marches on, new people settle the Cape Fear region, and the Indians disappear into the past. Still, the pageant organizers wanted to be accurate and authentic in their representation of the Indian episode.

The Pageant of the Lower Cape Fear offers an opportunity to explore the nineteenth- and twentieth-century white view of Indians. The dialogues and narratives about Indians shape the very nature of Indian identity in the Southeast. This chapter looks closely at the state of knowledge about the Indians and explores how that knowledge was used to tell the story of the Siouan Indians of the Cape Fear region. The pageant's authors relied heavily on the most highly respected anthropological and historical sources of their time. These sources came from authors working at the Bureau of American Ethnology of the Smithsonian Institution, the University of North Carolina, and other respected institutions of higher learning. Such prestigious places lent credibility to the story being told of the Indians of the Lower Cape Fear. The story of the pageant begins in 1920 as the Wilmington community prepared itself for the great effort it would take to mobilize support for the pageant. I shall review the community effort and the search for authenticity. Then I shall look at the details of the Springtime Gathering episode, examine the anthropological and historical sources used to support it, and follow the rationale for the use of tribal names, from Cape Fear Indian to Croatan to Cherokee. The narratives and dialogues about tribal movements and origins have practical importance. The stage was set for answering the question "Who is an Indian?" in the southeastern United States by 1920.

On May 6, 1920, a Wilmington newspaper reported that "Dr. Koch [is] coming here next week" to speak in support of giving a "pageant of the Lower Cape Fear in a dramatic presentation of the history of our vicinity from the time of the Indians until 1920" (*Morning Star* 1920a). Dr. Frederick H. Koch, professor of dramatic literature at the University of North Carolina since 1918, was well known for his work with the Carolina Playmakers, "a group of students who write and produce their own plays." Working with the Literary Department of the North Carolina (Wilmington) Sorosis Club, Koch inspired and guided the efforts of the members of this women's club to create a great dramatic event. The Pageant of the Lower Cape Fear divided the history into four major topics: "(1) the Early Inhabitants, Settlers and Adventurers, (2) Colonial and Revolutionary Wilmington, (3) Confederate Wilmington, (4) the Present and Future Wilmington." Complete with scenery, costumes, and music, the pageant offered a colorful rendition of the history of the region. According to the May newspaper report, Dr. Koch was in town to read the entire manuscript before the Wilmington Chamber of Commerce "and urge that they take upon themselves the production." Supporting the effort, the news story continued, "If the men seize the opportunity we shall realize indeed that very wonderful conception of drama 'of the people, by the people, and for the people.' And Wilmington and our Sorosis will have the distinction of being the state pioneers in community drama." Their efforts paid off when the Chamber of Commerce voted to support the pageant project on May 11, 1920 (*Morning Star* 1920a).

In promoting the Pageant of the Lower Cape Fear, Koch proclaimed this to be "the first play ever written that prophesies a vision of Wilmington and America in the future." The Wilmington pageant would serve as an example to all of America, which in Koch's view was ready for pageants because of "a spirit of restlessness" typical of Americans "who are seeking expression." Linking the urge to present pageants to the "spread of Bolshevism," Koch was quoted as saying that "Bolshevism is caused by a lack of means of expression and that sort of ferment is the basis of great work." The theater, he said, "has always been the instrument of the people for the expression of thoughts and desires." The pageant movement springs from a "desire of the American people to express themselves en masse democratic, and it is the song of America for which they are preparing" (*Wilmington Dispatch* 1921b).

Being new to North Carolina, Koch was impressed by the "remarkable ground-soil for pageantry" afforded by the rich history of North Carolina, an "untouched store of brave tradition—legends" (Koch 1921:7). Plays of

Figure 3.1. Corps of "trumpeters" heralds the Pageant of the Lower Cape Fear, 1921 (North Carolina Collection, University of North Carolina Library at Chapel Hill)

the people, as Koch saw it, were "folk plays," as in the German concept of "volk" or the common people (Seldon 1988). As such, folk plays drew inspiration from the "legends, superstitions, customs, environmental differences, and the vernacular of the common people." The Pageant of the Lower Cape Fear, written as it was by a group of citizens of Wilmington, members of the North Carolina Sorosis, qualified as a "genuinely communal drama," in Koch's (1921:8) view. A "genuinely communal drama" required the collaboration of many people. This group effort contributed to community spirit and "should have a widespread effect in enlarging the horizons of dramatic literature by stimulating the people en masse—not simply as participating actors in the pageant, but also as joint authors." Once the Wilmington Chamber of Commerce gave its support to the pageant on May 11, 1920, the people of Wilmington spent the next several months marshaling the needed woman and manpower for the production.

The authors wanted their pageant to be "authentic," so they turned to historical and anthropological sources. Authenticity required that "the characters will be persons actually associated with that development and many present citizens of the district will see the characters of their ancestors depicted and ancestral deeds re-enacted during the course of the pageant"

(*Wilmington Dispatch* 1921a). Thus, participation by Indians and "colored people" was essential to authenticity.

To ensure that the pageant be truly educational, the planning committee included "authentic" Cherokee Indians, music, and dance to represent the "Red Man." To sing the spirituals in the "Plantation Wedding" scene, the Colored Spiritual Singers of "the older colored people" were especially recruited because it was thought that only they, those people "remaining of the last generation," could "sing these peculiarly American folk songs in the way they should be sung" (*Wilmington Dispatch* 1921d). Since Indians and "colored people" were to participate in the pageant, the planners made sure that the "colored people of the city" could watch the pageant at the amphitheater, where a section was reserved for them (*Wilmington Dispatch* 1921f).

The Wilmington pageant was to be of particular interest because "some of the descendants of characters appearing would take part, and . . . the Indians from Cherokee island would be seen." Koch viewed the participation of the Cherokee in the episode of the Cape Fear Indians as essential to the reality of the scene as was the presence of the "daring little blockade runner, *Lilian,* a replica of the original" to the episode on blockade running (Koch 1921:9). Without such props, the pageant would appear far less authentic.

The title of episode one was "Springtime Gathering of the Indians, 1663." The major characters were Watcoosa,[1] Chief of the Cape Fear Indians; Mahaiwee, Watcoosa's daughter; Leelinaw, another daughter; Wahgegwanee, a scout and interpreter; and other Indians of various tribes who had come to Crane Island in the Cape Fear River for the Springtime Feast. Rehearsals began in May for the June presentation and drew considerable attention (*Wilmington Dispatch* 1921c): "Last night those who will take part in the Indian episode of the pageant assembled for rehearsal and splendid progress was made. The Indian episode will be the key to the situation and will be one of the most picturesque as well as interesting parts of the great event. It will be decidedly historic for the people of the Cape Fear section." The Indian episode included "over a score of mighty chiefs from Cherokee and Eyota tribes of Red Men of the city." Supposedly authentic music and dance was chosen for Springtime Gathering: the "Sun Dance" was "genuine Cherokee music, having been transcribed by Lily Strickland." Characteristic Indian music also featured a "Scalp Dance." The cast included "Indians and squaws," according to the *Wilmington Dispatch,* "warriors and children,

---

1. The pageant authors used "Watcoosa" in place of "Wattcoosa," which appeared in accounts of Hilton's voyages (see Chapter 1).

Figure 3.2. Scene from pageant showing Indians seated to extreme right (North Carolina Collection, University of North Carolina Library at Chapel Hill)

and the medicine man." The famous chief Watcoosa was portrayed by Lacy Hunt, and the "band" eventually included thirty Indian girls, thirteen Indian boys, ten Indian "squaws," and "Representatives of the Red Men" as the Indian men.

The "Springtime Gathering of the Indians, 1663" celebrated the transfer of land from the Cape Fear Indians to William Hilton of Barbados. "The Indians are gathering for their great Spring Festival," explained the program notes (Koch 1921:27). "The squaws are making yopon tea, and cooking fish and game which the men bring in" when they are interrupted by a "brave" crying out "Watcoosa, Chief Watcoosa" (Koch 1921:27). Watcoosa, seated in a place of honor surrounded by his two lovely daughters, has just delivered a brief speech to the gathered crowd. In Cherokee and then in English, the Chief says, "My children, the long winter is over, and the Spring Festival is at hand. Manitou has blessed us. The Cape Fear Indians, the mighty tribe of the Sapona, give welcome to you all, and ask that you will help them celebrate with dance and feasting the coming in of Spring. Let the dance begin" (Koch 1921:28).

We know that Koch's intention was to be true to historical and ethnological knowledge in the first episode. What was the state of knowledge about the Indians of the Cape Fear in 1921? How did anthropology and history underlie the community's interpretation of the 1663 events? Where did this interpretation put the contemporary Indians of the Cape Fear, who might very well have been watching from the section reserved for the "colored people" of the area?

The pageant's authors in the Literary Department of the North Carolina Sorosis Club drew heavily upon the historical publication *Chronicles of the Cape Fear River*, by Dr. James Sprunt (1992), a Wilmington resident and renowned historian, as well as on other standard historical works. The most notable of these were publications by Samuel A'Court Ashe, "one of the state's foremost scholars and historians," who was a close friend of James Sprunt; the archaeologist David I. Bushnell; and the noted ethnologist James Mooney. Both Bushnell and Mooney worked for the Bureau of American Ethnology of the Smithsonian Institution. A pageant notation credited Ashe with identifying the Cape Fear Indians as "Congarees, a branch of the Old Cheraws," and James Mooney (and Fred A. Olds, a journalist from Raleigh) as saying, "they are probably Siouan" (Koch 1921:27). Sprunt's (1992:14–15) own *Chronicles* relied on the authority of Ashe and other noted experts, too. Their work inspired the setting for episode one, Springtime Gathering, and when a group of these "Distinguished Men" (*Wilmington Dispatch* 1921e), including Ashe, Sprunt, and Koch, came to town to view the pageant, they saw their own theories and ideas presented through the dialogue and staging. We begin with the setting first.

Sprunt, as editor of the *Chronicles,* compiled a series of articles on the history of the Lower Cape Fear that included selections by Ashe, Bushnell, and George Davis. The volume was published first in 1916 and won praise from Sprunt's friend Samuel A'Court Ashe, who expressed his appreciation in a preface written for the second edition. He wrote, "the reception of the Cape Fear Chronicles, not only by friends of the author but by the general reader, and in particular by historical scholars, has been most unusual" (Sprunt 1992:v). The work of Sprunt was so highly thought of that the University of North Carolina conferred upon him the degree of doctor of laws. Thus, quite understandably, the authors of the pageant readily accepted the views of Sprunt and his associates on the Cape Fear Indian and based their first episode on its authority.

The historical context for "Springtime Gathering of the Indians, 1663" came from Sprunt's endorsement of the work of George Davis, whose paper on the exploration and settlement of the Cape Fear was included in the *Chronicles.* Originally published in the *South Atlantic Magazine* in January 1879, Davis's paper spoke authoritatively about the Indians of the Cape Fear. Although he acknowledged that "the tribal identity of the Cape Fear

Indians has never been firmly established," he put great faith in the "tradition, generally known to older inhabitants," that the "Indians from the back country came regularly in the early springtime to the coast of the Cape Fear" (Sprunt 1992:14). These "springtime gatherings" brought Indians to the coast to collect fish and oysters and for "copious drinking of a strong decoction of yopon leaves, which produced free vomiting and purgation" (Sprunt 1992:15). Quoting "Dr. Curtis, an eminent botanist of North Carolina," Davis stated that "Yopon I. Cassine, Linn" grows along the coast and is the plant basis of the "famous Black Drink of the Southern Indians." The preparation of the Black Drink drew large numbers of Indians to the coast, where "they made a fire on the ground, and putting a great kettle of water on it, they threw in a large quantity of these leaves, and sitting around the fire, from a large bowl holding about a pint, they began drinking large draughts, which in a short time caused them to vomit easily and freely" (Sprunt 1992:15). The drinking and feasting lasted several days "until they had sufficiently cleansed themselves, and then everyone taking a bundle of leaves, they all retired to their habitations" (Sprunt 1992:15).

The Springtime Gathering episode alludes to the natural attractions of the coastal environment—fish, oysters, clams, and the plant ingredients for the Black Drink. These natural attractions brought Indians to the region— but just who the Indians were remained a mystery. Two scientists from the Bureau of American Ethnology offered opinions upon which the authors of the pageant were heavily dependent. Archaeologist David I. Bushnell's paper "The Archaeology of New Hanover County," published in Sprunt's *Chronicles,* followed the opinion of his bureau colleague James Mooney when it concluded that the historic tribes of North Carolina—the "Woccon, Saxapahaw, Cape Fear and Warrennuncock"—represented the Siouan language family (Sprunt 1992:16). Bushnell wrote that although the Cape Fear were "presumably Siouan," they "remain a mystery." Bushnell (in Sprunt 1992:16) notes, "The name was first bestowed by the early colonists, upon the Indians whom they found occupying lands about the mouth of the Cape Fear River, and more especially the peninsula now forming the southern part of New Hanover County." Bushnell left open the possibility that the term "'Cape Fear Indians' was applied to any Indians found in the vicinity, regardless of their tribal connections" (Sprunt 1992:16). In fact, Bushnell's archaeological survey of the region convinced him that it was something of a crossroads ethnically and linguistically. The natural resources of fish, oysters, clams, and the plant ingredients of the Black Drink attracted family groups to the sounds, coastal islands, and beaches. Bushnell found abundant evidence of their brief occupation where shells and pottery pieces intermingled. W. B. McKoy had studied pottery fragments recovered from the coastal Indian sites as early as 1878. Bushnell based his conclusions on

McKoy's descriptions of the variation in design and construction technique of pottery recovered from the area: "The designs are characteristic of pottery of the interior and farther south; other pieces are undoubtedly the work of southern Algonkian tribes." Indeed, "within a radius of about one hundred miles were tribes of Algonkian, Siouan, and Iroquoian stocks." The Cape Fear Indians sighted by William Hilton and led by Chief Watcoosa may have represented any one of the different groups. Bushnell thought that "small parties of the different tribes were ever moving from place to place, and it is within reason to suppose that members of the various tribes from time to time, visited the Cape Fear Peninsula; thus explaining the presence of a variety of pottery discovered among the shell-heaps on the shore of the sound" (Sprunt 1992:17). The Siouan theory, however, received strong support from James Mooney, Bushnell's colleague at the Bureau of American Ethnology, and Bushnell concurred with his conclusion.

Mooney's *The Siouan Tribes of the East* (1894) was the standard reference on Siouan peoples. When Mooney stated that "the Woccon were Siouan; the Saxapahaw and Cape Fear presumably were Siouan, as indicated from their associations and alliances with known Siouan tribes," people listened (Mooney 1894:65). Bushnell relied heavily on Mooney's interpretation of the Cape Fear Indians, as did the authors of the Springtime Gathering episode. The sequence of events described in the episode paralleled Mooney's own rendition of these happenings (Mooney 1894:65–66). According to Mooney, "the proper name of the Cape Fear is unknown." We have only the reference of the "early colonists to the tribe formerly living about the lower part of the Cape Fear." First contact occurred in 1661, "when a colony from New England made a settlement near the mouth of the river, but soon incurred the ill will of the Indians by seizing their children and sending them away, ostensibly to instruct them in the ways of civilization, but really as the Indians believed, with a semblance of probability, to make them slaves." This first encounter led to "a determined war against the colonists." The Cape Fear successfully drove these early settlers out of the region, keeping their cows and domestic animals. Two years later, "in 1663 another party from Barbados explored the river and its branches." Close to the mouth of the river, the colonists, led by Hilton, found, Mooney (1894:66) continues, "an Indian settlement called Necos, together with numerous fields of corn." The Indians traded corn for beads. Leaving behind these "friendly" Indians, "the Barbados party" under Hilton's leadership pushed on into the river and land of Cape Fear, where they met "Wat Coosa." The settlements around Wat Coosa were more numerous than the settlements around Necos. Hilton bought the land and river from Wat Coosa and soon after left the area. This purchase of land led in 1665 to another "colony settled at the mouth of Oldtown Creek, in Brunswick county on the southern side of the river, on a tract of land bought of the Indians, who still remained friendly" (Mooney 1894:66–67). The Siouan designation connected the Cape Fear Indians with their more southerly neighbors, among whom were tribes like the Cheraw.

Samuel A'Court Ashe identified the Cape Fear Indians as Congaree, whom he believed to be part of the Cheraw tribe (Koch 1921:27). Ashe's *History of North Carolina* (1908) shaped the views of the pageant committee as well as the view of his friend James Sprunt. No doubt, he and Sprunt conferred on the subject of the Cape Fear Indians many times. Ashe's (1908:1:72–73) account of the settlement of the Cape Fear differs very little from that of Mooney. Ashe is clear about the tribal identities of the North Carolina Indians, noting the "many different tribes of Indian, each having its own language" (Ashe 1908:1:85). The Algonquians and Iroquoians moved south from the Great Lakes, residing north of the Cape Fear, while the "southern" Indians "came from across the Mississippi River" and "extended into North Carolina." Ashe declared the Indians of the Cape Fear were the Congaree and a segment of the larger Cheraw tribe (Ashe 1908:1:86).

The Congaree link is stated in Ashe's contribution to Sprunt's *Chronicles,* which was entitled "Indians of the Lower Cape Fear" (Sprunt 1992:24–25). Ashe wrote that the Cape Fear Indians were "of Southern origin," clearly distinct from those residing along the Pamlico and Albemarle, who were of northern origin. The Cheraw were a large tribe, whose territory supposedly extended along the Santee and Pee Dee Rivers and their branches all the way to the Cape Fear. Ashe distinguished the "Old Cheraws" from the Yamassee, another large coastal tribe but one that lived much farther south along the coast of South Carolina, and concluded, "The Indians on the lower Cape Fear are said to have been Congarees, a branch of the Old Cheraws" (Sprunt 1992:25). The Congaree lived from north of the Waccamaw River to the Lower Cape Fear. In 1733 Governor Burrington of North Carolina wrote a letter concerning the North and South Carolina boundary, noting "some South Carolina grants had been located on the north side of the Waccamaw River, on land formerly occupied by the Congarees" (Sprunt 1992:25).

In coming to his conclusions, Ashe apparently relied upon the authority of the Right Reverend Alexander Gregg's *History of the Old Cheraws,* originally published in 1867. Gregg was the leading authority on the Cheraw in 1867. "Of the tribes which dwelt upon the Peedee and its tributaries," he wrote, "the Saras, or Saraws, as they were first called—afterwards Charrows, Charraws, and Cheraws—occupied the region still identified by the name: their territory extended thence to the coast, and along the coast to the Cape

Fear to the Peedee" (Gregg 1967:2). Gregg trusted Albert Gallatin's opinion on locating the boundaries of Old Cheraw territory up to the Cape Fear. Gallatin, in Gregg's view, was "one of the most eminent ethnologists of America." Gregg furthermore surmised that the Cheraw were related to the Cherokee. He theorized that the Cheraw became isolated from the main body of the Cherokee tribe sometime before European contact. This isolation was attributed to the encroachment of the aggressive, warlike Catawba, who invaded the territory, fought a bloody battle, won, and forever split the Cheraw from the Cherokee (Gregg 1967:3). Thus, scholars thought that the Cape Fear Indians were Congaree, a segment of the Cheraw who originated with the Cherokee.

Sorting out the tribal identities of the Cape Fear Indians offered a challenge even to James Mooney of the Bureau of American Ethnology. Mooney reviewed an enormous number of sources for his *The Siouan Tribes of the East* (1894). On the Congaree he wrote that they "lived on Santee and Congaree rivers, above and below the junction of the Wateree, in central South Carolina." In the eighteenth century, "Lawson found them in 1701, apparently on the northeastern bank of the river below the junction of the Wateree; but on a map of 1715 their village is indicated on the southern bank of the Congaree . . . about opposite the site of Columbia" (Mooney 1894:80). Mooney wrote that "nothing is known of their linguistic affinities, but their alliances and final incorporation were with the Catawba" (Mooney 1894:78). The Congaree were Siouan, like the Catawba.

The Cheraw or Sara were of Siouan stock, too (Mooney l894:53). Mooney hypothesized, "Their name is probably from the Catawba word *sara,* signifying a place of *tall grass or weeds."* The history of the Sara is known back to the Spanish period when in 1540 Hernando De Soto traveled through South Carolina (Mooney 1894:57). The Sara probably lived "in the piedmont region about the present line between South and North Carolina, southeast of Asheville, North Carolina." The Sara (Cheraw) were found in the same general area in 1670 when John Lederer arrived in their villages "near the mountains" (Mooney 1894:58) on his way to the Waxhaw and Catawba. Beyond the mountains to the north of the Sara lived the Rickohockan or Cherokee (Mooney 1894:58). In the eighteenth century, the Sara removed northward, ending up on the Dan River, perhaps to avoid the Spanish. Along the Dan River, they traded with the English of Virginia. Facing increasing attacks from the Iroquois, the Sara abandoned their homes along the Dan River and moved southeast to reside with the Keyauwee. Consolidating with other tribes like the Keyauwee and Eno gave the Sara some protection from enemy raiders. By 1715, Mooney wrote, "the Sara, now known as the Cheraw, were located on the Upper Peedee where it crosses from North Carolina into South Carolina" (Mooney 1894:60). The Cheraw lived in what became known as the "Cheraw District" of South Carolina, whose history was described by Gregg in 1867 (Gregg 1967). Unlike Gregg, Mooney made no mention of a Cape Fear Indian–Congaree–Cheraw connection other than to include them all in the Siouan language family (Mooney 1894). Presuming that they shared linguistic traits, they very likely shared cultural affinities as well.

Despite all the uncertainties about the tribal identity of the Cape Fear Indians, the pageant authors declared them to be Cherokee. The Springtime Gathering episode opens with Watcoosa speaking in Cherokee:

WATCOOSA

Daw tah dun ni?

What news have you?

WAHGEGWANEE

[*Pointing to the river.*]

A ni you neg gah!

The pale faces are coming!

[*The other Indians take up the cry of lamentation.*]

WATCOOSA

[*Rising with dignity.*]

Ches di Wahgegwanee. Watcoosa guest ya dah sky e hah. Oo nul stite dah di nel li. E gah lee ge sest di.

Peace, Wahgegwanee, peace my children. Watcoosa does not fear the pale faces. We will give them fish and furs and they will be our friends.

WAHGEGWANEE

[*Pointing to the river where a boat is seen nearing the shore.*]

Ni!

They are here!

. . .

WATCOOSA

E jen nah. Di g ne hest sti. E jalk kest sti. E g yu wi yah hi.

Go, each in order with his gifts, remember you are Cape Fear Indians [Koch 1921:29–30].

A program notation explains the use of Cherokee participants and Cherokee language. "Although it is thought that the Cape Fear Indians were perhaps Congarees, or possibly Siouan, the liberty has been taken of putting their conversations in the Cherokee dialect, and also using Cherokee customs" (Koch 1921:28). The pageant authors reasoned that "if the Congarees were a branch of the old Cheraws, and if the Indian tradition is true 'that before the coming of the Englishmen the principal body of that tribe, called Cheraw (or Chero-) kees, after a long fight with the Catawbas, removed to the mountains' (Ashe in Sprunt's *Chronicles of the Cape Fear River*, p. 25), we are not far wrong in choosing this dialect" (Koch 1921:28). They continued, "Another determining factor in our choice is that we have a Cherokee Indian Reservation in our State, and the Cherokees are the only large tribe now remaining in the State." George Allen Owl of Ravensford, Swain County, North Carolina, did the translation of the Indians' lines in the pageant from English into Cherokee. Owl was described as "one of a few of the Reservation Indians who can speak and write Cherokee" (Koch 1921:28). Owl may have been from the "remarkable Owl family—mixed bloods who, through their own initiative, acquired good educations and satisfying careers both on and off the reservation" (Finger 1991:69–79).

What the pageant notation does not explain is that the name Cherokee was at that time used by all of the Indians of North Carolina. So, the program notation that "the Cherokee are the only tribe now remaining in our state" is accurate but needs clarification. In 1921, there were two meanings of "Cherokee." First, there were those living on the Cherokee Reservation represented by George Allen Owl, the translator for the Springtime Gathering. Second, there were those living in the Cape Fear region, in Robeson County and several adjoining counties, who were formerly known as the Croatan Indians. The uncertainty over the Indians of the Cape Fear region goes back to the story of the Croatan Indians and the "lost colony," which began in 1885 when the state of North Carolina legally recognized the right of the Croatan to attend publicly funded schools for Indians. The authors of the Pageant of the Lower Cape Fear and those they depended upon for historical and ethnological authenticity, such as Frederick Koch, James Sprunt, Samuel A'Court Ashe, and James Mooney, all knew the history of the Croatan Indians and their recent designation as Cherokee.

Just eleven years after the state law provided schools for the Croatan Indians, James Sprunt published *Tales and Traditions of the Lower Cape Fear* (1896), a kind of forerunner to the popular *Chronicles of the Cape Fear River* (1992; originally published in 1916). He wrote that "the Croatans of this vicinity" were descendants of Sir Walter Raleigh's Lost Colony of 1584–1585. As Sprunt explained it, the survival of the "lost colony" depended upon their mixing with the "once powerful Hatteras tribe" (Sprunt 1896: 54–55). "The Hatteras tribe numbered about 3,000 warriors when Raleigh's expedition landed on Roanoke Island in 1584, and when the English made permanent settlements in that vicinity eighty years later, they were reduced to about fifteen bowmen. The Cape Fear Coree Indians told the English settlers of the Yeaman's colony in 1669 that their lost kindred of the Roanoke colony, including Virginia Dare, the first white child born in America, had been adopted by the once powerful Hatteras tribe and had become amalgamated with the children of the wilderness" (Sprunt 1896:55). From Hatteras, they eventually reached the Cape Fear region.

Sprunt, whose family owned Orton plantation, located along the Cape Fear River, probably knew that there were Croatan Indians living in the area. In 1892, the Columbus County Board of Education minutes noted the allocation of a small sum of money for their education (Columbus County 1885–1964:I:67). In *Tales,* Sprunt (1896) included an entry on the Cape Fear Indians, hinting at links to local Indians living in the region. He wrote, "It is an interesting fact that the descendants of these Indians [Cape Fear] live in the same locality to the present day, and illustrate an unusual condition—an amalgamation of white, black and Indian races." Despite this "unusual condition," he wrote, "the Indian characteristics, however, predominate." Sprunt appears acquainted with these characteristics when he says, "the men are thrifty, industrious and peaceable; engaged principally in fishing during the shad season, and in cattle-raising upon the same range that was occupied two hundred years ago by their savage ancestors" (Sprunt 1896:54).

Thus, from 1885 until 1911, the Indians of the Cape Fear region were called Croatan. North Carolina provided public schools for them based largely on the "lost colony" theory of their origins. On February 1, 1900, John D. Bellamy, representative from North Carolina to Congress, explained this theory when he spoke in support of an Indian appropriations bill that would give federal assistance to the Croatan Indians. Bellamy (1900:2–4) argued that "Indians of the United States are peculiarly the wards of the nation, and very justly they should be so regarded and so dealt with." This right should be extended to the "Croatans or Hatteras Indians, inhabiting the State of North Carolina about 60 miles from the seaboard, in the counties of Robeson, Scotland, Richmond, and Columbus." They live in "the settlement in Robeson County, where they chiefly reside, about 3,000 souls, and with scattered families in adjoining counties. The number may run to 2,000 men, making the tribe about 5,000 people." Who were they? Bellamy answered, "They, beyond cavil or doubt, are the descendants of the lost colony of Sir Walter Raleigh." Bellamy's confidence came from the authority of a pamphlet written in 1888 by Hamilton McMillan, who he described as "my old friend and preceptor." The "lost colony" theory explained the discovery in 1730 by white settlers of a very acculturated tribe of Indians. They found "located on the waters of the Lumber River a large tribe of Indians, speaking English, tilling the soil, owning slaves, and practicing many of the arts of civilized life. They occupied the country as far west as the Pee Dee but their principal seat was on the Lumber River, extending along that river for 20 miles" (McPherson 1915:48). By the nineteenth century, historians wrote convincingly about the "lost colony" (Hawks 1857:228). In 1891, Steven B. Weeks, a historian of North Carolina, thought the "theory of survival" as described by "Dr. William T. Harris, when United States Commissioner of Education," was "the greatest historical discovery of the nineteenth century" (McPherson 1915:58). The "lost colony" theory appeared on solid ground in the nineteenth and early twentieth century (McPherson 1915:59). The name Croatan was widely understood to mean the Indians currently living in the Cape Fear region. The majority of the Croatan lived "principally in Robeson County, North Carolina," but many "settled in counties adjoining in North and South Carolina" (McPherson 1915:39).

The *Handbook of American Indians North of Mexico,* considered the state of the art knowledge when it was published, included this theory in its description of the Croatan Indians of North Carolina (Hodge 1907:1:viii, 365). James Mooney wrote the description for the *Handbook,* which states that Croatan is "the legal designation in North Carolina for a people evidently of mixed Indian and white blood, found in various sections of the state, but chiefly in Robeson Co., and numbering approximately 5,000." Their designation as Croatan in 1885 gave them "a separate legal existence under the title 'Croatan Indians,' on the theory of descent from Raleigh's lost colony of Croatan." Mooney himself, however, found the "theory of descent from the lost colony as baseless, but the name itself serves as a convenient label for a people who combine in themselves the blood of wasted native tribes, the early colonists or forest rovers, the runaway slaves or other negroes, and probably also of stray seamen of the Latin races from coasting vessels in the West Indian or Brazilian trade." Mooney pointed out that "the physical features and complexion of the persons of mixed stock incline more to the Indian than to the white or negro." Despite his qualification of the theory, Mooney did not reject it entirely. In his entry on the Hatteras Indians, he commented, "they showed traces of white blood and claimed that some of their ancestors were white." He added that the Hatteras "may have been identical with the Croatan Indians (q.v.), with whom Raleigh colonists at Roanoke id. are supposed to have taken refuge" (Hodge 1907: 1:537). Thus, despite these doubts, the Croatan–Hatteras–"lost colony" theory made it into the prestigious *Handbook of American Indians North of Mexico.*

The "lost colony" theory endorsed the possibility that despite the initial race mixture between white colonists and Hatteras (Croatan) Indians (and, later, African Americans, Latinos, and pirates), a mixed-blood group might hold on to its Indian identity. The word *Croatan* appeared to be synonymous with the French Canadian word *metis*. *Metis* or "mixed" was a "term used by the French speaking population of the N.W. to designate persons of mixed white and Indian blood." According to James Mooney, regional differences existed, as his entry on the *metis* in the *Handbook of American Indians North of Mexico* explained. He wrote, "among the Spanish speaking population of the S.W. the word *mestizo,* of the same derivation, is used, but is applied more especially to those of half-white and half-Indian blood" (Hodge 1907:1:850). In addition, further south, in the Gulf states, "the term '*mustee*,' a corruption of *mestizo*," was used, and "In the W. the term 'half-breed' is loosely applied to all persons of mixed white and Indian blood, without regard to proportion of each" (Hodge 1907:1:850). This entry in the *Handbook* recognized racially mixed groups that might embrace one particular line of ancestry over the others. For the Croatan, this was its Indian heritage.

The Croatan found their lives subjected to restrictions and deprivations when North Carolina made changes in the state constitution in 1835. The right to vote was denied to people of color, free Negroes, free mulattos, and all free people of mixed blood, "descended from Negro ancestors to the fourth generation inclusive (though one ancestor of each generation may have been a white person)" (McPherson 1915:223). A few years later, in 1854, the general assembly revised the legal code of North Carolina to make it a crime to "knowingly issue any license for marriage between any free person of color and a white person" (McPherson 1915:223). The state voided all marriages "since the eighth day of January, eighteen hundred and thirty-nine, and all marriages between a white person and a free negro, or free person of color to the third generation." One effect of this was to prevent the mixed-blood children of a white person from being protected by the state inheritance laws. The 1868 constitution was further amended to ensure that not only was the vote restricted to whites but also to men who were literate and taxpayers (McPherson 1915:224).

By 1885 Croatan Indian schools were funded by the state of North Carolina. The school law created a legal middle ground for Croatan Indians separate from whites and African Americans. The "lost colony" theory acknowledged the Indian ancestry of the Croatan Indians. The 1885 law read, as "Croatan Indians," they "shall have separate schools for their children, school committees of their own race and color, and shall be allowed to select teachers of their own choice, subject to the same rules and regulations as are applicable to all teachers in the secondary school law" (McPherson 1915:225). The Croatans' special legal status was further protected by an act passed in 1887 to "prohibit marriages between an Indian and a negro and an Indian and a person of negro descent to the third generation" (McPherson 1915:227–228).

For twenty-six years (1885–1911), the Indians of the Cape Fear region were called Croatan. Croatan stood for Indian status, separate schools, and legal rights for almost eight thousand people living in Robeson and the surrounding counties. After 1911, some of the Croatan Indians legally changed their name to Cherokee Indians, a name they would keep until 1953 (Blu 1980; Sider 1993). Based on that name change and a request for federal status in 1914, the federal government looked into the matter (McPherson 1915:5). The Senate charged O. M. McPherson, Special Indian Agent, with finding out "what tribal rights, if any, they have with any band or tribe; whether there are any moneys due them, their present condition, their educational facilities, and such other facts as would enable Congress to determine whether the Government would be warranted in making suitable provision for their support and education" (McPherson 1915:32). In a word, the government wanted to know whether the Cherokee, formerly the Croatan, were eligible for federal tribal status. McPherson reported that the "Croatan Indians (designated Cherokee Indians of Robeson County by an act of the General Assembly of North Carolina ratified Mar. 11, 1913) comprise a body of mixed-blood people residing chiefly in Robeson County, N.C." There were "a few of the same class of people" spilling over into the surrounding counties—Bladen, Columbus, Cumberland, Scotland, and Hoke Counties in North Carolina and Sumter, Marlboro, and Dillon Counties in South Carolina. The census of 1890 noted the "North Carolina Indians," describing them as "generally white, showing the Indian mostly in actions and habits" (McPherson 1915:18). Furthermore, McPherson wrote, the "Handbook of American Indians, Bureau of American Ethnology, Bulletin No. 30" described them as "people evidently mixed Indian and white blood, found in various sections in the eastern part of North Carolina, but chiefly in Robeson County." By the census of 1910, the 6,278 Indians of North Carolina were distributed in the following counties: Bladen (36), Columbus (12), Cumberland (48), Scotland (74), Sampson (213), and Robeson (5,895).

Perhaps another two thousand Indians lived outside Robeson County, where the census enumerators likely overlooked them or counted them in other racial categories. The total was probably closer to eight thousand (McPherson 1915:8). Thus, at least eight thousand Indians lived in the Cape Fear region when the Pageant of the Lower Cape Fear was performed in 1921.

When the authors of the pageant chose to represent the Indians by using the Cherokee language, they reflected the current usage and meaning of Cherokee in North Carolina. The Cherokee designation held for forty-three years (1910 to 1953), influencing generations of Indians in North Carolina who sought a way to maintain their Indian identity in the face of shifting historical and anthropological opinion about their tribal origins. Thus, the people depicted in the Springtime Gathering episode of the 1921 Pageant of the Lower Cape Fear, written in both Cherokee and English and acted by local whites and possibly some Cherokee from Robeson County, depicted the Cape Fear Indians who many scholars believed to be Siouan-speaking peoples of the coastal plain.

4
Tribal Names as Survival Strategies
Croatan and Cherokee

It has long been noted that North American Indians have refused to disappear from American life. The modern Waccamaw Siouan Indians are no exception; they adopted political strategies in a conscious attempt to gain recognition and rights as American Indians. Anthropologist Nancy Lurie (1971:418) calls such political activity an emerging "articulatory movement" among American Indians. The word *articulate* means to "join with or to give expression to a cultural identity as a minority" and is the opposite of *assimilate* or "to be absorbed into the system, to disappear as a cultural minority" (Lerch 1988:76). The ancestors of the Waccamaw Siouan of North Carolina survived more than three hundred years of contact with Euro-American society and still kept a hold on their Indian identity in spite of strong pressures to assimilate. While outsiders focused primarily on "blood" and "racial" descriptions such as "mixed bloods," "tri-racial isolates," or "racial islands," they clung to their Indian heritage and identity and attempted to articulate with the dominant society. In this chapter, which begins in 1921 as the Pageant of the Lower Cape Fear was being staged in Wilmington, we will use Lurie's concept of articulatory relationships to understand the actions of Waccamaw Siouan Indian leaders. Resisting assimilation, the leaders asserted the Indian identity of their community and negotiated "informal contractual agreements with white-dominated government agencies controlling the distribution of public resources and services" (Lerch 1988:77). From the Waccamaw Siouan perspective, the basis of these articulatory relationships was to be recognition as an Indian community. In this chapter, we explore how separate schools were contested, the goals of Indian education, how different tribal names were adopted, and how relationships between Indian leaders and non-Indians centered on the issue of Indian identity. We learn a great deal about how the Waccamaw Siouan community was organized politically and socially by tracking their fight for separate Indian schools and a tribal name, first as Croatan and later as Cherokee. The definition of Indian (Croatan, Cherokee, Siouan) had to fit the current political views of the white community who held the reins of power over the Indians. The local racial definitions of "colored people" must be seen as part of the white society's expression of social control over minorities. Since the state of North Carolina, through its educational policy and county governing bodies set the standards for racial classification, this review of racial politics is very relevant to Indian identity.

What was the Waccamaw Siouan community like in 1921? To begin with, it was not called Waccamaw Siouan. Within the community, people referred to themselves as the "Wide Awake Indians" when speaking of their council. Outside the community when articulating with non-Indians, they used "Croatan" and, later, "Cherokee." In this chapter, "Croatan" is used to refer to the modern Waccamaw Siouan ancestral community when discussing their actions from 1921 until 1928. At that point, the community changed its name to the "Cherokee Indians of Columbus County." Thereafter in the chapter, "Cherokee" is used to conform to that period in their history. The modern tribal name of Waccamaw Siouan was not used until 1948.

In the early twentieth century, the Croatan Indian community (ancestral of the modern Waccamaw Siouan) centered in two small settlements bordering Columbus and Bladen Counties, about thirty-five miles outside of Wilmington and across the Cape Fear River. People lived on small farms, supplementing subsistence agriculture with fishing, hunting, and logging. Most inherited their land from family members who had secured a land base through private deeds in the eighteenth century (Lerch 1988:78). For example, Abraham Freeman, an early settler whose descendants lived in the 1920 Indian communities, established a land base along two small branches running north out of the Green Swamp, just above Lake Waccamaw, by 1787. Freeman and others appeared in the 1800 federal census as "all other free persons" rather than as white or slave. Over the years, marriage within the community preserved a core of people who lived together as Indians. From this group, they chose leaders who would speak for them in their dealings with the white society.

Those leaders or "men of age" formally organized as the "Wide Awake Indian Council" in 1910 (Lerch 1988:80). "Men of age" came from dominant family groups and served at the will of their relatives (Lerch 1988:79). Oral tradition describes these men as being willing to spend long hours in service to the community goals. Such men "exhibited 'good sense,' 'a nice personality,' and the ability to communicate and get along with insiders as well as outsiders." "Mother wit" rather than formal education served the community well. Domains of leadership, such as the economic, religious, and educational, drew upon different skills. Indian leaders had to work with non-Indians, getting them to "act as brokers or mediators for the Indian community. These might be lawyers, businessmen, government officials, anthropologists, and others" (Lerch 1988:79). The names of these "men of age" are found in the recorded minutes of the county Board of Education and county commissioners, in letters, and in legislative reports. Robert Jacobs, W. J. Freeman, D. J. Jacobs, and Sam Graham served as leaders in the fight for Indian schools.

In 1920, the Croatan ancestors of the Waccamaw Siouan lived in the rural areas of the Cape Fear region lying across the river from Wilmington, North Carolina. In that year, separate Indian schools brought the Indians to the Columbus County Board of Education with a petition. In January, the news that the Indian community and their committeeman Robert Jacobs had barred the admittance of a "colored" child at their community school came before the school board. The school board gave the Indians two choices: they could let the colored child in their school or they could find some other school for her to attend. This overt challenge to the school board over race was temporarily resolved, but the problem came up again later that fall (Columbus County 1885–1964:I:563).

That fall, the Indians defied the local racial categories and returned the school census with all eighty-one children listed as Indian, rather than colored, according to the report filed by W. J. Freeman, the new school committeeman. The Public School Law required a school census each year so the school board expected a census, but they did not expect or accept the listing of the children as Indian. Foreseeing this, and to ensure the legality of the document, W. J. Freeman had his signature "sworn and subscribed by A. F. Clark, Justice of the Peace" (Registrar of Deeds 1920). When Freeman returned the school census that fall, the school board had evidence of the self-identity of the community. A test of wills and a struggle over the power to define one's racial and social identity quickly took shape.

The following January, in 1921, the Indians continued boycotting the enrollment of non-Indians at their school. A strongly worded rebuke was sent through the Indian school committeemen to the community. The board minutes read, "the County Superintendent [will] be instructed to write W. J. Freeman, D. J. Jacobs, and Sam Graham, committee of District #2, *colored race,* Bolton Township, instructing them that they are violating the law in keeping any colored children from attending school in their district. The County Superintendent is further advised to inform said Committee that unless such colored children are allowed to attend school, that they will be subject to indictment" (Columbus County 1885–1964:I:594, emphasis mine).

Did the Indian school committee have the legal right to prevent "colored children" from entering their school? The answer was "yes" if they were legally an Indian school. The school board clearly disagreed, insisting on referring to their school as a "colored school" in all its official meetings.

In order to resolve the issue once and for all, the Indians hired Donald McRackan to provide legal counsel to the community. McRackan, born in 1866 and a resident of Whiteville, North Carolina, graduated from Wake Forest College and studied law in Greensboro. He served in the General Assembly in 1907 and the State Senate in 1915, where he had a long political career as a democrat (Conner 1915:206, 1917:436). McRackan's legal skills and political savvy made him a good choice because he was well acquainted with the legal status of "Croatan Indians" within the state. When the Indians' petition for Indian schools was turned down, McRackan contacted Dr. E. C. Brooks, State Superintendent of Public Schools, in April 1921 to discuss the issue. Attorney McRackan wrote, "We have residing in our county a class of people known as the *Croatan Indians* who inhabit one school district exclusively, with the exception of one colored child who is within school age. Of course there are white people living in the same district, but I mean there are no Negroes living therein except for the one above mentioned. These Indians are asking the County Board to provide a public school for their children in their district, but the County Board is not inclined to grant their request" (McRackan 1921, emphasis mine). Presumably, the use of the tribal name "Croatan" reflected the attorney's legal advice as well as the wishes of Robert Jacobs and the Wide Awake Indian Council. It was, in retrospect, a good articulation strategy successfully applied in Robeson County as early as 1885.

McRackan attempted to convince the county board that it was "their duty" under the Public School Law to provide these people with Indian schools. He argued, "It is the duty of the county board of education to provide public school facilities for the Indian children of the county in which such children may reside. The Indian children should be treated as white and negro children in the apportionment of the school funds of the county, and separate schools under the law, must be provided for them, if they are taxpayers and the Federal Government has provided no school or inadequate school facilities for them." McRackan believed the reason the school board refused to grant the Indians' request had to do with doubts about their "pure blooded" status. He wrote, "For some reason the board is opposed to granting their request and requires that these people prove to the satisfaction of the board that they are Indians" (McRackan 1921). McRackan continued, "I do not know what evidence that can be furnished the board stronger than for the people to appear before the Board and show from their personal appearance, which it seems to me is sufficient to satisfy any board that they are not negroes. They have good features, straight hair and red cheeks and do not bear any negro resemblance." In his opinion, the "construction of the school law makes it the duty of the board to grant this request." In appealing to Brooks, McRackan asked, "Can you advise me what I can do that will convince the Board of Education that it is their duty to give these people a separate public school." Cost was not really the issue. McRackan wrote, "This can be done without any additional cost to the County [as] it will not cost any more to run a public school composed entirely of Indians than to run a mixed school composed of Indians and Negroes." In fact, the Indians were ready to build the school themselves but "not withstanding this, the Board will not grant their request." McRackan generally had no quarrel with the all-white school board. He said, "We have a splendid County Board, but in this instance I must differ with them in their views." But the dichotomous racial categories of the board's majority defined the situation. Still hoping for the State Superintendent's support, he continued, "I will thank you to advise me in this connection as I am anxious to see these people have what they want, and I believe in this instance they are entitled to it."

McRackan appeared quite certain that his clients were being held to a higher standard than other Croatan Indians. He stated, "When our general assembly enacted a law providing for separate schools in the Counties of Richmond and Robeson we did not require any such proof as is now required by our County Board in this instance." On April 27, 1921, McRackan got word from Brooks referring the decision to the local people and the majority view on race. Brooks answered, "The law does not compel the county board of education to provide separate schools for the Indians of its county. Therefore, the matter is entirely in the hands of the county board of education as to whether it will provide separate schools for this class of people in your section of the County" (Brooks 1921). We have no evidence of McRackan's immediate reaction to this response. But McRackan's appeal focused on the heart of the issue—separate schools meant a separate social category, accorded respect and rights by the larger society. Recognition as "Croatan Indians" by local authorities was necessary to getting the State of North Carolina to provide Indian schools.

Once the "lost colony" theory established the Croatan Indians of North Carolina, their rights to separate Indian schools had soon followed. On February 10, 1885, the general assembly of North Carolina had enacted a law providing for separate schools for the Croatan Indians of North Carolina. The 1885 law applied only to the "Indians now living in Robeson County" (McPherson 1915:225–226). After 1887, Croatan Indians could not be married to African Americans. According to law, "all marriages between an Indian and a negro or between an Indian and a person of negro descent to the third generation, inclusive, shall be utterly void: Provided, This act shall only apply to the Croatan Indians" (McPherson 1915:226–227). A separate school law covered each population of Croatan Indians. For example, schools for the Croatan Indians in Richmond County were allowed by 1889.

It was widely known that Croatan Indians lived throughout the region. The eleventh census of the United States in 1890 for North Carolina had confirmed their presence outside of Robeson County, noting that beyond the 1,514 people counted as Cherokee Indians, there were another 174 Croatan Indians. They were defined as "a body of people residing chiefly in Robeson County" and who "show the Indian mostly in actions and habits" (McPherson 1915:33). Local officials generally conceded that there were more Croatans than counted since they blended somewhat with their neighbors and were easily undercounted. In 1890, Hamilton McMillan, the major proponent of the "lost colony" theory, wrote T. J. Morgan, Commissioner of Indian Affairs in Washington, saying, "The Croatan Tribe lives principally in Robeson County, North Carolina, though there are quite a number of them settled in counties adjoining North and South Carolina" (McPherson 1915:39). In 1907, the *Handbook of American Indians North of Mexico* noted that the Croatan lived in Robeson County and "various sections of the state" (Hodge 1907:365). Then, the census of 1910 found the "Indians of North Carolina" in Bladen, Columbus, Cumberland, Scotland, Sampson, and Robeson Counties. Finally, by February 14, 1913, it was generally known that there were between 1,500 and 2,000 Indians living outside of Robeson County in adjoining counties in North and South Carolina (McPherson 1915:8). So, by 1920–1921 it was well established that Indians resided outside of Robeson County. The real issue was the willingness of local authorities to not only acknowledge their presence but also separate them from African Americans in the public schools.

In 1921, McRackan argued that his Croatan clients from Columbus County seemed to be held to a higher standard of proof regarding their Indian ancestry than those previously designated Croatan in either Robeson County (1885) or Richmond County (1889) (McRackan 1921). Indian agent McPherson agreed, saying, "It should be noted that the act does not declare that they are Croatan Indians, merely designates or names them Croatans." He found that the "same class of people reside in Bladen, Columbus, Cumberland, Scotland, and Hoke Counties, N.C., and in Sumter, Marlboro, and Dillon Counties, S.C." (McPherson 1915:7). Unless legally required to provide Indian schools, local authorities classified the Croatan

Indians with the larger colored population, ignoring the self-identity of the Indians.

Just what were the duties of school committeemen in 1920–1921? After the local communities elected them, the Board of Education installed them and gave them detailed written instructions. For example, for the 1908–1909 school year, Superintendent F. T. Wooten prepared *A Pamphlet of Information,* which listed all the new committeemen and described their duties. The committeemen and teachers were instructed to "get a copy of the public school law, read it, and preserve it for reference" (Columbus County 1908–1909:5). The committeemen had "the care, custody, and control of all school houses, grounds and property." They hired and fired the teachers and prepared a census of the pupils for the superintendent. Since the schoolhouses were within the rural areas they served, these committeemen were charged with the daily operation of their schools. The conduct of Robert Jacobs, whose name appeared in Wooten's pamphlet for the years 1908–1909, thus fell within this description. The actions of W. J. Freeman, the census taker in September 1920, also fell within this description. Both were taking charge of their school. Did Freeman and the other committeemen act improperly as the school superintendent believed or were they exercising their rights as school committeemen and as Croatan Indians? The actions of the committee represent a clash of views with the county Board of Education over race.

In areas like Columbus County where the Indian population was relatively small compared with that of Robeson County, the little communities of Indians elected Indians to the school committees and assumed managerial control of their schools. Although these elections had to be approved by the county superintendent and Board of Education, none of which were elected by the Indians, Indians did run the local Indian schools. However, of course, it was the county superintendent and the Board of Education that imposed the "colored" label on the Indian schools. Thus, between 1885 and 1921 the actions of Robert Jacobs and the committee for his district clashed openly with the county Board of Education and superintendent over whose views of race would prevail.

When new school districts were formed in 1885, the white social categories simplified the complexities of race to "white," "colored," and "Croatan." This separation of the races was entrenched in the social and political history of North Carolina (Franklin 1943). The first group of fifteen Indian students to attend the Croatan Normal School had to be of unquestioned Indian ancestry by law: "all children of the negro race to the fourth generation" were prohibited (McPherson 1915:227). After 1913, the name "Cherokee" replaced "Croatan" for the Indians attending the normal school in Robeson County. Some time later, in 1928, the "Croatan" Indians in Columbus County adopted the Cherokee name, too.

The law did not protect the social separation of Indian schools in Columbus County. The Wide Awake Indian Council, through people like Robert Jacobs, W. J. Freeman, D. J. Jacobs, and Sam Graham, worked with non-Indians to carve out a place for themselves as Indian people. They often acted without legal backing, expelling "colored children" from their community schools. As Robert Jacobs knew, by 1922 the white school board did not recognize their right to do this. Rather than accept the opinion of the school authorities, the Indians closed the public school and moved their children into their Indian church for school. This move to the church was noted the following August, in 1923, in the school board minutes (Columbus County 1885–1964:II:226). Shortly thereafter, the Indians built their own school with their own funds (Columbus County 1885–1964:II:269). When the school board heard of this, they let the Indians know that "The law did not permit in this county but two systems of schools, the white and the colored." Later, a small amount of money was given to the Indians for their school but the social category imposed by the board of "colored" was not changed.

The law referred to most likely was the 1923 "act to amend the consolidated statues and to codify the laws relating to the public schools." It provided for the reorganizing of the North Carolina school system by providing for a "uniform system of public schools." In this reorganized system, white and colored children were to be educated in separate schools. Furthermore, the law stipulated that the "Croatan Indians now living in Robeson, Sampson, and Richmond counties, shall have separate schools for their children" (North Carolina 1923:5). This important law provided for public funding, regulated the length of the school term, and offered opportunities for vocational education and the completion of a standard course of study for adults. Since the law identified the Indians eligible for separate schools, it was important for individual Indians to be recognized as belonging to one of these named groups. The law elaborated, saying, "persons residing in Robeson and Richmond counties, supposed to be descendants of a friendly tribe once residing in the eastern portion of the State, known as Croatan Indians, and who have heretofore been known as 'Croatan Indians' or 'Indians of Robeson County,' and their descendants, shall be known and designated as the 'Cherokee Indians of Robeson County,' and the persons residing in Person County supposed to be descendants of a friendly tribe of Indians and White's Lost Colony, once residing in the eastern portion of this State, and known as 'Cubans,' and their descendants, shall be known and designated as the 'Indians of Person County.'" The 1923 law covered those

Indians previously established in Scotland County in 1909, Cumberland County in 1907, and Sampson County in 1917. The Indians had rights to "separate schools for their children, school committees of their own race and color," and the selection of teachers. The law segregated Indians from "all children of the Negro race to the fourth generation" (North Carolina 1923:15).

Despite this 1923 law, the Columbus County Board of Education decided on February 24, 1924, to reimburse "W. J. Freeman committeeman of district #2, colored" for construction expenses and "rent of church for school purposes [for] two years" (Columbus County 1885–1964:II:289). That same year, the school committeemen of district #2 returned their school census cards to the Board of Education listing their children as Indian. The Indians carried on their school business under the assumption that, as Indian people, they had a right to be treated as other Indian people in the state.

"Try, try again," as Karen Blu (1980) recognized, was a common political tactic of North Carolina's Indians. The Columbus County school board had made it clear they would never fund Indian schools unless required by law, so despite the reimbursements made in 1924, the Indian leaders Robert Jacobs, W. J. Freeman, and others returned to their former attorney, Donald McRackan of Whiteville, who was now a state senator representing the Tenth District comprising Bladen, Brunswick, Columbus, and Cumberland Counties. In January 1927, Senator McRackan drafted a bill "to provide separate schools for the Croatan Indians in Columbus County." This Croatan version of the bill passed with a favorable first reading and was referred to the Committee on Education. Then, a few weeks later, McRackan revised the bill, striking out the name "Croatan" and inserting "Cherokee," as was in keeping with the current policy on Indians in the state. "Croatan" had been legally dropped as a designation for Indians in 1911, being replaced by "Cherokee" in 1913. The second version of the bill, dated February 2, 1927, passed on its first reading and was also sent on to the Committee on Education.

Senator McRackan's drafts described the Indians as "persons residing in Columbus County supposed to be descendants of a friendly tribe once residing in the Eastern portion of North Carolina and in Robeson County." The text of Chapter 213, "An Act to Provide Separate Schools for the Cherokee Indians in Columbus County," differed very little from Senator McRackan's draft proposals. However, Section 1 added a full paragraph defining the territory within Columbus County where the Indians resided. This paragraph reads in full as follows:

Beginning at a point near East Arcadia and runs south to Atlantic Coast Line Railroad, then with the Atlantic Coast Line Railroad west to the White Marsh, then with the White Marsh to the White Hall road, then with White Hall road to the Bladen County line, then with the Bladen County line to the beginning point, near East Arcadia [North Carolina 1927:194–195].

The second version of the bill identified Robert Jacobs's community as follows: "[those people] heretofore ... known as Cherokee Indians of Columbus County and their descendants shall be known and designated as the Cherokee Indians of Columbus County North Carolina."

The bill followed the format of the original Croatan School Bill of 1885 and the more recent 1923 Public School Law. Like the earlier legislation, the 1927 bill established "separate schools for their children, [a] school committee of their own race and color, and [they] shall be allowed to select teachers of their own choice ... and there shall be excluded from such separate schools all children of the negro race to the fourth generation." The Board of Education of Columbus County had to carry out the provisions of the act, among which were a school census and establishment of school districts. The state treasurer was to ensure that proper funding was provided to the county based on the school census. The county, in consultation with the Indians, was to tax the Indians and their descendants in order to raise money to build schools. The tax lists had to reflect the Indian race of those in Columbus County Cherokee schools.

The first step in the process of setting up the Cherokee Indian schools was taxation. The authority to tax the Indians and their descendants fell to the county commissioners. Then, the Board of Education was to select and approve the list of qualified Indians. Census takers were to "determine on [the] census role the names of said children as belong to the Indian race." Finally, an approved list for taxation and school enrollment would be completed and the schools could open. The bill passed on February 26, 1927, and it looked like the Indians had won the argument over race.

On one level they did. Technically, Robert Jacobs, W. J. Freeman, and Attorney McRackan succeeded in getting the Indians designated as "Cherokee Indians of Columbus County." But the newly designated Cherokee faced great opposition from the commissioners and the Board of Education, who were charged with carrying out the bill's provisions. The first issue became the listing of the people as Indians in order to establish an Indian list for future funding of the Indian schools.

The taxman refused to comply with the law, preferring instead to list the

Cherokee of Columbus County as "colored under protest" rather than as Indian. The reason given was that "by listing in this manner it does not necessarily class them as Negroes and would also give them the privilege of producing records to substantiate their racial lineage, after which a satisfactory plan of listing could be agreed upon" (Columbus County 1926–1933 [1930]). This created a roadblock in getting the tax dollars earmarked for the Cherokee Indian schools. The same tactic was used in 1928 and 1929 by the commissioners to prevent the Cherokee Indians from being listed on the tax lists as Indian.

There had been so little progress made and so much opposition against setting up the Cherokee Indian schools that by June 6, 1927, the Cherokee Indian leaders in Robeson County, perhaps in consultation with Robert Jacobs and W. J. Freeman of the Cherokee Indians of Columbus County, contacted a Lumberton lawyer to start mandamus proceedings against the board, requiring them to comply with the law (Columbus County 1885–1964:III:80). A Lumberton newspaper, the *Robesonian,* carried a brief story on June 20, 1927, about the reaction in Columbus County to the recently passed law. It noted, "For some time an effort has been made to secure schools for Indians of Columbus County and as many of these migrated from Robeson County the Cherokee Indians of this County have interested themselves in the matter and employed Judge T. L. Johnson of Lumberton." Judge Johnson, an attorney with Johnson, Johnson & McLeod Law Offices in Lumberton, spoke to the county commissioners and school board where, the newspaper report continued, "there was considerable opposition to establishing separate schools for these people" (*Robesonian* 1927a). The school board minutes revealed the hostile reaction of the board, saying that Johnson had requested them to "put into effect immediately such machinery as would insure separate schools for these so-called Indians" (Columbus County 1885–1964:III:80). The minutes showed the school board responded by raising questions as to the legitimacy of the Indians' request and tried to convince Johnson that "there were probably no real Indians" in Columbus County. The *Robesonian* reported that an agreement was reached and progress made when Johnson and the board agreed to settle the matter by calling in a "specialist" from the Department of the Interior in Washington, D.C. This specialist would judge whether or not "these people are in reality Indians." Based on the specialist's opinion, the board would grant their request or Johnson would drop his defense of their claim (*Robesonian* 1927a).

The identity of the specialist was revealed in the *Raleigh News & Observer,* quoted in the *Robesonian* on Monday, June 20, 1927. Senator F. M. Simmons assisted in the effort to secure an ethnologist named Dr. J. Walter Fewkes, who then headed the Bureau of American Ethnology at the Smithsonian

Institution. Fewkes was reportedly engaged in some work in South Carolina, giving Simmons hope that "Dr. Fewkes may be able to conduct the investigation in Columbus County himself while he is in that territory."

T. L. Johnson wrote to Senator F. M. Simmons on June 13 seeking his assistance on behalf of the Cherokee Indians of Columbus County (Johnson 1927). Johnson noted that Simmons was "thoroughly familiar with the status of the Indians residing in Robeson County, formerly known as Croatan Indians and more recently designated by statute as Cherokee Indians." The Cherokee of Columbus County were described by Johnson as having "migrated to Columbus County" from Robeson County, making them part of the same body of people. Johnson described their racial status, saying, "Up to this time they have had no recognized racial status and the only separate schools they have had have been maintained by private subscription." Despite the recent passage of the 1927 Cherokee Indian School Bill, Johnson explained, "the County Board of Education has ignored the statute and refused to provide separate schools and a budget, taking the position that it was the duty of these Indians to establish their race identity by a judgment of the court as to each family." Johnson continued, "Of course, this position is absurd, because the statute itself is conclusive in its provisions." Johnson expressed another concern as well, writing, "the statute is somewhat crudely drawn and, in addition to this, I have some misgivings as to its constitutionality, if it is challenged in the courts as private legislation under the amendment of 1917." Perhaps Johnson was concerned about a test of constitutionality that might have wider implications, including a review of the schools for Cherokee Indians in Robeson County and other parts of the state. Whatever he was worried about, he decided, "In order to avoid litigation, I have proposed to the Board of Education that [to answer] the question as to whether these people were of the same type of Indians as those of Robeson County . . . an expert in ethnology be obtained, whose investigation and report be accepted by both sides as conclusive." This compromise protected the Robeson County Cherokee and offered Johnson a way out of the case if the expert ethnologist ruled against the Cherokee of Columbus County.

On receiving the letter from Johnson, Simmons wrote to Fewkes on June 16, 1927, asking for attention to a matter concerning "the racial identity of the Indians of Columbus County, North Carolina" (Simmons 1927a). He wrote that "Honorable T. L. Johnson, Lumberton, North Carolina," had described the situation, saying, "these Indians migrated to Columbus County from Robeson County some years ago; and . . . there now reside in one township as many as 1,000 to 1,200 of them." Simmons continued, "Establishment and maintenance of appropriate schools for the Indians seems to be contingent upon the settlement of a technical dispute that has arisen as to the racial identity of the Indians; and the parties in dispute have agreed, it is indicated, to abide by the result of an investigation and report by an expert ethnologist." Bureau of American Ethnology expert advice had previously assisted the Croatan of Robeson County, so Johnson's strategy of seeking their assistance held the possibility of success for the Cherokee Indians of Columbus County.

A prompt reply to Simmons's letter came on July 10, 1927, from A. Wetmore, acting secretary of the Bureau of American Ethnology (Wetmore 1927). Time, money, and legal issues stood in the way of bureau involvement in the case. Wetmore replied, "though the problem concerned is difficult it is possible for an expert physical anthropologist to determine in an individual the presence of Indian, white or Negro blood though the amount of such mixture, and the closeness of racial affinity is hard to ascertain, and [this] is to be attempted only by one with great skill in such matters." It would take six weeks or more to complete such a study on ten to twelve hundred people. Wetmore brought up the legality of the bureau's involvement, writing, "It is noted that the matter of identity of these persons is one of contention between the County Board of Education of Columbus County and the legislature authorities of the State of North Carolina, and, therefore, possibly a matter for legal action." Wetmore continued, "It has been the policy of the Smithsonian Institution to avoid participation in such disputes, except where the national government has been concerned." Finally, Wetmore concluded, "In view of this, of the length of time required for the study, and of the fact that our financial resources are limited, I regret that we are not at this time in a position to give definite assistance in the matter. We have at present no one whose services can be available for such a length of time as indicated." Wetmore did, however, recommend Dr. Ales Hrdlicka, of the staff of the National Museum, who had experience in this kind of investigation. The very next day, Simmons contacted Hrdlicka, "requesting his consideration and advices" (Simmons 1927b).

In 1927, Ales Hrdlicka was curator of the Division of Physical Anthropology at the United States National Museum in Washington, a post he had held since 1903. He was by then one of the world's most prominent anthropologists and instrumental in establishing the study of physical anthropology in North America. Wetmore recommended him not only because of his world-renowned stature but also because in 1915 he had "assessed the racial makeup of Chippewa people on the Leech Lake and White Earth reservations in Minnesota and studied Dakota Indians" for the Department of Justice (National Anthropological Archives, listing for Hrdlicka at http://www.nmnh.si.edu/naa/guides.htm, August 9, 2002). Hrdlicka's experience with a variety of peoples made him the best choice for the kind of study Johnson and Simmons seemed to want the Bureau of Ethnology to conduct. Hrdlicka, however, refused to get involved.

Hrdlicka and Simmons exchanged correspondence about the Cherokee Indians of Columbus County between July 11 and August 25, 1927 (Hrdlicka 1927). Hrdlicka wrote, "The whole matter to which the enclosed correspondence relates is not very clear. I am not positive just what is desired and how large the task may be." He recommended that the parties involved come to Washington and discuss the matter further. He continued, "It would be of general advantage if some authorized and capable representative of the parties concerned could either explain with all details what the conditions are and what is needed or wanted; or still better if he could come here, to Washington, where everything could be properly discussed. The writer of the accompanying letters has evidently but little idea of the work that may be involved, as well as the necessary expenses." Who would bear this expense? The Columbus County Board of Education certainly would not consider this their responsibility. The Cherokee Indians of Columbus County might refuse to bear the expense to bring an expert from Washington to rule on their racial status when they believed, quite rightly, that the 1927 Cherokee Indian School Bill already designated them Cherokee Indians. The law firm of T. L. Johnson would not pay for the cost. And it was unlikely that the Robeson County Cherokee would pay for the expense of a physical anthropologist. There is no record that Hrdlicka heard from any of the parties again or that he ever came to Columbus County to conduct such an extensive and time-consuming study as he believed this would be. Six months later, a cheaper solution was sought.

By December 5, 1927, the school board faced a mandamus order directing it to "give its reasons for not establishing separate schools for Indians" in Columbus County as it was required to do by the "act passed at the last session of the Legislature" (*Robesonian* 1927b). The Cherokee Indians of Columbus County, represented by T. L. Johnson, were described as "Cherokee who had migrated from Robeson County." The case seemed to hinge on the reported link to the Cherokee of Robeson County. If so, then this proved to be a weak defense for the Cherokee of Columbus County. The Columbus County Board of Education refuted the claims of the Cherokee of Columbus County by stating that they were "part Negro." The answer seemed to lie in asking the Cherokee Indians of Robeson County their opinion of the Indian status of those in Columbus County. That is exactly what happened. According to a local reporter, "when an answer was filed in court setting up this defense, Senator T. L. Johnson, who was counsel for the plaintiffs, sent some representative Indians down to Bolton to make an investigation." Apparently Johnson relied heavily on the opinion of these "representative Indians." A negative report came back that "the plaintiffs were not genuine Cherokee Indians," prompting Johnson to file a non-suit. He refused "to prosecute the action further" (*Robesonian* 1928).

Those opposed to the 1927 Cherokee Indian School Bill succeeded in 1929 in getting it repealed. The county commissioners asked Representative Williamson to introduce H.B. 500 and on February 26, 1929, the repeal passed into law and stopped the opening of the Cherokee Indian schools of Columbus County for that fall (North Carolina 1929). A local newspaper hinted at the motivations of the commissioners. It was reported that the bill to repeal the 1927 Cherokee Indian School Bill would save the county taxpayers money and "nip in the bud untold troubles which would arise in future generations" (*News Reporter* 1929). The article went on to say that "one main trouble with the carrying out of that act was determining just who the Indians are." And it continued, "there are some families in which some of the brothers and sisters claim to be Indians; others in the same families claim that they are of the colored race." In the reporter's view, this might lead to a situation in which "the one would claim entrance into the Indian school, the other would not." This seems a spurious argument in light of the reporter's earlier statement about "saving the taxpayer money." The reporter reveals his/her own fears by asking, "what would this bring about twenty years from now?" The reporter answers, saying, "It could result in nothing but the forming of feuds." The reporter envisions a fractious future wherein "growing children might decide that they are as much entitled to the separate schools as their cousins who are in them." Well, then, the reporter asks, "Who would determine their race?" In the reporter's view, "the matter could never be boiled down to any satisfactory point." The reporter could not understand why the "self-styled Indians of this county," described as "not a bad set of folks," who "never have been notorious for crime as those of neighboring counties," should want to rock the boat. The reporter apparently approves the racial status quo, saying, "so long as they [the self-styled Indians] maintain their present standing, they are going to be treated as good and responsible citizens." But, the reporter cautions, "when they engender in themselves and their children a superior air over their fellows who in actuality are the same race, then there is no way of telling what trouble would arise." The preservation of the racial status as defined by the controlling white community safeguarded the moral and financial "good effect" of society.

The Cherokee Indian School Bill of 1927 dealt a blow to the rigidly defined racial system and met powerful resistance from some of the white community. Robert Jacobs, W. J. Freeman, and the Indian community had faced an uncertain future in this fight in the fall of 1927 because their political ally and supporter, Senator Donald McRackan, had passed away on October 20, 1927, as reported in the *News Reporter*. The Cherokee of Columbus County (later known as the Waccamaw Siouan) faced opposition from both local white power holders and Cherokee representatives from Robeson County. The opposition of the white county commissioners and Board of Education was predictable and understandable within the context of race of the 1920s. But clearly the white opposition was not monolithic, since McRackan, a Democrat, had pushed the legislation recognizing the Columbus County Indians as Cherokee in the first place. With his death, the Cherokee of Columbus County turned, perhaps mistakenly, to Senator T. L. Johnson, an attorney from Robeson County, where the large population known as the Cherokee Indians of Robeson County lived. Johnson initially was a strong supporter, but when confronted with opposition in Columbus County, he agreed to get "expert" opinion from the Bureau of Ethnology in Washington, D.C., and from the Cherokee of Robeson County. Both approaches failed the Columbus County Cherokee.

The Cherokee of Robeson County in 1928–1929 were insecure in their own Cherokee Indian designation, fearing perhaps a return to the ambivalent status of "Croatan Indians." As the gatekeepers for who was a "Cherokee Indian" in their part of the state, they sat on "blood committees" and oversaw the entry into their schools, as was their right by Public School Law 1929, Chapter 195. According to the law, "in order to protect the Public Schools in Robeson County for the education of the Indian race only, and the Cherokee Normal School of Robeson County, there shall be a committee composed of Indians who are residents of Robeson County, and all questions affecting the race of all those applying for admission . . . shall be referred to the committee." Gerald Sider, an anthropologist, thinks that this act was very important because it gave local Indian people and not the county officials control over the so-called blood committees (Sider 1993:73). The Cherokee Indians of Robeson County played out the racial stereotypes of the larger society, following the same rules of "blood quantum" and reducing Indian identity to the pseudo biology of "blood." These Indian representatives ruled against the Cherokee of Columbus County, playing into the hands of the dominant white power holders who also insisted that the Indians in their county prove they were free of Negro blood.

5
The Wide Awake Indians

The ancestors of the modern Waccamaw Siouan called themselves Cherokee between 1928 and 1940; thereafter, they started to publicly refer to themselves as the "Wide Awake Indians," a name they had long used for their council (1910) and their school (1934). Outside the community, they sought recognition as the Cherokee. The story of the Cherokee tribal name covers the Indians living in the North Carolina counties of Bladen, Columbus, and Robeson. Use of "Cherokee" was a good articulation strategy for all the Indians, at least for a while. The Cherokee tribal name, like the Croatan name before it, opened the way to Indian recognition and rights. Over the years, opponents to its use put up roadblocks, couched in racial dialogue, to achieving those rights. Eventually, the names "Waccamaw Siouan" in 1948 and "Lumbee" in 1953 replaced "Cherokee."

A 1927 statute entitled "Cherokee Indians of Columbus County" made specific reference to the ancestors of the Waccamaw Siouan, providing publicly funded Indian schools. Unfortunately, the statute was repealed two years later. In 1929 the stock market crash ushered in the Great Depression, which was felt all the way into the rural areas of North Carolina. With money tight everywhere, the Indian tenant farmers, day laborers, and loggers somehow managed to raise enough money to continue the fight for recognition as Cherokee. Scholars link the survival of the small Indian communities to their social isolation (Berry 1945, 1963, 1978; Dane and Griessman 1972; Frazier 1966; Gilbert 1945, 1946a, 1946b; Griessman 1972; Pollitzer et al. 1972; Price 1953; Thompson 1972). Although they may have been socially isolated, there is evidence that they were not politically isolated. This chapter explores the shifting political strategies and articulatory efforts like legislation, boycotts, civil disobedience, use of attorneys, and letter writing. The meaning of "Cherokee" is found in their acts of defiance, in their political strategies, and in their overt rejection of non-Indian racial categories. Largely illiterate and poorly educated, they have not left a written tradition

The Wide Awake Indians / 65

to study. Oral tradition, story telling, and acts of resistance recorded by non-Indians are our only evidence of how the Indians defined their identity.

As the new decade opened, the 1930 federal census reported 293 Cherokee Indians living in Columbus and Bladen Counties (Columbus County had 208 in Waccamaw Township and 17 in Bolton Township; Bladen County had 68 in Carver's Creek Township) (U.S. Census Bureau 1930). Entry after entry listed race as Cherokee Indian and parentage as mixed or "full blooded" and Cherokee. By implication, those listed as full-blood had full-blood Cherokee grandparents and great-grandparents. This satisfied the "fourth generation" stipulation included in all laws regarding Indian schools in North Carolina since the 1885 laws providing separate schools for the Croatan Indians, which required that "there shall be excluded from such separate schools all children of the Negro race to the fourth generation." Since race on the 1930 federal census was not self-reported but enumerator ascribed, we must conclude that the Cherokee Indian status had some acceptance among local whites. The political implications cannot be overlooked either. The Cherokee Indians of Columbus County were to some degree recognized as Indians. The 1930 census was a point of articulation with the dominant society based on Indian identity.

The Cherokee of Columbus County took every opportunity to articulate with non-Indians on the basis of their Indian identity. Indians did not lump together Indians and African Americans as "colored people." Indian children learned early to respect the dividing line between their people and black neighbors. One man recalled that his father insisted that he walk an extra four miles to an Indian school rather than allow him to go to a colored school "within hollering distance." He recalled, "I could've walked right across to that school everyday and went to school and been there on time and all but my daddy say no! You ain't going over there with them black people. You going . . . to Hickory Hill, which was four miles. And I had to tend to the cows first and do the milking and all and feed the mules . . . and then go to school. When I got there be 12 o'clock, after 12, be half done before I even get out there." This strict separation impressed the children with the distinction Indians made between themselves and "colored people." Indians had a right to their own schools.

Indians did not align themselves publicly or officially with "colored people," which is why they refused to be listed as "Negro" for tax purposes in 1930, drawing angry comments from the Columbus County commissioners, who referred to them as "so-called 'Indians'" (Columbus County 1926–1933 [1930]). This defiant act was reported in the local paper, in which a reporter wrote, "There is a settlement of the race which call themselves Indians in Welches Creek and Waccamaw townships, and some in Ransom.

They completely segregate themselves from the two other races, maintaining their own schools and churches" (*News Reporter* 1930).

Indians acted nonlocally, reaching out to politicians who agreed to the social distinction between Indians and "colored people." Under the strong leadership of W. J. Freeman, the Cherokee of Columbus County hired two Raleigh attorneys in January 1931 to begin procedures with the state legislature for the introduction of another Cherokee Indian school bill (*News Reporter* 1931). "A smoldering fire burned brighter," as the local newspaper put it, when word of the new bill became public. The 1931 Cherokee Bill asked for "legislative recognition of their rights as Indians" rather than "any radical changes to the system." The 1931 Cherokee Indian School bill would direct the Columbus County Board of Education to establish two Indian schools for the Cherokee Indians, Hickory Hill and St. Marks, where Indian children were then in attendance. As with earlier bills, this bill provided a way for Indian people to select the eligible students and appropriate Indian teachers. The student body would be composed only of Indians, excluding "all children of the Negro race to the fourth generation" (*News Reporter* 1931). The state superintendent of public instruction wrote to county officials informing them of a visit from W. J. Freeman and others from the Indian community, saying, "Your Indian friends were in the office yesterday, and we spent a long time talking over their situation," that is, their desire to be granted separate Indian schools and the local school board's resistance to this desire. The state superintendent proposed a solution, outlined in three parts. First, there should be a "recognition of the contention of these people who claim that they are of Indian descent in some such way as the Indians in Robeson County are recognized." Second, a commission could be set up "to be appointed by the Governor consisting of leading men among this alleged Indian group to determine what children should go to the separate school provided for them." And, finally, the proposal suggested "making it possible for them to secure teachers trained at Pembroke Normal." Pembroke Normal trained Indians to become schoolteachers in Indian schools (Allen 1931). The local newspaper printed this plan and the alleged response of the county school superintendent, who reportedly was "earnestly desirous of seeing the matter settled in an amicable matter" (*News Reporter* 1931). The article continued, "There were in truth a few members of the Croatan race in the Hickory Hill and St. Marks school sections" but there was also suspicion that there were those "intermarried with Negroes and other races." The Indian leader W. J. Freeman continued to pressure the state superintendent about the school issue (Columbus County 1885–1964:III:203).

The state legislature reviewed the Cherokee Bill in February 1931. W. J. Freeman wrote to the state superintendent of public instruction, saying,

"Our attorneys being now at a point of taking up the bill with the legislature concerning separate schools for the Indians of Columbus Co. we are asking your cooperation with them" (Freeman 1931). Freeman feared delaying the bill because it would mean one more school year gone by without Indian teachers. He appealed to the state superintendent's sense of fair play, writing, "I do think it is unjust for us as taxpaying people to be handicapped as we are in educational facilities." Freeman referred to the Indians' efforts to provide for schools within their churches with local funds. The results were poor, as he explained: "What little school we have been fortunate to have, was conducted in [a] poor equipped building furnished by ourselves." Indian rights included some limited sovereignty over Indian affairs, but being poor and tax-paying citizens, Freeman believed they deserved to receive a fair share of the local tax dollars reserved for education. His comments make clear that the Indians did not recognize the authority of the white officials to impose their racial categories on the Indians. Freeman's actions make it clear that Indians were not passive when faced with opposition to their goals.

Were the local officials afraid that if the state passed the 1931 Cherokee Bill it would be approving some limited sovereignty of the Indians? Indian tribes gained such status by treaty, executive order of the president, or by law. This might be the first feared step. In response to the bill, the Columbus County commissioners mounted an all-out effort to prevent the legislators from ever introducing another Indian school bill for the Cherokee or any other Indian group in Columbus County. Their minutes of January 13, 1931, made it clear they were opposed to schools for the Cherokee Indians of Columbus County, describing them as "certain free mulattoes." Prior to the 1929 repeal effort, they had reported on an investigation for the director of school accounting, J. L. Hathcock, "which disclosed the fact that these self-styled Indians are of mixed blood and were free previous to 1865, but were not then and are not now regarded as Indians." The commissioners collected affidavits from "citizens of Columbus County who have known the self-styled Indians for many years" declaring "that there are no Indians" in the area. Foreseeing quarrels arising from narrowly limiting the Indian schools to St. Marks and Hickory Hill, the county commissioners went on record emphatically opposing the 1931 bill. They did, however, leave open the possibility that the "self-styled Indians" might get Indian schools if "it has been proved . . . to the satisfaction of the Board of County Commissioners and Board of Education of Columbus County" that they are indeed Indians (Columbus County 1885–1964:III:241; *News Reporter* 1931). Nothing official came from the 1931 bill, but the "smoldering fire" of recognition did not completely die out.

In 1931, the Cherokee Indian leaders in Robeson County contacted the Office of Indian Affairs about obtaining federal status and access to government Indian schools. They pursued greater sovereignty over their affairs by seeking assistance from the federal government. This request prompted a federal review of the tribal name of Cherokee that in turn brought up questions about the implications for the Eastern Band of Cherokee. If the federal government granted the Cherokee Indians of Robeson County federal status, how would this affect the Eastern Band of Cherokee or any other Indian group using the name Cherokee? In 1931, United States Senator J. W. Bailey of North Carolina introduced bill S. 4595, "Providing for the recognition and enrollment as Cherokee Indians of certain Indians in the State of North Carolina." The bill referred to "those Indians in Robeson and adjoining counties, North Carolina, which were designated Cherokee Indians by the Act of March 11, 1913, of the General Assembly of the State of North Carolina, and which were formerly known as Croatan Indians." As written, this bill may have been interpreted as including Indians in other counties that were designated Cherokee by state statute after 1913. If that were so, then the Cherokee of Columbus County also would be included. Therefore, the 1931 state bill that W. J. Freeman was pushing for in the North Carolina legislature may have anticipated this.

The federal-level discussion continued into 1933 when alternative names to Cherokee were considered by the Indian leaders. What tribal name was appropriate for the awarding of federal status? Would it be Cherokee, Cheraw, or Siouan? These deliberations are important to the modern Waccamaw Siouan story because this is when "Siouan" became widely associated with the Indians of the region. John R. Swanton of the Bureau of American Ethnology was largely responsible for this. Swanton (1934:5–6) offered his opinion in a memorandum entitled "Probable Identity of the 'Croatan' Indians," writing, "the evidence available thus seems to indicate that the Indians of Robeson County who have been called Croatan and Cherokee are descended mainly from certain Siouan Tribes of which the most prominent were the Cheraw and Keyauwee, but they probably included as well remnants of the Eno and Shakori and very likely some of the coastal groups such as the Waccamaws and Cape Fears" (Swanton 1934:6). Swanton pointed out that while predominantly Siouan, "a few families or small groups of Algonquian or Iroquoian" could be present too. If Swanton had to pick one name, he favored Cheraw, because it was more well known than "Keyauwee," though the Keyauwee probably actually "contributed more blood to Robeson County Indians than any other." He wrote, "therefore, if the name of any tribe is to be used in connection with this body of

6 or 8 thousand people, that of Cheraw would, in my opinion, be most appropriate."

However, the name Cheraw failed to win support among the Cherokee of Robeson County, who instead selected the more general title of "Siouan Indians of the Lumber River" in bill S. 1632. In the end, Secretary of the Interior Harold L. Ickes expressed the government's view on granting federal status in a letter commenting on S. 1632. A tribal name was really secondary to his concerns, although he clearly preferred "Siouan Indians of the Lumber River" to Cheraw. He did not favor granting federal recognition nor "federal wardship or governmental rights or benefits upon such Indians." He raised the objection that the Croatan, as he called the Indians of Robeson County, never had a treaty with the U.S. government; thus, there was no prior obligation on the government's part to assist them. He did not accept the argument that the government owed them special support as Indians of the United States. The state of North Carolina had, in his view, an obligation to them, such as providing for their education. Ickes favored "clarifying their status," thus designating them Siouan Indians of the Lumber River. For some Robeson County Indians, "Siouan" seemed preferable to more specific names like "Cheraw" (Blu 1980:83); but if the original intention was to secure a "more precise identity" (Dial and Eliades 1975:18), then the Siouan Indian bill failed to deliver it.

How was this potential name change received within Robeson County? "Sentiment among Indians divided in change of name: Indians of Robeson aroused over passage of bill by Senate to change name from Cherokee to Siouan" shouted the front page of a local newspaper (*Robesonian* 1934a). Opposition from within the Robeson Indian leadership eroded congressional support for the bill and, while it passed in the Senate, it failed to pass the House (Sider 1993:148). Thus, the name Cherokee Indians of Robeson County remained the legal name of the tribe. However, the supporters of the Siouan name decided to go ahead and put it into use anyway when they formed the Siouan Lodge and the General Council of the Siouan Indians of the Lumber River. Under this title, they affiliated with the National Council of American Indians (*Robesonian* 1934b). The Siouan Lodge of the National Council of American Indians, Inc., involved people from Robeson County as well as those from surrounding areas. In this way, the Siouan Lodge was different from other organizations because "it explicitly sought participation from people throughout the countryside" (Blu 1980:82). Going a bit further, the "General Council of the Siouan Indians," an affiliate of the Siouan Lodge, wrote to request that it be recognized by the Department of the Interior "as the appropriate representative of the Siouan Indians of North Carolina in all future activities of the Department that may affect our people" (Blu 1980:82). By August 1934, the Siouan Lodge printed special letterhead carrying its name.

The Siouan Lodge and its General Council, as Blu (1980:83–84) pointed out, made an effort to reach out to the communities of Indians throughout the region. Just how far they went is not known but older men living in the Waccamaw Siouan Indian community in the early 1980s recalled attending meetings of the Siouans and hearing the reports about Siouan Lodge leaders who went to Washington to work on behalf of the Indians. How much influence did the Siouan Lodge have on the Indians in Columbus and Bladen Counties in the early 1930s? Were there meetings to discuss strategies for winning Indian schools, working with state legislators, or securing assistance from Washington? We cannot be sure, as there are few direct records available to look at. However, very likely W. J. Freeman, who spoke for the Cherokee Indians of Columbus County, participated in some of these discussions and heard and/or read about the activities of Indians in Robeson County in the local newspapers that constantly carried stories about them. Could it be coincidence that W. J. Freeman hired lawyers to help with a second Cherokee Indian school bill for Columbus County in 1931, causing the local educators to speculate that Freeman's intentions went beyond simply education for the children? Could they have been alluding to the fact that the Cherokee of Robeson County in 1931 were making efforts to gain recognition from the federal government and did they think the Columbus County Cherokee were planning a similar move? Parallel efforts were made, whether or not we can show a direct connection between the two Cherokee populations.

The Cherokee Indians of Columbus County faced a setback when the 1931 bill failed to pass into state law. Nevertheless, they continued to manage their schools by using the committee structure of the Board of Education. The Indian men appointed to sit on the school committee brought requests from the Indian community. Most of the children attended classes at St. Marks Church, owned and operated by the Indians, with a smaller number still at the public school known as Hickory Hill. Board minutes still referred to the schools and committeemen as "self-styled Indians" (Columbus County 1885–1964:III:297, 323). Until 1933, almost all of the efforts to win Indian schools focused on Columbus County. Now, the Indians residing just across the county line in Bladen County stepped up efforts to secure an Indian school in their county. However, they did not insist on being known as Cherokee Indians.

The issue of the Cherokee name never came up in Bladen County. In April 1933, "a group of Indians from Carver's Creek Township" re-

The Wide Awake Indians / 71

quested erection of a school for their twenty-five children, "some of whom formerly attended the school for Indians in Columbus County" (Bladen County 1931–1954:II:561). The "Bladen Indian Colony" continued these requests until "it was agreed that any or all material in the old Council school building be given for the construction of a building on a tract of land to be deeded to the Bladen County Board of Education by citizen or citizens of the Indian Colony" (Bladen County 1931–1954:II:583). By the 1934 school year, the Bladen Indian Colony's school opened under the name of Wide Awake Indian School. One story about those days suggests a playful origin for the school's name, hinting that the Indians thought of themselves as "on the ball and alert." Equally possible is that the reading material widely used in elementary schools at the time was the Wide Awake Third Reader (Murray 1920).

Despite success in the Bladen Indian Colony, those across the county line in Columbus County faced resistance by the Board of Education. Just before school opened in 1934, W. J. Freeman and James Jacobs came to the board's August 28 meeting requesting, once again, that St. Marks be designated an Indian school. Board minutes outline what took place: "After a general discussion by members of the Board . . . the County Superintendent was authorized to contact Mr. A. E. Lee, County Superintendent of Bladen schools, and ascertain the status of the Indian school in Bladen County, located near the proposed site for the above mentioned [St. Marks school] set up by the appearing delegation" (Columbus County 1885–1964:III:343). Negotiations with Bladen County eventually led to a consolidated Indian school located in Bladen County but open to children living in Columbus County. This took several years to settle. Older people recall these difficult times with a mixture of pride and some bitterness. Recalling the Wide Awake Indian School, an older Indian woman put it this way, "now that's the school that brought the worst operation, [I] liken it to [the] devil's work." Her mother was one of those who approached the Bladen school board about getting her children and grandchildren, who lived in both counties, into the Wide Awake Indian School. The racial status the whites assigned to the Indians in Columbus County again became an issue.

The St. Marks Church was still serving as a school on January 7, 1935, when "a petition by a group of the St. Mark's district was presented requesting the establishment of an Indian school in said community." The petition was "referred to the State School Commission" (Columbus County 1885–1964:III:351). Ten months later, the Indians returned to the board, making it clear that they "under no condition were agreeable to opening their schools under the same condition as they had operated during the past twenty or more years" (Columbus County 1885–1964:III:400). This time the board sought a "final solution" to the problem: they would request the State School Commission to transfer the Indians to Bladen County. If this request was denied, the board made it clear that nothing would change regarding the conditions, such as the racial status of Hickory Hill and St. Marks. Teachers would be provided and the school committees would carry out their duties just as before under the label "colored" or "Negro schools." Two years passed without any change in policy in Columbus County, while in Bladen County, the Indian Colony welcomed Wilton Lowry from Pembroke Normal to teach at the Wide Awake Indian School in 1934–1935.

It is clear that white challenges to Indian goals did not diminish the strength of the Indian's commitment to them. Their actions reveal just how they saw themselves. As Indians, they were politically savvy, tenacious, and stubborn in their rejection of white interference in their affairs. When the Wide Awake Indian School opened in Bladen County, the Indians in Columbus County pressed their school board even harder for their right to be recognized as Indian in public schools. In March 1936, they raised the question of Indian schools again before the school board. This prompted an annoyed response from a local reporter, who began his article by calling the Indian request for schools "as constant as the ever babbling brook." The reporter went on to say the "self-styled Indians are certainly persistent," raising this issue at "practically every meeting for the past several years" (*News Reporter* 1936a).

Their actions also demonstrated their willingness to suffer hardship for their beliefs. W. J. Freeman and thirty-one other Indian men were arrested, fined, and some sentenced to work gangs because they refused to list or report their property for tax purposes. They explained to the court that "they did not like the fact that their abstracts were listed in the same books as the colored people." The tax recorder could not guarantee them that it would not happen again, so they refused to list their taxes altogether. These acts of civil disobedience preceded the Civil Rights Movement by twenty years and challenged the racial system that imposed the category of "colored" on them (*News Reporter* 1936b).

Indian leaders in one Indian community were often very aware of how other Indian leaders battled for recognition. Leaders in Columbus and Bladen Counties knew about the efforts of the Cherokee Indians of Robeson County to obtain federal recognition. They were familiar with the name debate. They knew about the factions that developed between those favoring Cherokee, Cheraw, and Siouan. They knew that however the tribal name Cherokee might be perceived in Washington, D.C., it still opened

The Wide Awake Indians / 73

doors to Indian schools in North Carolina. Knowing all this, W. J. Freeman, leading spokesman for the Cherokee of Columbus County, returned again in 1937 to the strategy of getting the Cherokee name officially granted through state law. Freeman acted with full support of the Indian community, which raised the money for attorneys and trips to Raleigh. As a local reporter observed, "Once again in the churches, the Community box suppers and what not, funds have been raised to get what these people believe themselves entitled to" (*News Reporter* 1937).

Freeman must have known how the local white community would react. "The age-old Indian question" came up again in Columbus County, where there was "little surprise," was the local newspaper's response (*News Reporter* 1937). The paper reported that "Representative J. R. Williamson carried the matter before the North Carolina Legislative body in the form of a bill which provides that the board of education of Columbus County be required to furnish separate schools for the Columbus County Cherokee children when the State Board of Education finds that they are in fact Cherokee Indians." This looked on the surface to be a rather supportive bill but in fact it still gave the final say to the Columbus County Board of Education. W. J. Freeman and his people needed to prove to the board's satisfaction that they were Indians.

The Indians demonstrated a certain flexibility and pragmatism in their fight for Indian schools. Different contexts required different articulation strategies. The Indians recognized the complexity of their situation. So when the Bladen County school board agreed with a plan to allow "Indians living in Columbus County and near the Wide Awake Indian School of Bladen County . . . to attend the Wide Awake Indian School," they saw a way around white opposition to their goals (Bladen County 1931–1954 [1937]). However, the plan still faced difficulty with the racial categories imposed in Columbus County between 1937 and 1939 (Columbus County 1885–1964:IV:82, 109; Erwin 1937). Indian opposition to these racial categories led to the closing of Hickory Hill and St. Marks in 1938–1939 and the transfer of some children to the Wide Awake Indian School. Some Indian parents were so dissatisfied with the overcrowded and poorly funded Wide Awake Indian School by 1939 that they wanted to try to reopen their old school of Hickory Hill as an Indian school (Columbus County 1885–1964:IV:119). The Indians confirmed their allegiance to the principal of limited sovereignty over their affairs when they replied to the school board's request to submit proof of their Indian ancestry "for three generations" to the "satisfaction of the Board of Education" (Columbus County 1885–1964:IV:128). The Indians defined their membership to their own satisfaction. They realized that when they kept their children home, the board would likely close the school (Columbus County 1885–1964:IV:256). It was not until 1945 that the school board finally agreed to the Indian's position on racial classification and designated Hickory Hill an Indian school (Columbus County 1885–1964:IV:269). Then the Cherokee Indians of Columbus and Bladen Counties had two county-recognized Indian schools—the Wide Awake Indian School in Bladen County and Hickory Hill in Columbus County.

As the years passed, the Wide Awake Indian School prepared children for high school. By 1941 twenty-four were ready to go on to high school if they could find one to accept them (Highsmith 1940). Even though the students at the Wide Awake Indian School had Indian teachers like Wilton Lowry, Pembroke Normal School in Robeson County refused to admit them. Just as in the past, when the Indian leaders faced obstacles to their goals, they adjusted their approach to fit the situation. In this case, personal connections helped a few students get into already established Indian high schools. Indian pastors from Robeson County preached at the local Indian churches in Columbus and Bladen Counties, traveling between Indian communities, crosscutting the tribal boundaries, serving as links between the separate groups (Lerch 1992b:50). One woman recalled how her pastor helped her enter an Indian school in Robeson County in the town of Fairmount in 1943. Indian pastors had extended this help for many years, as in the case of one woman who went to an Indian school in Magnolia, Duplin County, during World War I. She continued into the eighth grade at a Robeson County Indian school. However, personal connections proved the exception, as most did not have this opportunity. The next focus of Indian activism of the Wide Awake Indian Council and its leaders turned on getting high school education.

A different articulation strategy was needed now that the tribal name Cherokee was controversial within the state. Indian leaders like W. J. Freeman had based their articulation strategy on acceptance of the tribal name Cherokee for more than a decade. Three separate Cherokee Indian school bills had been proposed, one in 1927, another in 1931, and yet another in 1937. While the Cherokee name carried weight with state school officials, it was also a useful articulation strategy for Indians. But by 1940, Indian leaders turned to other approaches to meet their goals.

The people who called themselves Cherokee in Columbus County and their relatives in Bladen County began publicly referring to themselves as the "Wide Awake Indians," extending the name of their council and school into their interactions with non-Indians. A 1940 memo from the "Wide Awake Tribal Council" of "duly elected councilmen, including W. J. Freeman, Chairman" appointed a young Indian man named Ossie Jacobs to the task of research on the "origin, birthright and habits of the Indians living in and around Bolton, North Carolina in Bladen and Columbus Counties." As he had in the past, Freeman demonstrated the ability of the Indians to adjust to changing times by carefully selecting the right name and adapting older strategies like letter writing, contacting state education officials, and lobbying state legislators to new goals.

In the 1940s the focus of Indian activism was going to be on secondary school education. W. J. Freeman brought a new generation of Indian men like Ossie and Lewis Jacobs and Alex Patrick in to serve as school trustees for the Wide Awake Indian School. Indian activism now involved joining forces with other Indians in eastern North Carolina who faced some of the same problems gaining entry into the state's secondary schools for Indians. An intertribal effort gained momentum when Indians from several counties requested assistance from the state (Jacobs et al. 1941). This intertribal effort resulted in the passage of Chapter 370, Public Laws of North Carolina, 1941, entitled "An act to provide better educational advantages for members of the Indian race in Eastern North Carolina not otherwise provided for."

Chapter 370 provided vocational and normal school education for several counties where Indian schools existed, including Sampson, Hoke, Scotland, Cumberland, Bladen, Person, and Harnett. Chapter 370 made no reference to entry qualifications based on white racial categories, purity of Indian blood, or lack of mixture with African Americans to the third or fourth generation. What was more important was prior attendance at an Indian elementary school. The state Board of Education commissioned a report on Chapter 370. They found there were 950 Indian children eligible to attend secondary school (Credle et al. 1941). The report recommended a site in Sampson County that was centrally located and close to other Indian schools. Although Chapter 370 provided for college instruction, including courses for teacher training and vocational education, the report suggested that the greatest need was for an accredited school offering basic elementary and secondary education.

The Wide Awake Tribal Council's decision to work with other Indians in securing a high school proved very effective. Chapter 370 provided an opportunity for higher education at an accredited school. The law seemed to confirm that Indian concepts of Indianness were more important than non-Indian racial categories. To enter this new Indian high school, a pupil needed only to have previously attended one of the county Indian schools. Thus, by 1945, most children in the Wide Awake Tribal Council's community had met this requirement.

The report on Chapter 370, Public Laws of North Carolina, 1941, recommended a "modern building of at least ten classrooms" (Credle et al.

1941:5). All modern features like an "auditorium and auxiliary facilities such as an office, book storage room, toilet facilities," and a vocational workshop for boys should be included. The report strongly recommended that the state consider building a dormitory and dining facilities for about fifty students, too. "Unless this is done," the report argued, "provision will not be made for the education of those high school students who are found in the counties outside of Sampson" (Credle et al. 1941:6). When Indian children came to the New Bethel School, one of the Indian schools near the site of the proposed new high school, many came from outside the county. Among thirty-five students enrolled there in 1940, there were "20 from Bladen, 9 from Harnett, and 6 from Person." This number was expected to increase with the opening of the East Carolina Indian School. Without the new dormitory, the children would continue to be housed with Indian people in the local community. The report observed, "Obviously this condition is very unsatisfactory. The Indian families are large and the houses are small. It is extremely difficult for these families to provide physical accommodations for anyone from outside the immediate family. Many of the Indian families could not take care of anyone, [and] undoubtedly the number of high school students would exceed the total number of Indian families in the New Bethel community." Besides provision of a place to live and eat in the dormitory, the report said, "These children moreover need these more desirable social and cultural contacts as part of their education." The report concluded, "the present problem is one of providing satisfactory elementary and high school education for the Indians" (Credle et al. 1941:7).

Indian youngsters from the Wide Awake Tribal Council's communities were among those planning to attend the new East Carolina Indian School. Without dormitory facilities, they would board with Indian families. Recruiters from Sampson County let the parents of the Wide Awake Indian School students know that they were welcome. In anticipation of the opening of the new high school, some children attended the Indian schools in Sampson County in preparation for the building of the consolidated East Carolina Indian School. The Indian students paid for their own transportation, books, and, if they could, their room and board. If not, as one man recalled, they would "work it out and act like one of the family." Sometimes, a student did not know the family until he or she arrived. "I went in there Sunday night," recalled an Indian man, "and it was just like letting down somewhere in South America. You might call it that way [because it was] just a strange place. It was night in the fall of the year and that a big cotton, potato, tobacco community, [with] strawberries, trucking crops, and when I woke up the next morning, I saw big fields of cotton and corn. Tobacco was harvested at that time, [and] I could see the big fields, where tobaccos come in. No, we familiarized ourselves somehow, blended in and got along good." If lucky, a young man might return home once a month. In addition to school, there were other things to do to earn some extra money. "We would help pick strawberries maybe of a morning, we'd help gather crops, truckin' crops [like] vegetables, evening, in wintertime, we'd cut wood [to] provide for heat in the home." The Indian families treated their boarders well, "like one of theirs." A man recalled, "I couldn't expect no better treatment and recognition. They'd share with us what they had as one of their own family without any distinction whatever." Indians from the Wide Awake Tribal Council's communities were welcome in Sampson County, where "they found out about us someway or nother [and] from all observations [they] seen we was Native American race and they were anxious to get us to go [to the East Carolina Indian School]." Sampson County encouraged the Indians from the surrounding counties to come to their schools. On the other hand, the Robeson Cherokee actively discouraged people from coming to Pembroke Normal School. "We wasn't encouraged to go there," a man explained, "and it was somewhat little dissension there, discrimination, at Pembroke [Normal School] at that time and date. They wasn't taking nobody into that facility but Robeson County Indians so that put a little barrier in our way [although some had] intentions to go to Robeson County." Without such encouragement, many headed toward the East Carolina Indian School, which operated from ca. 1941 until it closed in 1965.

6

"I Was an Indian, I Was Outstanding"

H.R. 7153 and H.R. 7299
A Bill to authorize the Secretary of the Interior to accept voluntary conveyances of lands owned by Waccamaw Indians in North Carolina and to issue trust patents for such lands, and for other purposes.
—U.S. House of Representatives 1950

For more than two decades, the ancestors of the Waccamaw Siouan hammered away at their goals, forging articulatory relationships with the non-Indian society. In the process, we glimpse the values central to their concept of Indianness. Indians define their members; distinctions are made between Indians and colored people. Indians do not align themselves publicly with colored people. Indians act nonlocally in pursuit of their aims, forging contractual relations with non-Indians based on acceptance of their Indian identity. They are persistent, stubborn, tenacious, and pragmatic in their choice of articulation strategies. So, as the 1940s came to a close, the Wide Awake Indian Council (WAIC) brought its fight for recognition to the federal level as Congress considered the Waccamaw Bill of 1950.

The story of the Waccamaw Bill of 1950 centers on the imagery of a "lost tribe" recently and romantically rediscovered. The imagery invokes an Indian culture untouched by civilization's corrupting influences. The theme of American Indians as objects of discovery, living disconnected from modern times, is linked to the very beginnings of American anthropology (Hoxie et al. 2001:268–269). The American public generally accepted the idea that American Indian cultures "could not have a modern existence." They were "lost" in the sense that native life and modern life were incompatible. On February 6, 1950, Norris Poulson of California, who was a member of the Subcommittee on Indian Affairs, explained to his colleagues that the Waccamaw Bill "will recognize what might be called a lost tribe of Indians in North Carolina. The story of these Indians is both interesting and tragic" (U.S. Congress 1950:A886).

It was the WAIC and its newly appointed leader, Reverend R. T. Freeman, who were responsible for getting Norris Poulson to introduce the 1950 Waccamaw Bill. R. T. Freeman was the younger brother of W. J. Freeman, who recently had "retired" as "chief spokesman" for the council after serving for many years. The time-tested articulatory strategies remained in place and R. T. Freeman continued to seek contractual relations with non-Indians in pursuit of Indian goals.

R. T. Freeman picked up the strong leadership tradition of his elder brother. A close friend described R. T. Freeman as "a born leader" (Lerch 2002:32). Like his brother before him, he established connections to Indian and white leaders outside of his community who could offer assistance and advice. For example, there are stories telling of the friendly and supportive relationship between R. T. Freeman and Governor Kerr Scott of North Carolina. One story narrates how the governor learned of the plight of the Indians through his brother, who once employed the young R. T. Freeman. Over the years, Freeman visited the governor, bringing before him issues concerning his tribe. Governor Scott trusted Freeman's word on the Indian membership of his community. Freeman carefully screened tribal membership by reviewing birth records and affidavits certifying Indian heritage. His actions were similar to those of the Indians of Robeson County, who since 1921 had had screening committees guarding entrance into their Indian schools (Blu 1980:81). Freeman often faced difficult choices "because he would have to tell some no, [some] that was awful good friends. I mean, you know, it caused a lot of heartaches, you know, when you had a person that worked for you for twenty-five years and always got on good, but was mixed-blooded for some reason, then he had to [say] no, you're not [an Indian]" (Lerch 2002:33). Yet, R. T. Freeman's actions demonstrate that Indians defined their own membership.

Indian leaders also acted nonlocally to accomplish their goals. R. T. Freeman remained friendly with men like Butler Prescott, the chief United States probation officer in the Eastern District of North Carolina. In 1943, Prescott handled the pre-sentence investigation of six "Indian young men" charged with failing to report for military duty at the local draft board in Whiteville, North Carolina. According to one account, "Early in 1943 six Indians from the settlement were drafted. They appeared on the specified day and learned they were classified as Negroes. They advised the head of the draft board that they would not be inducted as Negroes but sought the privilege of being inducted as Indian. When denied this privilege, they returned home" (U.S. Congress 1950:A886). They were then charged with violation of the Selective Service Act. Prescott (1949) concluded that "these young men . . . were Indians and that the efforts to designate and induct them as Negroes [were] due primarily to the prejudice of the white people in the vicinity." The charges against the Indian men were dropped but the "ultimate solution" was to classify all later Indian draftees as 4-F (unfit for military service). The WAIC and R. T. Freeman supported the civil disobedience of the six Indian draftees. They rejected any official racial classification by non-Indians that failed to recognize them as Indians. These narratives about Freeman tell of his political savvy, know-how, and connections to influential people outside his community. The context, both in 1943 and in 1949 when the groundwork was being laid for the Waccamaw Bill, was Indian rejection of white racial categories. As an elderly man put it, "We were always conscious that we were Indian, and . . . as a child coming up . . . I didn't think nothing of race being discriminated on from the whites and all, nothing like that. Because I was an Indian, I was outstanding, and my folks were" (Lerch 2002:33–34).

The WAIC was composed of "men of age" who counseled leaders like R. T. Freeman, reaching consensus on articulation strategies. In the fall of 1949, the WAIC included many old-timers like Robert Jacobs, who had represented the Indians on their school committee since 1917, and W. J. Freeman, who preceded his brother as "chief spokesman" and led the fight for Cherokee Indian recognition between 1921 and 1938. There were younger men like William Jacobs, Sylvester Jacobs, Ossie and Lewis Jacobs, Alex Patrick, and Sam Graham who took their turn on school committees and church boards as the older generation retired or died. In 1949, these men considered the possibility of gaining federal tribal status. The culmination of their efforts was H.R. 7153 and H.R. 7299, the Waccamaw Bill, originally brought to Congress on February 6, 1950. Getting to this point, however, brought them into contact with state and federal legislators, government bureaucrats, Washington lawyers, anthropologists, the Cherokee of Robeson County, and the Catawba of South Carolina. R. T. Freeman and his council worked with many people, but most importantly with James Evan Alexander. Alexander's involvement came about by accident when he visited his wife's family in Columbus County. As a writer, he came looking for a story about the local Indian peoples. But what began as a brief visit soon turned into a yearlong campaign to assist the Indians (Alexander 1950b:30). The anthropological advice that proved most significant came from Frank G. Speck, a specialist on the Siouan peoples of the Southeast. He advised Freeman and Alexander on the specific tribal origins of the Indians.

R. T. Freeman and the WAIC directed Alexander to search out anthropological opinion on the tribal name and origins of the community. No doubt, the WAIC felt it necessary to select a tribal name that non-Indians could support. The controversy over Cherokee was still fresh in their minds. In October 1949, Alexander corresponded with Frank Speck, an anthropologist at the University Museum of the University of Pennsylvania. Alexander wrote, "I am at the present time in an Indian settlement on the Old Indian trail that leads from the Cape Fear River to Lake Waccamaw located four miles north of Bolton, N.C." (Alexander 1949a). The Indians, he said, "lived here for many generations" and, he speculated, "are a remnant of the Siouan tribe that inherited the area, probably augmented by members of tribes from the Peedee, Congaree, and Cheraw." It seems highly likely that Freeman and the WAIC filled Alexander in on the Siouan name and its use in the 1930s as an alternative to Cherokee. Alexander described several customs he assumed to be surviving Indian traditions, such as head binding, herbal medicine, pottery making, and hunting with a "sparhawk" or a kind of slingshot. The presence of these "traditional cultural items," Alexander believed, would convince Speck of the genuine nature of this "lost tribe." This approach, as Hoxie and colleagues (2001:268–269) observed, reflected the widely held belief that real Indian life was essentially incompatible with modern life.

"Both Bob Ward and myself," Alexander continued, "feel sure that your findings in this community would add much to your already great contributions to the world's knowledge of the American Indian." Alexander's friend Robert Ward of Rock Hill, South Carolina, was acquainted with Speck's work with the Catawba and other Siouan Indians. Alexander explained to Speck that the Indians are "of a suspicious nature with regards to the white man" and "they begged me not to reveal my attempt to assist them to the nearby outside world." Alexander believed this fear was justified: "after investigation I can honestly state that I believe their fear to be well founded, even to the point of fearing physical harm." Speck wrote back, "I am excitedly interested in your letter regarding the Indians near Lake Waccamaw and urge you to go ahead with your opportunities to record all you can on their identity, history, and customs" (Speck 1949). The contents of these letters were reported at the WAIC meetings.

The WAIC listened to the questions Speck raised about their tribal identity. Speck wondered, "What tribal identity do they claim? (Are they part of the so-called Croatans of Robeson Co.?)." The WAIC knew that Speck's questions reflected non-Indian concern with purity of Indian blood. In the white view, Croatan was associated with mixed heritage and doubtful tribal origins. For Speck to ask about Croatan origins suggested he had doubts about their Indianness. The WAIC and R. T. Freeman considered their answer carefully, directing Alexander to reply, "What tribal identity do they claim? Waccamaw" (Alexander 1949a). He explained, "Older members of the tribe say they are of the Siouan nation. They pronounced it 'Soo-ine,' the last syllable 'ine as in mine.'" Furthermore, he continued, "These tribal members are vehement in disclaiming any relationship to the Indians of Robeson County." As he understood it, "Tradition among these people has it fixed that they have always been here. Certain segments of the tribe have from time to time, migrated from the Green Swamp, the upper reaches of the Waccamaw River and have invariably returned to the Islands in the swamp of this area." Alexander formed his own opinion as to their origins, "It is my belief that the road through the settlement which, according to the grants, was known as the Old Lake road at the time of the Revolutionary War, followed the Old Indian trail from Indian Wells on the Cape Fear River to Lake Waccamaw. [William] Bartram's estate, 'Ashwood' was located on the Cape Fear River just above the juncture of the trail and the river. This must have been the trail he followed when he visited the Lake in 1734, and the people in this settlement are without a doubt the ones he refers to in his 'Journal of Travels' as having told him that no Indians had resided on Lake Waccamaw for 50 years preceding his visit." Thus, Waccamaw became the accepted name.

The Waccamaw tribal name thereafter appeared in most correspondence on the Indian community's behalf. The WAIC, R. T. Freeman, and Alexander discussed the choice of tribal name until a consensus was reached in favor of Waccamaw Siouan. Alexander's letters to Speck hint at the pace at which this decision was made (Alexander to Speck 1949a). On October 19, 1949, Alexander referred only to "the Indians" on whose behalf he was working. Speck's reply of October 27, 1949, also referred to "the Indians," asking what tribal name they used (Speck 1949). The answer came back "Waccamaw" on November 2, 1949. From this it does not appear that the anthropologist Speck actually chose the name Waccamaw but learned of its use among the Indians from Alexander. The WAIC asked Alexander to give them advice but they remained the sole authority on the final decision to adopt Waccamaw Siouan. Alexander read widely, using standard works like Mooney's (1894) *The Siouan Tribes of the East* as sources for the tribal history he was writing to support the tribe's case. He certainly knew that Mooney included the historic Waccamaw in the Siouan language family. The tribe's leaders likely listened to Alexander's opinion as a literate and skillful writer. But without doubt Speck's advice had influence, too. In a letter to Robert Ward dated November 7, 1949, just five days after Alexander told Speck that the tribe's name was Waccamaw, Alexander implied to Ward that Speck did indeed have some influence. He wrote, "Just a note to bring you up to date on our Indian research. Thanks to you and many helpful people, we are about ready to present our data to the authorities in Washington. We took your advice and contacted Dr. Speck and have been corresponding with him. *We have found his opinions to be most helpful in determining the origin of these Indian people.* . . . These people are without a doubt descendants of the Waccamaws, members of the Siouan nation and closely related to your own Indians, the Catawba" (Lerch 2002:36, italics added). If Speck did write to

Alexander speculating on the tribe's identity, then those letters have been lost. But, by November 26, 1949, Speck sent a postcard acknowledging the receipt of some artifacts from the tribe. Alexander, who was eager to hear more from Speck, responded, "I am still very anxious to hear what you have to say about the customs, medical remedies, and of course the missing pottery fragments and arrowheads." Curiously, in this letter to Speck, Alexander refers to the Indians as "tribal members" rather than as "Waccamaw." One explanation could be that he is less confident in applying this name in his correspondence with Speck since he seems to be waiting for more analysis. Alexander's opinion was influential but secondary to that of the WAIC.

The word *Siouan* was not an entirely unfamiliar label to R. T. Freeman and W. J. Freeman in 1949. W. J. Freeman, the elder brother, led the community in the 1920s and 1930s when names like the popular Siouan and the legal names Cherokee and Croatan were applied to Indians in Robeson and adjoining counties. For a short time, the Indians of Columbus County were legally recognized as Cherokee. W. J. Freeman was comfortable with the names Croatan and Cherokee since he played a key role in having the group designated Cherokee in 1928. He fought for the name Cherokee well into the 1930s. Alexander may have been ignorant of the recent history on the use of Cherokee based on what he wrote Speck. He said, "One time in the past when attempting to get recognition, a white man made out affidavits which were signed by numerous residents of the surrounding area. These documents set them forth as Cherokee. My investigation leads me to conclude that the uninformed white inhabitants of this region believe all Indians are Cherokees." The label Siouan was widely used in Robeson County in the 1930s and 1940s, where the popular Siouan Lodge tried unsuccessfully to win federal recognition for the Indians of Robeson and adjoining counties.

Years later, an older Indian man, Mr. Joe, explained what he remembered about how the WAIC adopted Waccamaw Siouan. A transcript of our dialogue follows. Mr. Joe told me how James Alexander came to be involved in the whole matter. "Well," he said, "Alexander became interested in the people" through his wife who grew up in Columbus County, and "he just moved in and stayed . . . and he began to write. So we got busy with him . . . We got into it and we went to Washington." "Oh, then the name Waccamaw, it was used then? When you went to Washington?" I wondered. A little distracted by some outside road noise, Mr. Joe asked, "How was that?" "The name Waccamaw was in use in the community when Alexander was here?" "Yes it was." "Oh." Surprised, I wanted him to clarify this: "When was the first time that you used that name to describe the community?" "Well, this community here is . . . was due to Lake Waccamaw here . . . people always thought that they were to have the name as Waccamaw. And though we have been called over a period of time, you know, the Indian here, I heard 'em . . . How long have we been called Waccamaw?" I repeated my question hoping to make myself clear. Mr. Joe elaborated, "Well it was begun back in the 40s." "Oh, in the 1940s then. Do you remember how the name was decided? You said it was because of the area and the lake. You decided to use that name then officially?" After he said yes one more time, I continued by asking, "So it was a conscious effort by the people in the group to get together and choose a name?" Patiently, he continued, "Well, you know, this was the general run, whenever we found the people here, some had been called the Lumbees, some the Cherokees, some the Siouans, and so what they come out with was this, the Waccamaw Siouans." Mr. Joe's memory of this time hints that this issue was complicated in 1949 when the people got together to consider what name might be appropriate for this phase of their battle for recognition.

Once the WAIC selected a tribal name, they used it as a key articulation strategy. They then asked Alexander to contact Washington about federal status. In November 1949, Alexander began a letter-writing campaign to congressmen and representatives on behalf of R. T. Freeman and "the last of the Waccamaw Tribe of the old Siouan Nation." The WAIC advised Alexander to stress such issues as education and illiteracy, race discrimination, voting rights violations, loss of land, and recognition as Indian. For example, in a letter to Julius Krug, secretary of the interior, the major problem of the Waccamaw was identified as "the South's malicious practice of race discrimination [that] recognizes only two sides of the color line" (Alexander to Krug 1949a). The white side of the color line was not in jeopardy as, "These Indians, though not wishing to be classed as white, refuse to accept the classification as colored. This refusal to accept a destiny imposed upon them by the white man has caused them to be the victim of many abuses." The Indians dictated narratives of abuse for the congressmen and bureaucrats. For example, one story concerned voting rights violations. The narrative described the events: "[Several men] went to the [school] to register for voting. On arriving at the school they found [the white official] was not there, so they preceded to his home and his wife said he was at [a local drug store]. This was about 10:30 A.M. As [the men] entered the store [the official] was registering others. He advised the Indian men that he did not have time to register any more people but that he would be at the [school] from 1 P.M. to 6 P.M. that day. [The Indians] returned to the school about 3:30 P.M. Finding [the official] was not there, they proceeded to his home and was told by his wife that he was in another township registering people. She suggested they come back the following Saturday. [The Indian men] waited in the vicinity of the school until 6 P.M. but [the official] did not return to the schoolhouse. The following Saturday [the same men] returned to [the official's] home. [The official] told them he could not register them inasmuch as he had already turned the books in." In another story about trying to register to vote, another obstacle, a literacy test, prevented an Indian man from registering. In this story, the Indian man was made to recite the Preamble to the U.S. Constitution from memory and to write a letter to the President of the United States to demonstrate his literacy. When he completed both tasks, the registrar told him, "This is fine. It would be all right if you were writing to me, but the law says you must satisfy your pole holder (meaning himself) and it doesn't satisfy me." Narratives of abuse and stories of such incidents relayed the "troubled existence" of the Waccamaw.

Another story related an incident involving the "collection of fines without trial." In this story, a young Indian man told of being fined by the local sheriff for trespassing while he was out looking for his runaway hunting dogs. Walking along the right-of-way of the then Seaboard Railroad, the Indian man was confronted by a "woods rider" from a local hunting club. The "woods rider" advised the Indian man that he was trespassing. The Indian man tried to explain that he had been hunting on the "Indian hunting reservation" when his dogs took off to join those heard in the distance at this all-white hunting club. Later in the evening, the Deputy Sheriff came to the Indian man's home with a warrant for his arrest. Finding only the man's wife at home, the Deputy Sheriff informed her that he "didn't want any trouble," and that her husband had better come over to see him that evening. When the Indian man arrived in town to find the Deputy, he was told to pay a fine for trespassing. Fearful of defying the Deputy, he paid the fine although he had done nothing illegal nor had his "day in court."

Other stories told about land lost by Indians to white neighbors. Most of the losses came about due to poverty, illiteracy, and irregular land transactions. Two land claims, one in 1867 and another in 1908, linked Indian men of different generations in a long fight to keep their land from being taken from them (Eddy and Harmon 1949). In 1867, two brothers-in-law, Eli Jacobs and E. L. Patrick, and their close friend John Jacobs joined together to prevent the sale of land they believed they had already purchased. The story of their efforts came out on November 30, 1908, when Eric Norden bought a large tract of land located in the center of the Indian community, lying on both sides of the Bladen/Columbus County line. The Indian men lay claim to a large tract of land that was originally owned by Shadrack Jacobs and Abraham Freeman. Abraham Freeman began buying land in the Buckhead/Ricefield area as early as 1787 and Shadrack Jacobs joined him there, buying land in 1805 and 1806. A large section of the original Shadrack Jacobs tract came eventually to be owned by a family of Mitchells. Margaret Mitchell, perhaps Shadrack's daughter and certainly an acquaintance and neighbor, acquired a portion of Shadrack's tract in 1828. E. L. Patrick, Eli Jacobs, and John Jacobs came from families who were friends and associates of Shadrack Jacobs, Abraham Freeman, and Margaret Mitchell. Bythel Mitchell owned the tract in question in 1856 and he mortgaged the land to David B. Gillespie, a non-Indian. The Gillespie family argued that Mitchell lost the land after a judgment was made against it and David Gillespie purchased the property. No record existed of this transaction; however, the Gillespie family stated this to be the origin of their claim to the land. The land became known in court records as the Gillespie Tract; the Indians referred to it as "Mitchell Land," recalling its earlier connection to their ancestors who settled the area in the early nineteenth century. E. L. Patrick, Eli Jacobs, and John Jacobs made an agreement to purchase the Mitchell Land in 1867 for one thousand dollars from David Gillespie. Payments were made from time to time until David Gillespie sold the land in 1883 to George S. Gillespie, who conveyed the land to Eric Norden in 1908 (Eddy and Harmon 1949:354). Hearing about this transaction, the heirs of E. L. Patrick, Eli Jacobs, and John Jacobs brought a counterclaim to the court, described in the records of the court as an "unrecorded agreement made between them and David B. Gillespie sometime in the year 1867." George Gillespie made an effort to clear up the matter several years prior to 1908 when he "instituted suit against all of the claimants in the year 1899, and a Restraining Order was issued against them August 28, 1908." The Indians were prevented from any further use of the land, such as "cutting, removing, or selling any timber, trees, cross-ties, wood, [or] poles." Gillespie eventually won his case, and "a judgment in favor of Gillespie and against the claimants was rendered by the Superior Court in the year 1910." The heirs of E. L. Patrick, Eli Jacobs, and John Jacobs made "a motion in Superior Court to set aside the judgment and the case was pending in October 1914." However, eventually the court ruled in favor of the Gillespie claim, especially to lands lying north of the Bladen/Columbus County line. This story of land loss was linked directly to members of the early WAIC because men like E. L. Patrick and his brother-in-law Eli Jacobs both served on the school committees: Patrick served in 1885 and 1892 and Jacobs in 1885. School committeemen often represented their families on the WAIC. These same men were only one generation removed from earlier ancestors like Shadrack Jacobs and Abraham Freeman, who secured the land base of their families by acquiring deeds and land grants in the late eighteenth and early nineteenth centuries.

Many people lost land to missed mortgage payments; irregular land transactions, poverty, and illiteracy left entire families to face a grim future as sharecroppers. Such stories supported the need for federal status.

On November 14, 1949, the secretary of the interior received a letter from "the Council of Wide Awake Indians, Waccamaw Tribe of the Siouan Nation" petitioning "for recognition and acceptance as Indian Wards of the Government of the United States." The great-grandsons of E. L. Patrick and Eli and John Jacobs—Reverend R. T. Freeman, Hezzie Patrick, Clifton Freeman, Ossie Jacobs, and Lewis Jacobs—signed this letter as members of the WAIC. The council asked the secretary for practical help with road improvement, schools, medicine, hospitals, and field drainage. They continued, "In as much as we are uneducated people, we further pray that the skilled guidance of our Government will teach us to make our lands prosper. We are not begging alms. Our only desire is to be accorded the same conveniences and necessities our neighbors enjoy, which we are denied, for the taxes we pay." Finally, they asked for "protection from those whose greed would see us destroyed."

Just how much help could they expect from the government? They found out at their first meeting that help would be difficult to obtain. R. T. Freeman and a delegation of Indians met with John Provinse, assistant commissioner of Indian affairs, in mid-November 1949. Provinse explained that the government's Indian programs were reserved for federally recognized tribes. Simply asking to be made wards of the government was not enough; they had to get support from Congress. Provinse suggested to Freeman and the delegation that they seek help from their North Carolina congressmen. Freeman took Provinse's advice, asking Alexander to make these contacts as soon as possible. Consequently, Hon. F. Ertel Carlyle, Hon. Clyde R. Hoey, and Hon. Frank P. Graham received letters about the Indians' request for federal status. Later, on December 8, 1949, Provinse summarized what he told the Indian delegation in a letter to Frank P. Graham: "I informed Mr. Alexander and the delegation that the United States evidently has never recognized the group in question, and has assumed no responsibility for legal protection, welfare, or other matters. Usually such recognition is based on a treaty between the United States and the Tribe of Indians, or it may be based on an Act of Congress authorizing the Secretary of Interior or the Commissioner of Indian Affairs to perform certain acts or provide certain services for the tribe in question. There is neither treaty nor statute covering the Waccamaw Indians." He continued, "Congress, of course, has authority to provide for the welfare of the people in question by legislating in their behalf. I should be happy to discuss the problems of those Indians with you, if you desire. It is my impression that the group is in need of educational facilities, and perhaps some assistance in making better use of the resources they now possess."

Shortly after R. T. Freeman and the Indian delegation met Provinse, Norris Poulson sought information for the Subcommittee on Indian Affairs. Provinse responded to Poulson that while he had the historical material on the Waccamaw written by Alexander he had had no opportunity to "verify" it. He wrote that it "can be assumed that the present inhabitants of the area are descendants of a tribe or tribes whose existence has long been unknown." He describes the "so-called Waccamaws of today" as "remnants of a group that was overlooked or assumed to have disappeared." Provinse made it clear to Poulson that the state of North Carolina had the major responsibility for providing schools, health care, and other services to the Waccamaw. As he said, "in the absence of a treaty obligation or legislative direction the Department of the Interior is without any authority to expend public funds in behalf of these or *other similarly situated Indians*" (italics mine). As this latter phrase shows, Provinse was beginning to think of the wider implications of extending federal status to the Waccamaw. Later, he came out against the Waccamaw Bill.

The November meeting with Provinse was on Alexander's mind when he wrote to his friend Robert Ward of South Carolina on November 29: "The case of the Waccamaw Indians has been presented to the Office of Indian Affairs and they have been assured of as much assistance as the Bureau can offer them." The Indian delegation presented Provinse with Alexander's history and "much documentary evidence." Perhaps somewhat disappointed, Alexander lamented, "The amount of aid these people can be given without congressional action appears to be quite limited." Alexander hoped that Ward might offer him some direction on what to do next. Ward did have valuable experience to share with Alexander and the WAIC. He had served as executive secretary for South Carolina Senator J. P. Richards "during the period of time the Catawbas were seeking recognition." He published a short historical piece on the Catawba, too (Ward, cited in Brown 1966:17). Alexander told Ward, "it would be helpful to know as much as possible about the problems of the Catawbas in their effort to gain recognition" and asked Ward to send him a copy of the Catawba Bill, constitution, and bylaws. The Catawba recognition effort would prove useful to the WAIC.

R. T. Freeman learned from Provinse that the government helped tribes with whom they had treaties. Neither the Waccamaw nor the Catawba ever had a treaty with the federal government, so the Catawba case might be of interest. Both depended on state governments for assistance with education, health care, and economic development; the Catawba had a state reservation and federal protection as wards of the government. Freeman and the WAIC listened to Alexander's report on the Catawba as they waited for word from Congress about federal status. Perhaps the Catawba would serve as a model on how to proceed.

The WAIC authorized Alexander to meet with the Association on American Indian Affairs (AAIA) in New York. On December 16, 1949, Alexander Lesser, executive director of AAIA, made a report to the executive committee on the Waccamaw (Stevens 1949–1950:1949:2). Lesser explained to Oliver La Farge what approach might work, using the Catawba as a model. La Farge agreed: "There is precedent for the action required (which at this writing seems likely to be favored by the Bureau) in the 1940 legislation which gave similar status to the isolated Catawba group. I have taken the position that if the people themselves want it, we would support if not sponsor the necessary legislation" (Lesser to La Farge 1949). Lesser sent Alexander to Felix S. Cohen, the AAIA's lawyer, "who knows a lot of the background." Lesser cautioned La Farge that "[u]ntil very recent years there was no schooling at all for these people—none have an education beyond third grade—and health services were also virtually nil." These were good reasons to help them, but Lesser continued, saying, "There is little Indian in culture about these people now, but there is no doubt of documented proof that they are still living on the land area which their aboriginal ancestors inhabited in the 17th-18th centuries." Lesser was alarmed by what he termed "some pretty brutal treatment" of the Waccamaw, saying, "I believe we should find out all we can about this, legally and otherwise—I have read Alexander's long historical and contemporary summary . . . and then, if it makes sense, [we should] support their rights and use them as an appeal issue. It has many dramatic angles."

Three days later the AAIA executive committee passed a resolution to sponsor legislation giving the "Waccamaw Indians recognition as an Indian tribe and such rights as they be entitled to as a tribe, providing that proposed legislation meets the approval of the Waccamaw people." Two days after that Alexander Lesser wrote to the WAIC via Alexander informing them of this support (Lesser to Alexander 1949). Attorney Felix Cohen, already personally acquainted with Alexander and his wife after a recent visit by the couple to Washington, discussed the wording of the proposed bill by telephone with Alexander on December 23, 1949 (Alexander to Lesser 1949b). Alexander thought highly of Cohen, saying, "I enjoyed very much meeting Mr. Cohen. I feel the Waccamaws are extremely fortunate in having so fine and able a man representing their interests." Alexander then informed the WAIC of these developments.

Earlier in November, R. T. Freeman and the WAIC had made it clear they sought some type of ward status, recognition as Indians, and protection from the federal government. The two thousand or so acres of land they offered included parcels ranging in size from three to three hundred and fifty acres. Eighty percent of this land was described as swampy and unsuitable for cultivation. The lands were "located in the Waccamaw Township, Columbus County; Carver Creek Township, Bladen County, approximately four miles north of Bolton and two miles off highway 211. These lands are adjoining the Seven Mile Bay and lie in the Swamps of . . . Ricefield, Doehead, and Buckhead. These lands are almost entirely surrounded by the properties of large paper companies" (Alexander to Cohen 1949b).

The WAIC approved the final wording of the Waccamaw Bill, 157 adults signed on in support of the effort, and Freeman made a certified copy of his request for the legislation (Alexander 1950a). On December 24, 1949, R. T. Freeman authorized Alexander to mail the package containing the necessary documents to the AAIA. The WAIC had discussed the wording at length in their meetings during December 1949. Alexander explained to the Waccamaw two proposals outlined by Cohen, both of which would lead to congressional action giving federal recognition and some federal assistance. The first plan suggested a bill for recognition of the "Waccamaw as Indians and giving them the privilege of borrowing money from the U.S. Government under the Indian Reorganization Act (IRA) of 1934." The IRA assisted tribes by helping them to organize their governing body and to write their constitution. It also granted them status as federally chartered corporations. As such, they were then entitled to employ their own legal counsel and issue charters of incorporation for business purposes (Deloria and Lytle 1983:100). The format that emerged from the IRA of 1934 was a model of tribal government that followed the European legalistic form. In the Waccamaw case, this meant replacing the old informal method of choosing the "men of age" who spoke for the major family groups on the WAIC with a formally elected tribal council. The position of "chief spokesman" would become one of tribal chief.

No matter which proposal the Waccamaw favored, the leadership position of Reverend Freeman would undergo a slight redefinition that very likely would have resulted anyway from the interaction of the Indian and the white interpretations of words like "tribe" and "chief." In all the correspondence written by Alexander on behalf of Freeman and the Indian community, Alexander refers to the group as a "tribe" and in the views of most white people, tribes must have "chiefs." It is not clear that this is the Indian view because Freeman signs the first letter from the "Council of Wide Awake Indians, Waccamaw Tribe of the Siouan Nation" to the secretary of the interior on November 14, 1949, simply as "Reverend R. T. Freeman" (Freeman et al. 1949). The more informal reference to leaders as chief spokesmen by Indians themselves becomes simply "chief" by the 1950 hearings on the Waccamaw Bill. Reverend Freeman's testimony is listed as "Statement of Chief R. T. Freeman of the Waccamaw Indians of North Carolina" (U.S. House of Representatives 1950:29). In his letter to Felix Cohen on December 19, 1949, reporting which of Cohen's plans the community favored, Alexander described Reverend Freeman's leadership position as "the Chief of this Tribe." Alexander summarized the consensus of the community, saying that this first proposal would not "accomplish anything toward their rehabilitation other than, as the Chief of this Tribe put it, give their white county officials a 9 ft. stick to beat them with" (Alexander 1949b).

The Indians favored Cohen's second proposal for a procedure to place the Indian land in trust and to confer the "privilege of being accepted as Wards of the Federal Government." The WAIC felt this clear change in their status would be preferable to the status quo. But several questions came up about the actual transfer of land to federal trust status. Since their landholdings were small, the Indians wanted to know whether in the future additional lands could be put in trust. Most important, they wondered whether putting their lands in trust under the federal government would indeed lead to the desired schools, medical attention, and other privileges accorded to federally recognized tribes. The WAIC listened as Alexander explained how "under Federal protection it would be slow in gaining many of the things they need and [being accepted as wards] would not create an ideal situation." More discussions took place after Christmas in 1949.

At that time, as an older man recalled in 1990, there was growing concern among some in the Indian community about the meaning and consequences of accepting ward status. The WAIC approved a visit to the Catawba of South Carolina to gather information about ward status. "At this time, we had our meeting at the church," the man recalled. "There was some question about being wards of the government and being placed on a reservation. So, we decided to let [some of us] go and look at this group in Rock Hill, South Carolina, that had just been made wards of the government. So we went and our finding was that the people looked like they had just quit working, setting on the doorstep. So we didn't go for that and we came back and told . . . and all that that wouldn't work" (Lerch 2002:38).

The delegation visited the home of Catawba leader Chief Blue after Christmas of 1949. Chief Blue may have been Samuel Taylor Blue, whom anthropologist Frank B. Speck described as *the chief* "because of his unique personality and friendly cooperation with white friends and others seeking information" (Brown 1966:349). Chief Blue maintained a traditional style of leadership and had an air of authority that surrounded him even when he was not the officially elected chief of the moment. Indeed, he served as elected chief for twenty years and president of the Catawba branch for forty more. Even in his seventies, he continued to lead his group. Blue's mother was a full-blood Catawba and his father was white. Speck thought highly of Chief Blue (Brown 1966:350).

But to one Waccamaw visitor in December 1949, his white appearance was remembered, not his chiefly bearing. The story of that visit continues: "The first place we visited was Chief Blue's house. And they [the federal government] built him a little small, wooden home. His son had on a new suit of clothes cause it was Christmas. He was carrying wood in . . . for a fire and it [was] right smelly with that new suit on. I said . . . to myself, how's these people think? Well, [one of the Indians from Waccamaw down for the visit] he looked just like a white man, so [as a joke] we introduced him to Chief Blue as "Chief . . . " cause both of them looked white. Actually, by them being recognized and wards of the government, it showed us the picture. And we could see that regardless to what the government said we was in the white man's ways and it was time to accept the white man's ways. And that's what me and my family and most everybody else around have going ahead and accept, being Indians, but working" (Lerch 2002:39).

The contrast between being a ward of the government and an independent citizen and private property owner was striking. One young Indian saw enough to make him reject wardship status outright. For some of the younger generation, a reservation was out of the question: "Several men of my generation who had worked hard to get ahead . . . more so than many others who did nothing to help themselves, rejected the idea of pooling all of their resources so everyone own everything in common" (Lerch 2002:40). After visiting the Catawba of Rock Hill, these men were even more against the idea than ever. However, they were in the minority. One man reported his view as follows: "When we had the meeting there was so many that was just thrilled to death because they wanted the reservation. But here's where I came in. I'd been out there stuffing from the time we got married. When we got married, we did not have any place to build a house. My folks didn't have nothing and her folks wouldn't give us nothing. And so there we was, kids without any land. We have worked hard, I loved sawmill work. But there was folks that had never done that in the community. They would take my land, take everybody's land and set it up as wards of the government. Each one of us would start with the same thing and I couldn't see that. From my personal feeling, not from my feeling whether I was an Indian or white, or what, I felt, what . . . am I doing[?] I am giving away all of this hard work [that's what] I am doing. And I had a cousin who had never in his life tried to do that and I used him in the talk that night. I said [my cousin] will have the same thing I got. He's got the clothes on his back and what he can steal. I got this land, this farm, new car, four or five trucks, thirty two different people that works for us, and now I going to come down and be a ward of the government and equal with him. I can't see that. And I got a few to seeing it my way" (Lerch 2002:40).

The WAIC worked over the final wording of the Waccamaw Bill, taking into consideration this young man's objections. Eventually, the wording included the phrase "voluntary conveyances" of land to reassure the opposition that no one was being forced to give up their land. The council also had to consider the opinions of attorney Cohen and Alexander Lesser of AAIA, who favored the first plan recommending the incorporation of the tribe under the provisions of the IRA of 1934. The final version of the bill included this provision. Apparently, by January 3, 1950, Cohen (1950) convinced them that "further aid might be secured if the legislation were broadened to include recognition of the Waccamaw Tribe as entitled to all the benefits of the Indian Reorganization Act of June 18, 1934." The next day Lesser added his support to Cohen's proposal because "the Waccamaw people should have the advantages of rights under the Indian Reorganization Act, and, if one piece of legislation can do the whole job, it would be well to get it done that way." Lesser feared that it would be even more difficult to go back to Congress and ask for more bills as such a process is "always hazardous and entails the same difficulties all over again."

The WAIC faced congressional difficulties; local white opposition grew as soon as word got out about the bill. Three days after H.R. 7153, known as the Waccamaw Bill, was formally introduced, white opposition mounted against the Indians. "Commissioners Reject Plan for Indian Reservation in County" ran the headline in the *News Reporter* on February 9, 1950 (*News Reporter* 1950). The Columbus County board of commissioners had "disapproved a petition for an Indian reservation in the Bolton area." The paper cited a drawback to the plan in "the smallness of the tribe" of sixty or seventy families. Another obstacle, the article continued, was that "[t]he response of the Department of the Interior has been that the Federal Government recognizes Indian tribes through treaties or statutes, and is trying to shed responsibility for Indians as rapidly as possible rather than take on new groups." Another newspaper report said that the Waccamaw were just one of many such groups wanting federal recognition. The paper quoted the attorney for the Bureau of Indian Affairs who, while unfamiliar with the

Waccamaw, said he knew of "similar requests" from some "15,000 Croatan of North Carolina—west of Lake Waccamaw" and "groups in Louisiana, and other Southern and Eastern States" (*News and Observer* 1950).

The wheels were set in motion, grinding forward with their own momentum. The Waccamaw Siouan Indians found both support for and resistance to their plan. Their plea for help touched a nerve in Congress—many hoped to completely end all federal obligations to Indians. A new era of termination had begun.

7
The Waccamaw Bill and the Era of Termination

On Wednesday, April 26, 1950, the Waccamaw Bill received congressional review before the House of Representatives Subcommittee on Indian Affairs, Committee on Public Lands. The text of the hearing preserves the "voices" of the principal parties. The committee chairman, Toby Morris, noted that Congressman Norris Poulson of California and "our colleague, Justice Bosone, of Utah" (U.S. House of Representatives 1950:1) sponsored the Waccamaw Bill (known as H.R. 7153 and H.R. 7299). The Waccamaw leaders who participated in the hearing included Chief R. T. Freeman, Lewis Jacobs, William Jacobs, Sylvester Jacobs, W. J. Freeman, and Robert Jacobs. Their advocate, James Evan Alexander, was also present. The North Carolina senators and representatives were absent but Chairman Morris would contact them at a later date (U.S. House 1950:2).

The Waccamaw Bill (H.R. 7153 and H.R. 7299) authorized the secretary of the interior to accept "voluntary conveyances of lands owned by Waccamaw Indians in North Carolina and to issue trust patents for such lands, and for other purposes." The Indian trust lands became "inalienable, except with the approval of the Secretary of the Interior, and non-taxable until otherwise provided by Congress." The bill called for a tribal membership and guaranteed the same "rights which are enjoyed by all other Indian tribes, including the right to participate in Indian educational facilities, Indian health facilities, Indian loan funds, and all other privileges extended to Indians and Indian tribes by the Act of June 18, 1934 (49 Stat. 984), as amended, without prejudice to the rights of citizenship now held by the said Waccamaw Indians."

The Waccamaw Bill would establish federal status for the Indians. This was the clear intent of the Wide Awake Indian Council (WAIC), Chief R. T. Freeman, Felix Cohen, James Alexander, and the Association on American Indian Affairs (AAIA). The congressmen also understood this; their questions focused on two important qualifications for federal Indian status. First, was the tribe in question a distinct political community that governed itself? Was the tribe socially and politically distinct from non-Indians? Second, had the federal government acknowledged "that it had both a political relationship with the specific tribe and a responsibility for it[?]" (Roth 2001:50). These two qualifications had been in place since 1830. The answers given by the Waccamaw demonstrated their eligibility; however, the congressmen were in no mood to accept another tribe into federal status. The policy of termination of Indian rights was gaining momentum in 1950, involving many of those who sat in review of the Waccamaw Bill.

The act of June 1934 was the Indian Reorganization Act (IRA). Passed under the Roosevelt administration, the IRA ended the unpopular policy of allotment of Indian lands initiated by the 1887 General Allotment or Dawes Act. John Collier, Indian commissioner during the Roosevelt administration, championed the IRA, believing it gave Indians greater say over their affairs and strengthened their tribal governments. Under its provisions, tribes organized for the common welfare of the tribe and adopted federally approved constitutions and bylaws. This organization, Collier believed, made tribal government more effective in dealing with local, state, and federal governments. Power was shifted to the tribal governments and away from the federal government and the Bureau of Indian Affairs (Deloria and Lytle 1983:14). The Waccamaw Bill was written on the recommendation and encouragement of the anthropologists and lawyers of the AAIA using the same guidelines as the IRA of 1934 (Stevens 1949–1950: 1950:1). The previous chapter discussed the Waccamaw leaders' role in shaping the IRA provisions to meet their local needs and fears. They particularly stressed that land conveyances would be voluntary under the Waccamaw Bill.

The historian Alvin M. Josephy, Jr., notes that Collier conceived the IRA of 1934 as a move toward Indian self-determination and assimilation. It strengthened tribal government while at the same time it encouraged the kind of assimilation that would reflect "an accommodation without coercion between the dominant society and Indians who were managing and running their own affairs" (Josephy 1998:204). Josephy says Collier and his anthropological supporters like Oliver La Farge, who later headed the AAIA, which advised the Waccamaw on the Waccamaw Bill, "practiced a kind of paternalism that considered the Indians too untutored in the white man's ways to be able to cope with the dominant society on an equal basis" (Josephy 1998:205). After World War II, the IRA and other New Deal programs for Indians suffered from lack of funds and support in Congress. The text of the hearing on the Waccamaw Bill of 1950 hints at this loss of support. When the hearing opened, the extent of support from the Indian Office was unknown (U.S. House 1950:1).

Chairman Morris clarified the meaning of the bill saying, "this bill in substance seeks to put these particular people in the same category as other Indians." We see why he used the phrase "these people" rather than calling them the Waccamaw Indians when he continued: "My understanding is that the *theory* behind the bill [is] that these people are *actually Indians* and should be treated as such and they have been discriminated against by not receiving the benefits that other tribes have received, and I take it that is the main issue." The main issue centered on Indian rights and government responsibility, and it was considered on the eve of a shift in Indian policy toward federal termination of all tribal responsibility (U.S. House 1950:6, emphasis mine).

James Alexander represented the WAIC of the Waccamaw Siouan tribe in the first half of the hearing. Alexander's statement before the committee sought to establish the Waccamaw Siouan as a small remnant Indian population, surviving from colonial times to the present, in relative isolation in swampy land in southeastern North Carolina. This explained why they did not already have federal relations with the government. He established the need for federal tribe status when he described how many families lost their ancestral land to speculators and developers in a controversy over legal title to these ancestral lands (U.S. House 1950:8).

This loss of land in the twentieth century aroused the interest of the congressmen, who probed deeper into the issue. Alexander reported what he learned from the Indians about the ancestral lands. There were "two blocks of land that some of their ancestors had foresight enough, having learned the white man's ways, to possess and had filed patents upon" that anchored the community to lands deeded in the eighteenth century (U.S. House 1950:9). The WAIC hoped the congressmen would extend federal protection from unlawful seizure to their lands similar to that granted Indians generally. Alexander pointed out that like many Eastern Indians, the Waccamaw had no prior treaty or agreements with the federal government, "[s]o they were never accorded any recognition as an Indian group and never accorded any privileges or rights due the Indians as the original possessors of the land" (U.S. House 1950:9).

The congressmen learned of certain surviving Indian traditions distinguishing them from non-Indians. Alexander testified, "Now, taking statements from the individual members of the tribe, as far as their memories and customs are concerned, the older members of the tribe remember that their ancestors placed their deceased on scaffolds so that the 'fowls of the air' might carry the remains away. The vultures would pick the bones clean, in other words." He continued, "Certain other Indian traits are retained in their methods of cooking. Some of the members of the tribe still roll their food in corn meal and cook it on the hearth on the open fire. Their medical traditions are of Indian origin, and [involve] the use of roots and herbs concocted into brews for the purpose of curing ills." He added, "An interesting sidelight is that there is evidence of many of the Indians having been bitten by rattlesnakes, and I cannot find one instance where any one so injured has died after partaking of a brew prepared by [a certain woman] . . . being the medicine woman of the tribe, from certain herbs" (U.S. House 1950:10). Alexander's narrative intended to establish that the Indians had a long history in their current settlement. Alexander said, "They have been there in the swamp. They have always been there. They can take you to old sites right there on the land. For example, one of them took us up and said: 'This is where my forbears [sic], my ancestors, lived, on this little hill right over there.' And we dug around in the field and found innumerable arrowheads and pottery fragments, and evidence of Indian culture, on that hill. Now, you could hunt those fields over for years and not find anything if you had not been directed to the site—and they had no way of knowing about those Indians being there if it had not been handed down to them from their own ancestors" (U.S. House 1950:10–11).

The congressmen gathered facts about the community, asking, "How many are there altogether, as you understand it, of this tribe, of these people—how many are involved?" Alexander responded, "There are approximately 340 of these people. I have not kept up with the recent births. But there are 127 adults 21 years of age or over, and that has been broken up into 71 families." "Where do they make their money?" asked Mr. Poulson, to which Alexander replied, "They do some work in the woods and they cut pulpwood, and some of them have some income from very small tobacco allotments. But due to the nature of the soil and the need for drainage in that area, they frequently lose their crops from excessive moisture." To the question, "Do they own their property in common or individually?" Alexander responded, "They own the property individually, although some of the property, for example, which one man may claim he owns he does not hold a deed on; it is some other member of the tribe who holds the old deed. In other words, they have not actually transferred the land. But the deeds do exist for all of the lands" (U.S. House 1950:13). Land tenure followed a quasi-communal land principle among the Waccamaw Siouan. Family land was informally divided among heirs without the legal transfer a deed represents. The Indian system resulted in confusion about ownership that may have contributed to land loss. Another question about landholdings followed, "Do they all live in one compact area or are they scattered out?" Alexander explained, "They all live in one compact area consisting of about 2000 acres. Actually the settlement is divided by the branch of a swamp. In other words, part of them live on Ricefield Island, and the others back on Buckhead Island . . . These 'islands' are simply higher patches of ground. However, they are about equally divided on those two islands, but they are all an integrated community. In other words, they live close to the land they till." These lands badly needed drainage to increase their productivity. Impassable roads also compounded the problems of drainage (U.S. House 1950:140).

The congressmen heard evidence about illiteracy and education next. As proof that there was need of federal intervention, the testimony of Joe Jennings, the superintendent of the Cherokee Reservation in North Carolina, was offered. Concerning the local school known as the "Wide Awake School," Jennings reported, "The windows are poorly spaced and furnish only about one-half of the light needed. Dark, dirty walls aggravate this condition. The blackboards are poor and insufficient. The seats are old, and not of the proper sizes. Especially in the class room used by the seventh and eighth grades the desks are so crowded together that there is hardly leg room for the pupils, and desks designed for one person are occupied by two. There are no instructional supplies. The rooms are absolutely cheerless. There is no attempt at beautification or decoration, and nothing in the classrooms to stimulate thought or interest. The building is supported by brick stilts with no underpinning, and hogs wander freely beneath it. There is no provision for the noon lunch; pupils and teachers bring their lunches from home. It is apparent that the teachers have no supervision. It is a sad fact that after the people have worked so long and hard, and have put forth so much of their own labor and money to secure a school of their own, they have only this wretched building with its shallow well and three unsightly and unsanitary outhouses" (Jennings 1950).

The welfare of the Waccamaw came under state jurisdiction because the tribe lacked federal status. State taxes supported public education but Alexander believed this to be the major problem. Tax dollars supported only white and colored schools except in cases where state law recognized Indian rights (U.S. House 1950:17). In the Waccamaw Siouan case, this had come only recently and the literacy levels were low as a consequence. To make matters worse, voting rights had been denied, too (U.S. House 1950:19). An incredulous Congressman White asked, "Do you mean that they deprived these people of their rights of citizenship, if they are citizens?" (U.S. House 1950:20). Alexander responded, "That is right." American Indians had been granted citizenship rights in 1924; however, many Southern states resisted

Figure 7.1. View of front of Wide Awake Indian School described in Jennings Report of 1949 (Natl. Arch., Bureau of Ind. Affairs Coll.: RG 75, CCF GEN. SERV. 1940–56, Box 13)

Figure 7.2. Chief R. T. Freeman (on right) in front of Wide Awake Indian School, 1949 (Natl. Arch., Bureau of Ind. Affairs Coll.: RG 75, CCF GEN. SERV. 1940–56, Box 13)

"in law and/or in practice" recognizing citizenship rights of Indians (Roth 2001:51). To overcome these discriminations, the WAIC wanted federal protection.

Congressman D'Ewart asked, "You do not think that making this an Indian reservation would improve the situation, do you?" (U.S. House 1950: 21). On behalf of the WAIC, Alexander answered that yes that is exactly what they want. D'Ewart replied, "On these Indian reservations, you have no law and order. You have no school regulations, you have no marriage laws, you have no school attendance laws, and all the rest of it. All that is waived when you make an Indian reservation" (U.S. House 1950:22). The reservation symbolized a degradation of the human spirit, backwardness, and stood as an icon of the antimodern. The incredulous congressman could not accept the reservation as a solution to the Indians' problems. Alexander's narrative countered the antimodern imagery by evoking an idyllic tribal society: "These people have no crime among themselves, sir. They have their own tribal council . . . the council of old men; and whatever they say is law and the young men will enforce that which is set down and enacted. And it is very effective. These people do not need protection from themselves. They live together very harmoniously" (U.S. House 1950:23). There was a political community here that articulated with non-Indians.

Modernity or modern life threatened the harmony of tribal life portrayed in this description. First, from the perspective of the Indians, the failure of modernity to deliver the promises of development threatened the very existence of the tribe. Second, from the perspective of the congressman, reservation life corrupted individuals by forcing them to live communal, pseudo-tribal lives. Alexander added, "I have known these people morning, noon and night, Sundays and weekdays. I have watched them work, seen them die, run around for somebody to take care of a new-born baby. I know these people personally and intimately. I know them to be as fine, good, upstanding, cleanliving people, in short, *good Christians,* as you will find anywhere" (U.S. House 1950:23–24, emphasis mine). The dialogue's emphasis on Christian conversion, a product of the colonial encounter between Indians and Europeans, testified to their relation to modernity at an earlier era in their history. That brush with Christianity molded them into the clean-living people portrayed by Alexander, qualifying them for protected tribal living under the federal gaze.

The sentiment against creating another reservation was strong on the committee. Congresswoman Reva Bosone of Utah, one of the bill's sponsors, summed up the feeling, saying, "I suppose it is true . . . that if this becomes an Indian reservation, it would be one step towards what the members of this committee want to guard against, and that is placing the

Indians in wardship. But I am just wondering whether that is the answer . . . As I gather from the testimony of the witness, nothing has ever been done with them. They are a *lost tribe,* and if we leave them that way, the State of North Carolina is not going to help them. So to get jurisdiction so that we can have a survey made of them might be the answer, because the assistance that the Federal Government could give might be of great benefit" (U.S. House 1950:24, emphasis mine). The question then became how to help the Indians "establish themselves as Indians" without going all the way toward establishing the hated reservation. Bosone offered a middle ground in setting up a reservation temporarily, then terminating the federal relationship at a later date. Helping the Waccamaw Indians, who were described as "a horrible example of what civilization can do," was disconnected from the establishment of a reservation.

Even Alexander seemed to agree in principle, but he reminded the committee, "The provision asking that their lands be placed in trust, these Indians want that. They have discussed it. They have been losing their land. They feel if they lose much more of it they will not have enough land for their children" (U.S. House 1950:28). Tribal life was difficult to maintain without some federal protection. The tribal elders had lost the authority to prevent even "a wild youth" from selling off their ancestral land. They now found themselves in the position of arguing for a reservation and ward status in order to maintain a tribal authority over the next generation. Leaders from the Waccamaw community spoke to these and other issues in the second half of the committee hearing.

The first Indian leader to speak on behalf of the WAIC was Chief R. T. Freeman. Chairman Morris greeted him, saying, "You understand what the whole thing is about: to determine whether you folk are entitled to be taken under the regular jurisdiction of the Bureau of Indian Affairs. That is the substance of it—whether or not you are entitled to certain rights and privileges *as an Indian tribe,* and *whether or not you have need for the services* of the Bureau of Indian Affairs, for your tribe" (U.S. House 1950:29, emphasis mine). Chief Freeman began, "Mr. Chairman and members of the committee, I know we need to be under the Federal Government. We feel as though we are going to lose all of the little land we have title for today. That is the reason I know that we should be under some Government that will take care of us and lead us in the right way. We are in bad shape" (U.S. House 1950:30). Freeman focused on need, which he knew and felt was basic to their plea for federal tribal status. Since he did not initially address the issue of entitlement *as an Indian tribe,* he was interrupted with another question. "Why do you want to wear the yoke and not remain free, the same as I am?" asked Mr. Lemke. Freeman answered, "[W]e need somebody to help us protect our land, because it is being taken away from us so fast." The Indians' tie to land and community was at the basis of Freeman's argument. But the committee pressed Freeman further, getting him to pin down the cause of this loss of land as a lack of education. "That is the real trouble, Chief, is it not: lack of education?" asked Mrs. Bosone. But a school alone would not solve the problem in Freeman's view: "We would be glad to have the school, but love to be under the jurisdiction of the Government." Freeman understood the difference between federal tribal status and their current situation; he sincerely doubted better schools alone would change very much.

The Indians and the congressmen held two entirely different views on the solution to the problem. Chief Freeman wanted the jurisdiction of the Bureau of Indian Affairs extended to the Indian community by the means of federal recognition. Some of the committeemen favored ending all government responsibility to Indian tribes. As the questioning continued, the committee members tried to establish a reason the Waccamaw never had a previous relationship with the bureau and whether or not there was sufficient need to warrant extending federal recognition now. Other solutions would be proposed and discussed.

Chairman Morris asked, "Do you know why you folk have not been accorded the same privileges, as you term them, at least, that have been accorded to other Indians?" (U.S. House 1950:31). Morris surely did not expect Freeman, a man who admitted to having no formal education and who could barely read and write, to understand the history of Indian relations with the federal government and the application of Indian law. Morris had already heard Alexander address this issue earlier in the day. So what was he after? Was he asking what was wrong with Freeman's people? What did they lack or have that might prohibit them from this relationship? Freeman seemed to interpret Morris's questions this way because he had heard them all before from white power holders at the local and state levels. He responded, "One thing is that the lawmakers of the county and state, we have been after them for years and years, and session after session, to build us a school. Of course my dad never went to school, and I never went to a day's public school in my life. So it came up to my own generation, and I did the same. Still they did not do anything for us, *unless we would receive the rights of a colored person and be recognized as colored.* And of course we live on our own land. We try to pay our taxes as best we can, and we feel as though we are entitled to a proper school and proper schooling" (U.S. House 1950:31, emphasis mine). Freeman linked his own efforts to those of the previous generation of leaders. They had carried their fight to the local authorities for many years, resisting the racial classifications of those in power that extended the privileges of modern life to those who conformed and accepted their place in society. Mr. Poulson, one of the bill's sponsors, established their social distinctiveness from non-Indians by asking, "Is it not true that there have been no intermarriages between members of your tribe and the colored folk?" Freeman answered, "No, there has not been." White intermarriage "way back" was a possibility. Chairman Morris, still unsatisfied, repeated his question, "do you know why, originally, or maybe up to this time, you have never been taken under the Bureau of Indians Affairs?" Although Freeman already identified racism as a major factor, he responded, "we never found a friend educated to lead us till we found Mr. Alexander, and he saw the conditions, the suffering, the terrible conditions—no doctor, no help in any way, no schools" (U.S. House 1950:32). Chairman Morris dropped the point, turning instead to a series of questions about the lifestyle of the Indians and exploring the second basis for granting ward status—need. "What is the general condition of your people, chief, in regard to their general living conditions?" Freeman replied, "Very poorly, very poorly." Morris asked, "Do you live in modern homes?" Freeman said, "One or two of us have modern homes. But they have nothing extra. Most of them have little." Morris learned that the Indian people had "enough food" but not enough land, worked "a little pulpwood and a little sawmill logging," had meetings and assembly places, churches, and a separate social life (U.S. House 1950:33). They needed so much that the committee members seemed frustrated.

Mr. Morris finally asked, "What would you say in your judgment is the most pressing need here? Would it be the school, schooling?" (U.S. House 1950:34). Freeman replied, "Schooling; recognition, drainage, and such as that." While Freeman returned repeatedly to federal recognition, the committee members steered him toward other economic issues like drainage, the productivity of their land, roads, and their ability to live in a self-sufficient manner. The committee members hoped to discover in Freeman's answers that the Indians had overlooked the possibility of getting assistance from the county and state governments. But Freeman made it clear that they had been to those agencies before. At the end of Chief Freeman's testimony, Mr. Morris summarized the committee's position: "I don't know, and I don't think any member of the committee knows, just what the results will be, yet, or what solution to this problem will be forthcoming, but certainly we are going to give it every consideration to determine, if we can, what we can do" (U.S. House 1950:38).

Some hints at what the committee might decide came with the questioning of the next Waccamaw Indian, Lewis Jacobs. When asked whether he thought a good school for the community might be a solution to their problems, Jacobs said, "Yes, sir; if we could get a school and get the help to get our land drained, I think that we could—if we got help to take care of it and help to manage it like it ought to be, I think we could make a living" (U.S. House 1950:39). Committee member Mr. Lemke expressed a negative view of federal recognition, saying, "if you come under the Bureau of Indian Affairs, you are just jumping out of the frying pan into the fire. You would have a boss from the Bureau of Indian Affairs here in Washington down there telling you what to do and what not to do. Would you like that?" Jacobs's response probably surprised Lemke: "A good captain would be better." The sentiment against a reservation and full federal recognition was strong on the committee. The members discussed ways of helping without establishing federal tribal status. Chairman Morris reflected, "*Certainly if these people are Indians—and I certainly say from their appearance they are Indians,* why, I think we very probably owe them some consideration more than they have received, because of the fact that we originally took the land away from them, and I doubt if we have treated these particular people with the justice that they are entitled to receive at this time" (U.S. House 1950:41, emphasis mine). Lewis Jacobs was asked to verify that his people have always lived in their present area. He said, "they have been there all of their days, as far as I can remember." He was further questioned: "More than a hundred years?" He responded, "Yes." Another question: "Well, say 200 years?" He said, "Yes, sir."

Before adjourning the hearing, the committee explored several other issues including the language of the Indians, the governmental organization, and the views of committee members on the contents of the Waccamaw Bill. Alexander explained that the Indians spoke only English now but that their ancestral language was "Eastern Siouan." An anthropologist established that "they were of Eastern Siouan origin, and the fact is that Waccamaw means 'Ball Knock' in Eastern Siouan" (U.S. House 1950:74). Alexander elaborated on the meaning of the word Waccamaw saying, "Lake Waccamaw in Indian legend was formed by a ball of fire that fell out of the sky and made that depression. Indians are usually named after the place they resided, so these people are the Waccamaw or 'ball knock'—or, 'where the star fell.' That is the interpretation by Dr. Frank Speck of the University of Pennsylvania, who was the authority on Eastern Siouan Indians and the Siouan language" (U.S. House 1950:75).

The Waccamaw Bill did not specifically design a particular form of tribal government. One committee member voiced concerns about how the tribe would govern itself and work with the Bureau of Indian Affairs. Alexander elaborated upon his earlier comments on tribal organization: "Yes, they have two councils. One is a council of old men, or as I call it, a council of elder men, who make the policy; they are the policy making group among the tribe. Then there is the council of younger men, who are the more active ones among the tribe, who actively control the tribe's activities, although they are influenced almost entirely by the older men. . . . They have a chief, and the first witness I put on today is Chief R. T. Freeman" (U.S. House 1950:75–76).

A Mr. Murdock stated his position that "there are Indians and Indians . . . with reference to their claim upon the justice of our Government. . . . That is why I asked the witness [Lewis Jacobs] a moment ago how long have your people lived on this land[?] . . . Are these Indians, and have they occupied the land before the coming of the white man, as well as, is it expedient and wise to do justice to them by the establishment of a reservation[?]" (U.S. House 1950:78). As for circumstances in North Carolina, committee member Mr. White thought the Cherokee served as a precedent for offering help to the Waccamaw (U.S. House 1950:79). Then Mr. Lemke, who questioned Chief Freeman earlier in the morning, stated, "Mr. Chairman, I am not in favor of creating any more reservations or taking in any more wards of the Government by the Government of the United States. I am in favor of giving them the help they need and of putting them on their feet." Mr. Lemke questioned the legality of turning citizens into federal wards; even if it was legal, he was opposed (U.S. House 1950:80). As the morning passed without clear consensus on what to do, perhaps many agreed with the sentiment of Mr. White when he declared that he wanted to hear the opinion of Mr. Zimmerman, acting commissioner of Indian Affairs (U.S. House 1950:27). The hearing adjourned at 1:05 P.M.

The sentiments toward wards and reservations expressed by Mr. Lemke reflected the growing support for termination of all federal responsibilities for American Indians. At the end of World War II, there were 250 reservations, many of which were widely believed to be impeding the progress of their inhabitants. Between 1945 and 1950, 1,365,801 acres of Indian land and an estimated 13,263 Indians had been affected by termination (Cowger 1999:100). Termination was the "final drive to assimilate the Indians once and for all in the dominant society." It meant the legal end of all federal trust obligations and administrative responsibilities to the tribes. The ideal situation was to transfer these responsibilities to the state and local governments. The tribal assets would be distributed to the tribes or individual tribal members. The termination movement began under the Truman administration. In 1947, William Zimmerman, the acting commissioner of Indian Affairs, complied with a directive from the Senate Civil Service Committee to draw up a plan for termination (Cowger 1999:52). The Zimmerman plan divided the tribes into categories based on their readiness for termination. The first group included the Flatheads, Klamaths, Menominees, Osages, Iroquois of New York, Potawatomis of Kansas, several California groups, and the Turtle Mountain. These tribes were the most prepared for termination in Zimmerman's view. Those in the second group would be ready in ten years and those in the third group probably never. Zimmerman evaluated the tribes on their degree of acculturation, economic readiness, and willingness to assume independence, as well as on the states' eagerness and ability to provide needed services. Zimmerman's plan suited the conservatives in Congress who hoped to proceed quickly with termination. Termination was a backlash against the policies of the New Deal.

The postwar period brought significant changes in Indian policy and the liberalism of John Collier and the Roosevelt administration (Cowger 1999:101). Collier promoted cultural pluralism and strengthening tribal government and supported a reduced role for the Bureau of Indian Affairs in the lives of American Indians. The new postwar climate favored an assimilation of ethnic groups and minorities and an even greater reduction of the role of the Bureau of Indian Affairs and an end of the federal support for tribes and reservations. The slogan became "set American Indians free" (Cowger 1999:101). This was a popular notion among western senators and congressmen like Burton K. Wheeler of Montana, Elmer Thomas of Oklahoma, and Harlan J. Bushfield of South Dakota (Cowger 1999:101). Americans needed similar values of individualism, competition, capitalism, and private property. American Indians, whose values of spiritualism, communalism, and community participation, appeared too "communistic" in this Cold War era.

While termination was popular with many congressmen, it was popular among some American Indians, too. The National Congress of American Indians (NCAI) accepted some aspects of termination while rejecting others (Cowger 1999:102). They disliked the use of force but favored the idea of ending federal regulation of Indian affairs. They liked the ideas of self-determination and the gradual elimination of the Bureau of Indian Affairs. The NCAI worried about state jurisdiction over criminal and civil Indian affairs (Cowger 1999:103). Would this be an infraction of Indian sovereignty? If termination came, some tribes favored establishing tribal rolls to determine who would share in tribal assets. Many tribes opposed the wording of termination documents claiming to "set them free" because they did not see themselves as slaves to the tribal system (Cowger 1999:104). Still others feared that termination took them backward, abolishing strong tribal governments, constitutions, and corporations established under the Indian Reorganization Act of 1934. Many of the termination-minded officials played key roles in the fate of the Waccamaw Bill of 1950.

As mentioned, the federal government put the fight against communism at the top of its postwar agenda. President Truman made it a higher priority than the funding of social programs like the Indian New Deal. John Collier resigned as commissioner of Indian Affairs in 1945 and the Bureau of Indian Affairs was set adrift under a series of short-term leaders. Roosevelt appointed William A. Brophy, a non-Indian, to the post. Although he supported the Indian New Deal, Brophy did not push these programs with much enthusiasm (Cowger 1999:51). Harold L. Ickes, the secretary of the interior and a supporter of Collier, soon followed Collier in retirement in 1946. Truman put Julius Krug into the position despite the fact that he had "little knowledge of Indian affairs" (Cowger 1999:51). Krug had less enthusiasm for cultural pluralism, diversity, and liberal reforms than Secretary Ickes. Commissioner Brophy's term as head of Indian Affairs was marred by his lingering illness between 1946 and 1948. William Zimmerman, assistant commissioner under John Collier and Brophy, acted as commissioner in Brophy's place. He continued in the post of assistant commissioner into May 1950 (Zimmerman 1950). As mentioned earlier, Zimmerman's plan for termination failed to protect the Indian New Deal gains from being reversed (Cowger 1999:52).

Secretary Krug received the first letter about the Waccamaw Indians from Alexander on November 7, 1949 (Alexander 1949a). A week later, the Council of Wide Awake Indians, Waccamaw Tribe of the Siouan Nation, forwarded their plea to Krug "for recognition and acceptance as Indian wards of the Government of the United States" (Freeman et al. 1949). Krug's reputation with the NCAI suffered in 1947 when he appeared to sell out "Indian interests to the large timber corporations" in Alaska. Many Alaskan natives opposed Public Law 385, known as the Tongass Timber Bill, as did the NCAI (Cowger 1999:60). Then, in 1948–1949, Krug "prepared to sponsor the Krug Indian Land Confiscation Bill to extinguish all native land claims in Alaska. He suggested that if Indians relinquished claims to the land, in return the government would provide sufficient land for them to live on" (Cowger 1999:62). The NCAI also opposed this action. So the Waccamaw leaders submitted their pleas to a man whose reputation was being formed as someone who weakly supported native and indigenous rights. Krug forwarded the material to John Provinse, assistant commissioner of Indian Affairs, who handled the appointments and meetings with James Evan Alexander, Reverend R. T. Freeman, and the Waccamaw delegation. Correspondence between Alexander and John Provinse in November and December 1949 shows that Alexander was aware of the antitribal sentiment in Congress (Alexander 1949a). Alexander obtained a copy of a speech by Senator Hugh Butler of Nebraska disparaging "mixed blood in Indian tribes." Butler was also known as an opponent of tribal rights and

The Waccamaw Bill / 109

reservations (Cowger 1999:61, 71). When chairman of the Committee on Public Lands in 1948, Senator Butler, along with Albert A. Grorud, clerk of the Senate subcommittee on Indian Affairs, Utah senator Arthur Watkins, and Montana congressman Wesley D'Ewart, "proposed legislation (S.J. 162 and H.R. 269) to repeal the 1936 act authorizing the secretary of interior to create reservations" (Cowger 1999:61). Butler tried unsuccessfully to link the leadership of the NCAI with communism in the 1950s. Wesley D'Ewart's opinions on reservations and his line of questioning during the hearing on the Waccamaw Bill revealed that he had not changed his position in 1950.

Throughout December 1949, John Provinse, acting Indian commissioner, handled correspondence on the Waccamaw Indians. Provinse asked Joe Jennings, superintendent of the Cherokee Agency in North Carolina to make a site visit in the Waccamaw community and report his findings (Provinse to Jennings 1949). He also answered correspondence from Norris Poulson concerning the Waccamaw Indians and their requests (Provinse to Poulson 1949). Poulson was gathering information from Provinse and the Bureau of Indian Affairs before making the decision to sponsor the Waccamaw Bill. Provinse advised, "The so-called Waccamaw of today are probably remnants of a group that was overlooked or assumed to have disappeared. The United States made no treaties with these Indians and neither has Congress directed that benefits be provided for them. In the absence of a treaty obligation or legislative direction the Department of the Interior is without any authority to expend public funds in behalf of these or other similarly situated Indians." Provinse described the situation in North Carolina: "The primary responsibility for the welfare of such a group now rests with the State of North Carolina. Some years ago the state, by motion of its Legislature, recognized as Indians a body of people residing primarily in Robeson County and established a school and other facilities for the group. It is conceivable that similar action might be taken in the present instance if proper representations were made to the State Legislature. I suggested this course of action to Mr. Alexander." Provinse's direction to Alexander to explore options on the state level clearly fit within the termination climate of the day.

The AAIA threw its support behind the Waccamaw Bill of 1950. Darcy McNickle, a Flathead Indian and co-founder of the NCAI, described the AAIA as "a predominantly white reform organization, an exception, truly sympathetic to the needs of Indians" (Cowger 1999:35). The AAIA was created in 1937 when the American Indian Defense Association and the National Association on Indian Affairs merged. John Collier had a hand in founding the American Indian Defense Association in 1922. The original name of the AAIA was the American Association on Indian Affairs, which was changed to its present name in 1946. Oliver La Farge, an anthropologist and author, was its first president. The AAIA worked to protect and secure the constitutional rights of Indians (Cowger 1999:36). When James Alexander approached them on behalf of the Waccamaw, they agreed to help. Oliver La Farge wrote letters on the Waccamaw case to the major congressional leaders, seeking their support (La Farge 1950). The Waccamaw Bill was described in La Farge's letters as "a just and honorable step for the United States to take."

After Norris Poulson and Reva Bosone introduced their Waccamaw bills, congressmen requested information about the Waccamaw. Some of these requests came to the desk of John R. Nichols, commissioner of Indian Affairs in February 1950. John McCormack, majority leader of the House of Representatives, wrote Nichols of his support for the Waccamaw, describing their plight as "the saddest and most pitiful I have ever read" (McCormack 1950). Nichols assured McCormack that they knew of the case and said, "we know that there are many other similar groups in North Carolina and in other states for whom the Federal Government has assumed no responsibility. I have no doubt as to the authority of Congress to extend Federal jurisdiction to this group. The Department has been requested to submit its report on Mr. Poulson's bill for the consideration of the House Committee on Public Lands. I shall be glad to arrange to have a copy of the report sent to you" (Nichols 1950). As we know from the hearing testimony above, Nichols's promised report had not reached Poulson and the committee by April 26, 1950. Nichols's views on the Waccamaw Bill, however, were expressed in a letter to North Carolina Senator Frank P. Graham (Nichols 1950). Nichols wrote, "You asked specifically for anthropological information as to whether the Waccamaws are Indians or Negroes." Here we find no inquiry into the need for recognition or the entitlement to services of the Bureau of Indian Affairs. Rather, it is race that is paramount. Apparently, Graham's position on the Waccamaw Bill depended in part on how Nichols responded. Nichols reported, "We have searched through such literature as is available and regrettably find very little published material in connection with this people. I am enclosing a quotation taken from John R. Swanton of the Smithsonian Institution, and the foremost expert on the Indian tribes of the Southeast." This anthropological testimony to the tribes in the Southeast came with the reports submitted by James Alexander and Joe Jennings, superintendent of the reservation of the Eastern Band of Cherokee Indians. Nichols reminded Graham that "[t]his material, in any case, would not be classed as expert testimony on the question of the racial designation of the Waccamaws. Both men have indicated that in their opinions the people in question are of Indian descent, or at least show evidence of having Indian

The Waccamaw Bill / 111

blood. Some individuals in the group also give evidence of having Negro blood. As I say, however, these are personal impressions of the men, neither of whom is a trained anthropologist." These inquires reveal the context of racial categories of the 1950s and how politics and anthropological authority informed who was and who was not an Indian. Joe Jennings's site report of February 16, 1950, detailed the extent to which Indian identity was situated in geographical, regional, and racial contexts.

Superintendent Joe Jennings of the Cherokee Indian Agency in North Carolina visited the Waccamaw Indian community in February on behalf of John Provinse, assistant commissioner of Indian Affairs (Jennings 1950). He limited the scope of his investigation to contemporary living conditions and racial discrimination. The letter Jennings wrote is hereafter referred to as the "Jennings Report." The Jennings Report situated the Waccamaw within the context of North Carolina Indians and reviewed the state's Indian schools in Sampson and Robeson Counties, racial discrimination, factionalism within and between the Indian communities of the state, the drainage and productivity of the land, tobacco allotments, living conditions, and local schools, and it offered possible solutions. Jennings noted "this group of people [Waccamaw] is a small segment of the approximately 30,000 persons whom the State recognizes as Indians, particularly in the matter of education." Jennings noted that Waccamaw Indian high school students rarely attended the Robeson Indian schools, where there is "a self-perpetuating committee in Robeson County that passes upon the eligibility of pupils seeking to enter the Indian schools of that County." Jennings explained, "I mention some of the ramifications of the race issue in order to show the complexity of the problem involved." Indian and non-Indian racial attitudes shaped the discourse within the Indian category, too. The Jennings Report commented that "[t]here is plenty of prejudice in all the counties concerned regarding the Indian groups, and not one of the counties will admit pupils from the various groups into the white schools." Indian bias against sending their children to "schools for Negroes" was also strong. The "complexity of the social problems involved" impressed Jennings.

The Jennings Report then turned to the social and economic conditions of the Waccamaw Indian community. "The people are very industrious," he wrote, making a living from "saw milling and other lumbering activities" that required them to "pay stumpage to cut timber on non-Indian land" hundreds of miles from home. Sometimes they worked "on the large contiguous tracts owned by paper companies." Indian homes "average somewhat better than the homes of colored people and tenants, but below the homes of the white people." Local prejudice created bitterness "against

Figure 7.3. Old home of wood construction in Waccamaw community, early 1990s (photo by Patricia Barker Lerch)

county officials, particularly those of Columbus County." Their history made them reluctant to contact state and federal agencies for assistance. Jennings was willing to offer his help even if the Waccamaw Bill failed to pass in 1950. There was indeed need for some federal protection, but with the sentiment for termination of federal relations with all American Indian tribes growing stronger, the bill's future was in doubt.

President Truman appointed Dillon Myer commissioner of Indian Affairs in 1950, replacing John Nichols. Myer strongly supported the termination policy. He purged the Bureau of Indian Affairs of all Collier's appointees, clearing the way for the new policy (Cowger 1999:106). He replaced Collier's group with his own from the War Relocation Authority (WRA), where he had previously served as director. At the WRA, Myer oversaw the internment of 120,000 Japanese Americans from the Pacific Coast in detention camps. He "ran camps in an atmosphere of forced compliance" (Cowger 1999:71). Although he was an experienced administrator, he had not previously worked in Indian Affairs. Myer spearheaded the drive to diminish the role of the Bureau of Indian Affairs in Indian life and to force a new lifestyle on Indians. The bureau was decentralized into regional offices under the direct control of Myer. Myer foresaw a gradual diminish-

Figure 7.4. Tobacco farming near Waccamaw community, early 1990s (photo by Patricia Barker Lerch)

ment of bureau control of Indian affairs, ending in a complete termination of federal service. The NCAI supported Myer's position on Indian self-determination at least initially. The NCAI also wanted the Bureau of Indian Affairs out of Indian affairs but did not want the "complete end to federal supervision of Indian affairs" (Cowger 1999:72). Their vision of the new relationship between the Bureau of Indian Affairs and Indians included "federal trusteeship that included improvements in education, health care, and employment opportunities before the federal government relinquished its responsibilities" (Cowger 1999:72). Myer's position on self-determination differed from the NCAI's. He "believed democracy meant individualism but also conformity" (Cowger 1999:72). His "dictatorial style" of leadership at the Bureau of Indian Affairs "challenged Indian legal rights, integrity, sovereignty, and the right to exist as separate cultural units" (Cowger 1999:79). The NCAI found itself at odds with Myer on the meaning of self-determination.

With Myer in charge of Indian Affairs and conservative congressmen set to reverse many of the liberal policies of an earlier era, termination seemed almost certain to become federal policy. Reva Bosone of Utah, one of the sponsors of the Waccamaw Bill, introduced in 1950 "one of the first resolutions calling for legislation to end federal supervision of Indian Affairs" (Cowger 1999:107). Her state's senator, Arthur V. Watkins, was one of the chief congressional architects of the new federal policy (Cowger 1999:106). Described as a "devout conservative" and member of the Church of Jesus Christ of Latter-day Saints, Watkins ascribed to assimilation as a path of development for American Indians. It is remarkable that Representative Bosone of Utah ended up advocating on behalf of the Waccamaw in 1950.

Nothing could be done for the Waccamaw until the commissioner of Indian Affairs finalized his report on the bill. Weeks passed, commissioners came and went, and the Waccamaw waited. Others got involved, muddying the waters. For example, Acting Commissioner Zimmerman wrote to Chairman Toby Morris concerning the "large number of Indians in North Carolina situated similarly to these Waccamaws" (Zimmerman 1950). With such a large group of Indians from Robeson County in town inquiring about federal recognition, the Waccamaw's supporters knew they needed to act fast on the Waccamaw Bill. Urgent letters and telegrams from Alexander Lesser of the AAIA and Congressman Poulson asked the office of Indian Affairs to conclude its report (Lesser to Myer 1950a; Lesser to H. Rex Lee 1950b; Poulson to Nichols 1950; Poulson to Myer 1950). Finally, a report came.

Dale E. Doty, assistant secretary of the interior and Commissioner Myer's immediate supervisor, sent the long-awaited decision to J. Hardin Peterson, chairman of the Committee on Public Lands, House of Representatives (Doty 1950). The letter began, "Further reference is made to your request for a report on H.R. 7299 and H.R. 7153, identical bills 'To authorize the Secretary of the Interior to accept voluntary conveyances of lands owned by Waccamaw Indians in North Carolina and to issue trust patents for such lands, and for other purposes.'" The conclusion was clearly stated: "I recommend that these bills be not enacted." The conclusion rested on two factors: (1) the fact that the Waccamaw Indians were one of many similar groups in North Carolina and the eastern and southeastern United States "who could and doubtless would, if encouraged, present like requests for recognition and aid by the United States" and (2) they did not need protection of their lands since landownership was minimal and no serious threat of loss of land from failure to pay taxes existed. The Waccamaw case could not be separated or singled out from that of "30,000 persons" regarded as Indians by the state of North Carolina. Doty believed it was better to leave things alone; "that this group should continue to be considered a segment of the population of the State of North Carolina and that the responsibility for the welfare of the group should continue to rest with the state." Because of fears that the Waccamaw case would open the floodgates for other requests, his decision had to be negative. Even though, as Doty noted, the Waccamaw owned land while most of the other North Carolina Indians sharecropped, they had suffered no serious loss of their land base: "Conveyance of the land to the Secretary of the Interior to be held in trust would not, of itself, contribute materially to the welfare of these people. Apparently the difficulties which these people experience are similar to the difficulties in many rural areas where people are living on a substandard level." Doty's decision seemed consistent with views on termination. Why take in more and more Indians at a time when sentiment favored terminating federal responsibilities to the Indians it did have under its protection? Were the abuses and discrimination the Waccamaw faced any different from those of other illiterate rural people? The way North Carolina handled its Indian population apparently fell within the acceptable range from Doty's assessment. The Bureau of Indian Affairs continued to defend Doty's decision later in the year when critics asked "why no assistance is being given to the Waccamaw Indians of North Carolina" (Hastings 1950). The bureau's answer was "that the Waccamaw Indians of North Carolina have never been under the jurisdiction of the Bureau of Indian Affairs but have been considered a responsibility of the State of North Carolina. As a segment of the population of the State they are entitled to State services, and North Carolina does maintain specifically for Indians some schools including a small normal college."

The Waccamaw Bill managed to resurface in the 83rd Congress, 1st Session, when H.R. 262 was introduced on January 3, 1951. The text of the bill was identical to that of the 1950 Waccamaw Bill. Norris Poulson, a true and faithful friend to the Waccamaw, introduced the bill, which was referred to the Committee on Public Lands. This time John R. Murdock, chairman of the Committee on Interior and Insular Affairs of the House of Representatives, waited only a couple of months to learn of Assistant Secretary Doty's negative reply. Doty literally sent the exact same memo from 1950 and simply changed the date to March 21, 1951 (Doty 1951). The issue was dead by then and can only be remembered years later as a valiant if impossible goal. Oliver La Farge, president of the AAIA, in writing to anthropologist Sol Tax of the University of Chicago on July 27, 1962, reflected on the question of "who is or who is not an Indian" (La Farge 1962). He contemplated the question after reading a draft of a new study by sociologist Brewton Berry entitled *Almost White* (Berry 1963). La Farge remembered, "About 1950, we tried to get recognition for the Waccamaws of [North] Carolina, a group that is lower than a snake's belly in relation to its neighbors, but we did not get to first base. I think that a group such as this probably has a stronger claim than many of those in the East, if only on the strength of the fact that it retains the name of a historic tribe of Indians that lived in exactly the same place at the time of first white contacts. Federal recognition, however, calls for a degree of Indianness that really pokes one in the eye." One might add that the political climate of termination made it doubly hard for the Waccamaw. They sought protection just at the moment when congressional sentiment favored ending its federal responsibilities to Indians.

8

The Powwow Paradox

The Wide Awake Indian Council (WAIC) of the Waccamaw Tribe of the Siouan Nation returned from Washington, D.C., disappointed by the defeat of the Waccamaw Bill. Ahead lay the turbulent decades of the 1950s and 1960s during which national social and political trends would bring major changes to their lives. The 1954 Supreme Court decision in Brown v. Board of Education forever reorganized the way Indians were educated. Within ten years, the local Indian schools closed and new integrated public schools opened. The Civil Rights Movement centered on issues like desegregation and voting rights important to African Americans. Indians, however, did not immediately embrace these goals (Lurie 1971:457). The WAIC viewed desegregation with grave misgivings since they preferred to "self-segregate" in many public contexts. To compensate for the loss of the Indian school, they turned to the powwow to "revive their culture" and to Pan-Indian activism to facilitate communication with other Indians.

Powwows are social dances, largely secular events, bringing together men, women, and children from Indian communities (Powers 1990:271). They originated in Oklahoma and spread quickly throughout the country (Howard 1955). In this chapter, we will see how the powwow became an essential annual event in the Waccamaw community. Powwows replaced the Indian school as a key Indian institution, reinvigorating and infusing new energy into the participants.

Robert K. Thomas, who was an earlier observer of Pan-Indianism in Oklahoma in the 1950s, defined it as "the expression of a new identity and the institutions and symbols which are both an expression of that new identity and a fostering of it. It is the attempt to create a new ethnic group, the American Indian; it is also a vital social movement which is forever changing and growing" (Thomas 1972:128–129). As powwows spread across the nation into Indian communities, they presented a paradox. On the one hand, a certain amount of mixing of traditions in music, song, and dance made it appear that powwows might be replacing local tribal traditions. Even more threatening to some, this intertribal mingling had the potential to erase specific tribal identity and replace it with a general Indian ethnic identity (Howard 1983:71). Pan-Indian social and political activities embraced leaders from many tribal backgrounds who joined together to find effective approaches to deal with the federal government and solutions to their common problems (Lurie 1971). Would all these Pan-Indian activities blur tribal cultural differences? On the other hand, many saw powwows as a healthy combination of traditional and Pan-Indian elements that could strengthen American Indian communities and infuse new energy into local practices (Powers 1990:108). At powwows, there was room for both Pan-Indianism and tribal identity (Browner 2000; Campisi 1975; Conklin 1994; Corrigan 1970; Dahl 1994; Dyck 1979; Ellis 1990; Gelo 1999; Hatton 1986; Herle 1994; Heth 1992; Hoefnagels 2002; Hughes 2001; Kavanagh 1982; Kracht 1994; Krouse 1991; Lassiter 2000; Lerch 2001; Lurie 1971; Mattern 1996; Paredes 1965; Powers 1990, 2000; Rynkiewich 1980).

Oklahoma-style powwows spread from coast to coast. The first powwow in North Carolina was sponsored by the state-recognized Haliwa-Saponi in 1966, followed by others held in the Lumbee, Coharie, and Waccamaw Siouan communities in 1969/1970. Since that time, the annual powwow cycle has grown to include more than thirty powwows sponsored by the state-recognized tribes and smaller communities and student groups in North and South Carolina (Goertzen 2001:63–67). My study of the Waccamaw Siouan powwow (Lerch 1988, 1992a, 1999; Lerch and Bullers 1996) and the work of Marty Richardson, a Haliwa-Saponi drummer and singer with the Stony Creek Singers, on Haliwa-Saponi powwows and history provide the only in-depth community studies of the powwow. Chris Goertzen (2001) looks at the use of the powwow by the Occaneechi, who are trying to convince the North Carolina Commission of Indian Affairs of their Indianness and, by emphasizing the powwow, trying to overturn a negative ruling from the commission in the state-recognition process.

The Waccamaw Siouan powwow illustrates some of the general contributions that powwows have made to the Indian communities of North Carolina. Powwows entered the state in the late sixties, an especially turbulent time socially and politically. They offered an opportunity to "revive the culture" and advertise the Indian presence to visitors. In an earlier publication, I offered social drama analysis as a model for understanding the process of change leading up to the adoption of the powwow. What follows is the core of that description (Lerch 1993).

Social drama analysis focuses attention on the dynamics of cultural and social change (Turner 1974:37–41). In this model of social change, there are four distinct phases known as the breach, crisis, redressive action, and reintegration. A breach erupts in the normal way of conducting everyday life and a crisis results in the unveiling of social tensions. People are fearful and anxious in the crisis. These tensions and anxieties largely dissipate when new social relationships are worked out during the redressive phase. People are reintegrated into the reorganized social system, eventually returning to a routine existence. The social drama model provides insight into the Indian response to desegregation and the Civil Rights Movement.

A breach in normal social relations came with the 1964 Civil Rights Act and the desegregation of North Carolina's school system. The WAIC learned from the Columbus County school board of its intention to comply with this act on March 3, 1965. The board announced, "In Compliance with the 'Civil Rights Act of 1964,' every child in the Columbus County School System shall have the right to attend a school freely selected without regard to race or color, effective with the 1965–1966 school year" (Columbus County 1885–1964:IV:3).

A crisis developed within the Indian community as parents pondered the implications for their Indian schools. One member of the class of 1967 remembers those days, saying, "I had mixed feelings. Some of the first feelings I had [were] we do not want to go [to the integrated school] and be with other groups because they know nothing about us and we know nothing about them. But then after reading some of the materials that had been presented about things that would be offered [at the new school], I had a change of view."

The fears and anxieties facing the children of the first years of integration are captured in the memories of a thirty-eight-year-old woman whom I interviewed in 1993. I refer to her as Alicia.[1] Alicia attended Waccamaw Indian School in Buckhead for her seventh- and eighth-grade years. In 1969 the Waccamaw Indian School closed forever, and she transferred to the integrated high school. We met late in the afternoon in her office to talk about those times. I had known Alicia for many years; we enjoyed talking about the Indian community. "Alicia," I began, "you know I am looking into the experiences of Indians in the schools in the county." "Yes, I know," she replied. I said, "I hope to write a book someday featuring these experiences. I want to thank you now for agreeing to share them with me." I assured her that "as we agreed, I will not use your real name when quoting your remarks." Alicia explained that she came from a large family in which grandparents, uncles, aunts, cousins, siblings, and parents lived and worked in

1. While she gave permission to include her words in any publication on Indian education, Alicia did not wish to reveal her real name.

close proximity to her home. Her early education at one of the Indian elementary schools and at the Waccamaw Indian School for the seventh and eighth grades was often under the direction of one of her aunts or other well-known Indian people. So, when she recalls transferring to the integrated high school in 1969, her memories are filled with feelings of loss, disconnection, and disorientation: "Major things were happening to our schools, as far as integration. And that affected my age group quite a bit . . . We were caught right in the middle of it. We were awfully young and we didn't fully understand what was going on." I interrupted her to ask whether she was in the very first class to be integrated. She replied, "No, they went the year before I went. But we knew that we were next because they were closing the Waccamaw Indian School the next year." That last year, Alicia's eighth-grade year, was a complete waste of time because her teacher doubled as the principal of the Waccamaw Indian School. Without an assistant, he spent most of his time preparing the paperwork for the closing of the school and the transfer of the students to the integrated high school. Alicia felt the county neglected the Indians, saying, "I kinda blame the county for leaving us in a predicament like that because I feel like I missed the whole eighth grade."

The shock of transferring came from feeling unprepared academically, socially, and culturally. At the Waccamaw Indian School, Alicia explained, "We were still in one classroom; you didn't get up and change classes. You had twenty-five kids in the room, all eighth graders. Nobody prepared us for the transition. It was just everybody catch the bus and go to the Hallsboro [High School]." "What was that first day like?" I asked. "What happened to me, after we got on the bus and went to the high school that very first day, they called us in for general assembly. We didn't even know what a general assembly was, not until somebody else told us, you know. Everybody was to go to the meeting in the auditorium and be assigned to classrooms and teachers. Things like gym class we had no knowledge of. I'd never been in a gymnasium until I was in the ninth grade at Hallsboro High School. I knew nothing about actual dressing out for gym class. We'd had recess [and] we'd played a couple of games of ball but never actually studied a lot of health and PE." As Alicia talked, I tried to remember the tense days of the 1960s and 1970s; but my experiences were those of someone in the white majority. Alicia continued, saying, "At the beginning of the integration, in the late sixties, it was difficult for the Indian students to adjust. Some of my classmates went through ninth grade, maybe tenth, and just as soon as they turned sixteen on their birthday, they quit. A lot of them quit. They just had a hard time dealing with the integration." "Do you think integration made them drop out?" I asked. She replied, "We really won't blame it on integration alone. It was orientation. If we had been prepared for so many other things that we were just not used to. Prepared for changing classrooms, changing teachers, a separate cafeteria from the library. You know, here at our school, at the Waccamaw Indian School, the cafeteria, the auditorium, and the general assembly—everything was in one big room. It was just as hard for some of the black students, too. But we were just not prepared. Even two days of orientation from a county official might have helped." "Did you get any help from the school?" I wondered. Her answer surprised me because I thought she would say no, but Alicia responded that "[t]he instructors at Hallsboro were fantastic! We had some well-known people who are still prominent in the Lake Waccamaw–Hallsboro area, who are retired teachers now and I give them credit for putting forth an effort. One English teacher was quite honest with us when she told us that we were probably about a year behind some of the other students in the ninth grade. We were in the ninth grade but only on the seventh or eighth grade level. She told us from the very beginning that we'd have problems and that she was going to do everything she could to help us overcome it." Behind in English and math, many Indian students gave up frustrated and embarrassed.

Alicia and I turned to other differences between the integrated high school and the old Indian school. At the old Indian school, she said, "We did have a May Day Program, a fall carnival, but we didn't have any ball games or activities or any sports. I had never been to or seen a football field until I was at Hallsboro. Our Indian community had its own ballgames." Thinking back on those times from our current perspective at the turn of the twenty-first century, the public often looks nostalgically to the days before integration, before the loss of community and close family involvement in schools. So I asked her, "Alicia, do you wish you never went to an integrated school then?" Again, her answer surprised me a little, as I expected her to long for the old days. Alicia said, "I'm thankful for the integration and the school. I sometimes think we would have been farther behind if the school had not closed. Mainly because we probably didn't get the proper equipment that we deserved to have based on county funds. We probably got some books, supplies, reading materials, but we got the leftovers, or last year's books. Integration gave us an opportunity, a chance to continue, and to grow. And I think if we had remained at this Indian school, we probably wouldn't have had as many opportunities as other schools would have had."

Alicia transferred to the integrated high school in 1969, just five years after the passage of the Civil Rights Act. The deaths of John F. Kennedy, Jr., Martin Luther King, Jr., and Robert F. Kennedy are drilled into my own memories of those turbulent years. Would Alicia have experienced these same feelings, I wondered? So I asked her, "Did your teachers, either at the Waccamaw Indian School or the integrated high school, ever talk about the death of Martin Luther King, Jr.?" "No, not really," Alicia said. "I remember the exact day that President Kennedy was killed. I remember because a parent came into the classroom and told us. She was a parent who dropped in from time to time and she made an announcement that President Kennedy had been killed. It was kind of sad for us but we didn't know what was going on in the world. The death of Martin Luther King, Jr., was some time after that. Was it the same year? Anyway, we knew that Martin Luther King, Jr., had died or was killed or assassinated like President Kennedy. Somebody shot Martin Luther King. But to go on about civil rights and all the causes Martin Luther King preached about, nobody ever went into any detail about Dr. Martin Luther King. Later on, as we grew up and were exposed to more TV and read about it in books, or heard the news, well, that is when we learned about civil rights and Martin Luther King." Alicia's isolation, youth, and Indian identity all played a role in how she remembered those times.

Alicia expressed the concerns of a whole generation of students and parents fearful about the changes taking place in society. The Waccamaw Indian School symbolized the Indian battle for recognition (Lerch 1988, 1992a). Generations of parents had presented petitions through their school committees to secure public funding for Indian schools and the recognition that this brought to them. Many people experienced discrimination firsthand in the surrounding towns and sought to isolate their children as much as possible from its humiliating effects. Families feared the loss of a sense of community that their schools represented, a loss of their traditions, and a loss of their identity. The parents of the graduate quoted above were afraid that their children would not be treated fairly or offered the same opportunities in school as others or would drop out of school. In their community, with few telephones or cars, if a child stayed out of school, the parents were visited by teachers or alerted by neighbors. This closeness, it was feared, would be lost.

Alicia discussed her parents' reaction to the changes. As we sat talking, I asked her to recall her parents' feelings at the time. She began, "Oh, they were kind of sad in a way. My parents believed that Indian people should stick together. They were disappointed but they were also kind of excited that we'd have a better opportunity. My Mom was happy that we'd be able to have the things we needed. She had only had jobs in sewing factories. That's what she didn't want us to have. You know, we decided we wanted to go to college, a school that offered more subjects, more English, reading, typewriting, and things like that. They were pleased that we were going to be exposed to more but sad that the Indian school that for a number of years they had worked really hard building ... sending their children to fund raising events, that [it] would close so soon. I think the Indian school existed maybe ten or twelve years. So that was a little bit disheartening. Somebody else changes the rules then changes your lives. But I think they were pleased as far as knowing that we'd have better opportunities." "So," I asked, "Are you saying then that your parents' generation knew that their Indian schools were inadequate?" "Well," she replied, "my uncles knew because they thought about sending us to other schools some years earlier. One uncle mentioned that other schools had better teachers, books, everything. They had a wider variety of things to study. If children in the community wanted to go to college, then they had better be prepared to go. That is one of the things that they actually looked at. They considered our lifetime goals, what we wanted to be. We talked about it at home. They saw that we probably needed more than we were getting." "What did you think about the quality of education at the Indian schools?" Alicia thought about it a minute, then said, "Now the school was fine. But to me, it was a pretty good elementary school. Now, I don't know what was happening at the high school level. I do know that they had home economics at the Waccamaw Indian School. They had agriculture, biology, and a typing class. I remember my older sister talking about these classes when I was in elementary school. But I'm pretty sure that there was a lot that they didn't have."

The fears expressed by parents were well founded. How would the Indian identity of children be reinforced if they went to integrated schools? Of the 12,043 students in the Columbus County schools in 1965, 56 percent were white, 41 percent were African American, and only 3 percent were Indian (Columbus County 1885–1964:IV:527). With the Indians a tiny minority, what would prevent the school officials from classifying them as "colored" or "Negro" as they had consistently done in the past? How would the parents be represented on the school committees of these integrated schools? Would their committeemen be as effective in making their concerns heard as in the past? The school board administered the schools through a series of school committees representing the local schools. This system was established in July 1885 (Columbus County 1885–1964:I:5).

The Waccamaw Indian School had been a powerful force for the socialization of Indian identity. The children who attended the school were Indians. The teachers who taught at the school were Indians, although not always Waccamaw. The school committeemen were leading men from the Indian families. Education was filtered through the lens of Indian culture and values. Since discrimination and prejudice faced all non-whites in the surrounding towns and cities, the Indian school did its best to deflect the worst blows by teaching the students not only how to read, write, and compute, but also how to evaluate and defend their self-identity as Indian.

News of desegregation provoked a crisis in the Indian communities. Indian leaders met statewide, seeking redressive actions to meet this crisis. The Waccamaw chief, Clifton Freeman, discussed with Indian leaders from throughout the state the possibility of creating a government office to handle Indian affairs within the state. The result was the formation of the North Carolina Commission of Indian Affairs (Lerch 1993:79). The desegregation of the public schools threatened the small Indian communities with social extinction. The commission members included the larger Indian tribes like the Cherokee and the Lumbee, as well as the smaller Indian tribes like the Waccamaw, Coharie, and Haliwa-Saponi. Soon state recognition followed for the Waccamaw Siouan, the Coharie, the Haliwa-Saponi, and three urban Indian associations. The commission strengthened Indian life by offering information and assistance with grants, leadership skills, and economic development (Lerch 1992b).

The powwow was another important redressive action. Chief Clifton Freeman and his daughter Pricilla Freeman Jacobs were instrumental in organizing the first powwow in 1970. Reflecting on those days, Pricilla Freeman Jacobs described that first powwow with a mixture of nostalgia and sadness. She recalled why the powwow was adopted, saying, "We needed that here to try to revive our Indian culture. This was a way of doing it—letting other people see. Mostly we had always had a problem with recognition as Indians anyway. Most people (non-Indians) didn't know anything about Indians—[we were just] a group of people out here in the woods that nobody knows much about, never even thought about too much. It was our intention to bring [Indian] people together for fellowship; to see what each other was doing [other tribes], to share our arts and crafts with one another, [to share] the progress. At that time, all the Indian tribes were doing the same then, we were all getting started in it at the same time, trying to revive our culture. That was the purpose of the powwow at that time."

The early powwows felt like a family gathering to Pricilla Freeman Jacobs. She remembered, "Back then [1970–1976], we didn't have to worry about paying someone to come do drums or do dancing—it was mostly a sharing thing then, we were sharing with each other, and it was real good then. The purpose somewhere down the line got from the culture and tradition to a moneymaking festival. That's the way I see it." A strong community feeling, a kind of "communitas" was generated by the powwow in response to the crisis of desegregation. Powwows soon marked important community events like the acquisition of five acres of tribal land in the early seventies. A neighboring paper company donated land to the Waccamaw, who had earned a reputation within the forestry industry as hardworking and industrious people. The presentation of this land was celebrated with a small powwow.

The North Carolina Commission of Indian Affairs brought Indian leaders together to discuss new articulatory strategies like the incorporation of tribal development associations. Waccamaw Chief Freeman, Pricilla Freeman Jacobs, and other Indian leaders filed incorporation papers with the state in 1976 to organize the Waccamaw Siouan Development Association (WSDA). The articles of incorporation stated that "the corporation will itself undertake demonstration and ongoing projects to serve the health, education, general and economic welfare needs of the Waccamaw Siouan Indians, in particular." The WSDA consulted with an elected tribal board on all programs it applied for from private, state, and federal agencies. Powwow planning and preparation became the responsibility of the staff of the WSDA, where once it had been that of the chief's family.

In 1992, I published a description of the 1991 Waccamaw powwow (Lerch 1992a). A brief summary is presented here, written in the present tense, from the perspective of a visitor to the powwow grounds. The powwow opens on a Friday night.

As one approaches the powwow grounds, formerly a parking lot for the WSDA, the air reverberates with monosyllabic chants, drum beats, and occasional sharp cries and shouts. Exciting sounds and images of feathers and beads, multicolored and attractive, fill the night air with a tinge of excitement. Traders advertise their wares of wooden tomahawks, blue feathers, beaded bands, silver jewelry, leather belts, arrowheads, and an assortment of "country craft" (Lerch 1992a:28). Colorful lights hang from the framework holding up the traders' booths, casting their hues across the crowd. One gets the definite impression that the night will be special.

The welcome address, prefaced with a Christian prayer led by Chief Jacobs, begins the evening. Chief Jacobs looks out at the Indian people sitting and standing before her and says it is good "to be alive again at the 21st annual powwow" (Lerch 1992a:29). The past year was saddened by the deaths of several Indian elders. She reminds people of their lives and how much they will be missed tonight and every night. Chief Jacobs touches upon an important part of life in the community. Family and kinship ties hold the people together. Moving on, she welcomes the Indian people from "tribes throughout the state" to the powwow. She says, "[L]et's not forget our people, especially those in leadership positions that help Indians." Prestigious guests from the North Carolina Commission of Indian Affairs are introduced and asked to say a few words to the assembled crowd. The com-

Figure 8.1. Chief Pricilla Freeman Jacobs delivers welcome address, 1992 (photo by Patricia Barker Lerch)

missioner, who is a Lumbee Indian, recalls the past and the former leaders who were so instrumental in organizing the commission. He says, "It's good to be back with you today, it's enriching to be with you. I remember the early powwows, I remember Chief Freeman, Chief Jacobs's father, who gave his time, energy, and effort in helping get the Commission started. We owe a great debt to Chief Freeman" (Lerch 1992a:29). The commissioner's words will be heard echoed in speeches made the following afternoon.

The commissioner's message carries a common theme in the Indian world. Indians must "walk in two worlds." The powwow is the "Indian world here tonight" and the "other world is the world of shirts and ties." The commissioner enjoins the assembly "to be proud, to have self-esteem." He tells them that the powwow does his "heart good" and "recharges his batteries."

At ten o'clock Saturday morning, the parade participants gather at the old Waccamaw Indian School that was once the pride of the Indian community. The first to line up is the marching band of the regional integrated high school where the Indian children now go to school. Behind the band, there are carloads of special guests and dignitaries like the first Indian elected sheriff in the county. Behind the sheriff's car, a van carries the North Carolina commissioner of Indian affairs and the first Waccamaw woman lawyer

Figure 8.2. Waccamaw Indian School in 1992 where powwow parade began; view of administrative offices (photo by Patricia Barker Lerch)

Figure 8.3. Waccamaw Indian School in 1992; view of classroom wing (photo by Patricia Barker Lerch)

Figure 8.4. Parade car carrying Little Miss Waccamaw Siouan Princess 1992–1993 (photo by Patricia Barker Lerch)

to be employed in the state attorney general's office. Another car carries the all-white school board. After the dignitaries, the Indian princesses wave to the crowd from convertibles of every color and make. The girls from the Waccamaw community represent three age levels: Tiny Tot, Little Miss, and Senior Miss. Their proud families have supported them all year, making financial contributions to pay for their Indian regalia. At each level, the girls must demonstrate some particular talent (miming song lyrics, singing, reciting poetry or folklore, dancing, etc.) before a panel of judges. The judges are chosen from other Indian tribes and from the non-Indian community. Most of the girls are members of the Indian dance team and perform at public events and fairs during the year. They may also compete for the cash prizes awarded to their age grades at the powwows. Indian princesses from other tribes, mostly from around the state, ride by, proudly waving to the crowd. Finally, the core of the competition dancers brings up the rear, riding in flatbed rigs drawn by tractors and trucks.

After the parade, the powwow grounds once again become the focus of attention. Chief Jacobs welcomes the guests and visitors to the powwow, stressing the themes touched upon the evening before. The Indian princesses from the surrounding tribes are introduced. The powwow has a county fair feel to it during the afternoon as the princesses demonstrate their talents by

Figure 8.5. Color guard begins the Grand Entry (photo by Patricia Barker Lerch)

singing and dancing for the crowd. The Waccamaw are Christians, primarily Baptists and Spiritual Baptists. Gospel singers from the local Indian Baptist Church entertain friends and relatives with sentimental religious songs typical of "country-western" shows.

After the singing, the powwow grand entry parade begins the afternoon of competition and exhibition dancing. Traditional and fancy dancers break out into age- and sex-graded groups of Tiny Tots, Junior Miss and Junior Boys, and Adult. The afternoon and evening events climax with the adult men's traditional and fancy dance competitions.

The powwow paradox—introducing something new and reinforcing something old—is central to the adaptability of the Waccamaw powwow. Susan Bullers and I analyzed survey data collected in May and June 1990 in

Figure 8.6. Grand Entry (photo by Patricia Barker Lerch)

the "Little Branch" area of the Waccamaw Siouan community (Lerch and Bullers 1996). We found that the annual powwow appeared to be firmly linked to Indian identity (Lerch and Bullers 1996:394). Participating in community activities such as the annual powwow was closely associated with other more traditional community-level identity markers such as living in the community, attending one of the local Indian churches, owning land in the community, and marrying someone who was also Indian. We concluded that local powwows have become an important part of traditional Indian identity among the Waccamaw (Lerch and Bullers 1996:395). We also considered the pull of assimilation that might come with marrying outside the Indian community. We wondered whether those Indian people who married non-Indian people would also strongly embrace the powwow because of its association with a cultural pattern introduced from the outside. However, we found this not to be the case at all. In our sample, the people who married other Indians more closely associated powwows with traditional Indian ways within their Indian community than did those who married outside the community. We concluded, "The most traditional Waccamaw are endogamous [marry in] and they embrace the local Indian powwow" (Lerch and Bullers 1996:395). We thought this might be explained by the fact that the local Indian powwow is now "so embedded in the individual's self-identity as a symbol of the group that it has become reinterpreted as a local emblem of Indian identity." We recognized that the powwow was first introduced as a way to "revive the culture" and was therefore possibly seen as a traditional pattern right from the beginning. The powwow is of course not the only important marker of Indian identity in the Waccamaw community. It shares that privilege with such traditional markers as family, community, heritage, and parentage.

A lot of what ethnographers do involves talking to people, engaging them in an ongoing dialogue about events, places, things, and people. Traditionally, this dialogue remains out of sight or behind the scenes, written only in the field notes of the anthropologist. More recently, the dialogue itself has come to form the content of some ethnographies (see Lassiter's *The Power of Kiowa Song* [1998]). I am choosing to reveal the following dialogue here so that the reader can see just how I learned about the changing nature of the powwow. The dialogical narrative includes the ethnographer as an actor in the text, inserting her thoughts, views, and senses as a way to reveal her in the process of fieldwork. However, this is not done in order to write a story about the ethnographer but to demonstrate how consultants and ethnographer work together to create a narrative about events, places, objects, and people. Some anthropologists reveal the identities of their field consultants; this is quite appropriate under some circumstances and in some field sites. In southeastern North Carolina, I do not think it is appropriate because of the strong history and climate of racism surrounding the Indian people. Most of my consultants are fearful of revealing their identities, so I shall respect that fear and offer pseudonyms in the dialogue.

It was Friday, October 15, 1999, when I got into my car to drive the thirty-five miles to the Waccamaw community, where a School Day was being held on the eve of the Waccamaw powwow. The sky was bright blue, the sun glaring on my windshield, the water of the Cape Fear River and the Northwest Branch glistened like a series of shiny diamonds in the sun. It was going to be a perfect day, I mused, as I headed out. I had visited the powwow many times since 1982 but could only get away from my university responsibilities a few times over the years to attend the School Day events. I really wanted to go today because I felt that this would give me better insight into how the Waccamaw presented themselves to their neighbors. Anyway, I had heard that Pricilla Jacobs[2] was to be there and I always liked to talk to her when I could. Just as I parked my car and walked toward the powwow arena, I heard Pricilla's voice coming over the public-address

---

2. Pricilla Jacobs is the current chief of the Waccamaw Siouan.

system, offering a warm welcome to about five hundred children bused in for the day. They came from the elementary and middle schools in Bladen and Columbus Counties and represented the diverse population living in the area, including whites, African Americans, Hispanics, and Indians. I noticed that Pricilla's regalia consisted of a long-sleeved red calico shirt, a scarf tied around the neck, and a long blue calico skirt tied at the waist with a belt. In her late fifties and a proud great-grandmother, she is slightly taller than I am, about 5 feet 6 inches, slender, with shoulder-length black hair and a youthful face. I greeted her when I could and, as always, Pricilla said, "Hi Pat, how are you? Glad you could make it today." Pricilla has always made me feel welcome. Knowing she is a busy woman, running a business and a large family, preaching part time, and representing her people, I try to see her whenever I come out. Pricilla handed the microphone over to Ray Little Turtle,[3] the emcee from the Lumbee-Cheraw Tribe, who is a regular at the Waccamaw Siouan powwows. Ray is well known to the older men of the community, many of whom knew Ray's father when he owned a barbershop near Lumberton. Ray did a good job educating the school children about the Indians, the Waccamaw, and the powwow. He explained what the powwow was all about, what regalia and dance styles would be seen. I noticed that there were mostly girls dancing that day; Ray noticed this too and jokingly said, "The boys are lazy." The low number of boys turned out to be true on Saturday, too, when a census of the dancer registration (Table 8.1) confirmed the gender imbalance. On Friday afternoon, the dancers were also younger, drawn from the lower age sets of "Tiny Tot" and "Boys and Girls." In the older age sets, the gap between male and female participants narrowed. I saw two teenage daughters of another old friend named Carol,[4] both of whom are fancy dancers. One of the tribal board members, Nancy, and her teenage daughter were also present. This year's Miss Waccamaw Siouan welcomed the children to School Day, something she would do many times throughout the coming year at fairs, festivals, and powwows throughout the region. As I greeted Carol, I asked her who was playing the drum in the afternoon. She explained, "It is a group from here, a young group of boys who call themselves the Falling Star Drum group. They are playing for us today; they are new at this and just play locally." I told Carol that the new location for the powwow looked like it would work out okay. She answered, "Yes, we all hope so." Then she and I looked around

---

3. Ray Little Turtle is a well-known emcee at powwows. His comments are public and spoken to the entire audience at powwows.
4. Besides those of the two public figures mentioned above, all of the other names used in the dialogue are changed to protect anonymity.

Table 8.1. 1999 Powwow dancer registration by tribe and gender

TRIBE	GENDER Female	Male	TOTAL
Waccamaw	37 39.4%★	7 7.4%	44 46.8%
Lumbee	14 14.9%	10 10.6%	24 25.5%
Coharie	7 7.4%	5 5.3%	12 12.8%
Haliwa-Saponi	4 4.3%	2 2.1%	6 6.4%
Cherokee	1 1.1%	2 2.1%	3 3.2%
Tuscarora	--	2 2.1%	2 2.1%
Combination	1 1.1%	1 1.1%	2 2.1%
WS/Lumbee	1 1.1%	--	1 1.1%
Total	65 69.1%	29 30.9%	94 100.0%

The original sample size was 97, of which 3 were missing.

★Percent of total for tribe.

together at the arrangements. I took out my notebook and made a quick sketch of the positions of the major activities and events. Later I drew a formal diagram of the grounds.

Until 1999, the parking lot of the day-care center doubled as the powwow ground. When the powwows were fairly small, the parking lot provided enough room for everyone but as the powwows began to attract larger crowds, space became an issue. So the decision was made to try the baseball field with its newly built concession stand and ticket booth. Now, with plenty of parking and a large spacious area, the powwow seemed to grow into the space. Metal bleachers surrounded the dance circle's folding aluminum chairs reserved for the dancers and their families. Visitors, family,

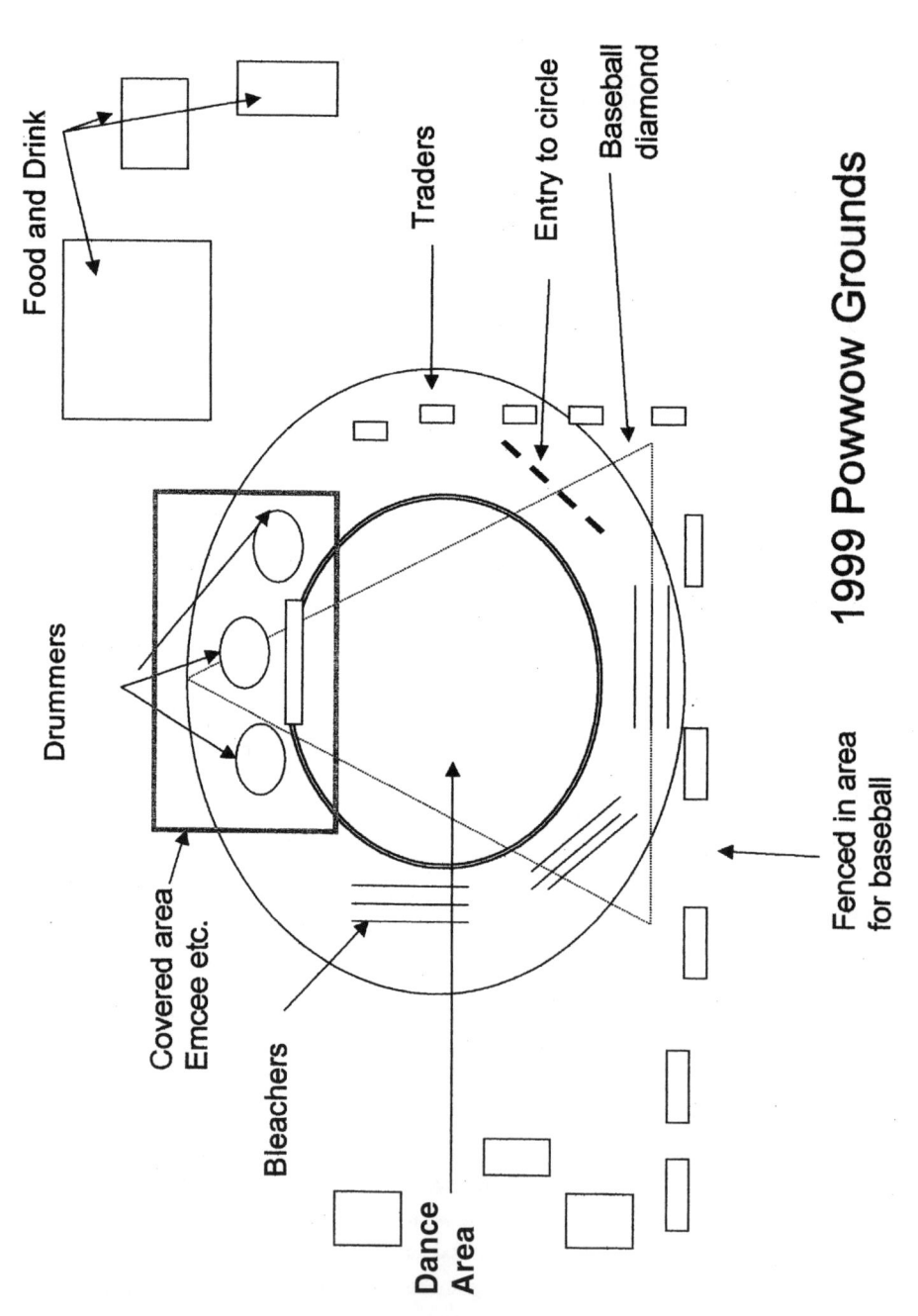

Figure 8.7. The 1999 powwow grounds (diagram by Patricia Barker Lerch)

Figure 8.8. Dance circle on eve of powwow (photo by Patricia Barker Lerch)

and friends could now look out over the seated dancers, gaining a good view of all the activities within the circle. The drummers played under a covered shelter, keeping both heat and rain off of them. The traders could now be placed spaciously around the outside of the circle of visitors and dancers, allowing people to walk leisurely through the area and to browse freely.

In 1991, I had noted that the traders were mostly whites. That may have been true then, but by 1999 things had changed. Carol was in charge of the traders. She and I chatted about the new space for the traders and I asked her how the traders were recruited or contacted for the powwow. That's when she told me about the new requirement of the traders being Indian. "When did this change take place—this year?" I wondered. "No," Carol replied, "actually for the past five years we have been asking that the traders be Indian. In fact, today, with this powwow, we've asked for the tribal enrollment cards of each trader before a contract could be given out. Most of the traders came from the Coharie, Lumbee, or Haliwa-Saponi tribes." "How strictly do you check?" I asked. "Well, we check them out. One of the traders was turned away because even though he claimed Cherokee affiliation, he didn't have a card." Carol explained that she checked out his affiliation on the Internet and even called Georgia but could not confirm that his group was even a state-recognized Cherokee group. "We check—all traders must come from state or federally recognized groups," she said. "Really, why—I know in years past that wasn't the case. What has changed?" I wanted to know. Carol explained, "They are doing this because Indian traders feel they get unfair competition from non-Indian traders. Sometimes non-Indian traders bring in cheap goods made in Taiwan or items that are not handmade." So, I noted, this was a change—now all traders must be Indian with a tribal enrollment card and with handmade crafts. Powwow traditions change over the years reflecting the current feelings of the community.

Young powwow dancers often grow up to become dedicated members of the community like Carol and Nancy. Carol worked in the area of community affairs for more than twenty years. She helped her community with economic development, job placement, summer educational programs, and a host of other programs for youth sponsored by the state government. As a college graduate, Carol is among the middle generation of leaders working on community affairs and serving as a member of the powwow committee. Nancy is a more recent college graduate, representing a slightly younger generation of community-minded leaders. Since Nancy was recently elected to the tribal board, I asked her how she got involved in tribal government. "I was asked to run for the tribal council," she explained. I commented that that seemed to reflect an older pattern of leadership in the community when years ago families would ask young men to fill a vacant position within a family line on the informal council or among the "men of age." Today, women lead the tribe in many arenas, including that of tribal chief, board member, and executive director of the WSDA. However, in 1998, only two of the seven people elected to the tribal council were women.[5] Both Carol and Nancy danced at powwows in their youth and now they have teenage daughters dancing at powwows. We chatted about the changing traditions at the powwows. Nancy explained that when she danced, "it was at Lake Waccamaw." It was different, she said, "because people danced as a group, not in individual competition." "Yes," Carol said, "that's true. I used to dance, but not in competition." Neither said whether competition was good or bad but simply noted that the dancing tradition had changed.

Another change in 1999 was in the food booth. I experienced the advantages of this change firsthand as I volunteered to work there from 11 A.M until 1 P.M. The new food building was built with a grant from Columbus

---

5. The council chairperson for 1998 was one of the two women, according to the 1998 Powwow Booklet.

County. All the labor came from community volunteers. Mary, a new staff person at WSDA, explained that the younger generation formed a Community Improvement Committee. "It's not affiliated with WSDA nor appointed by the tribal council," she explained. "Everyone is proud of this building—it has a full kitchen inside, a drink cooler, a freezer, sinks, counters, and electric plugs." I could see why they were so proud after spending several hours in it—it was certainly better than the old-style food booths with their simple structure. But I remember the food served at the earlier powwows as being very good—catfish dinners, barbeque, chicken and rice, cole slaw, fried chicken, green beans—despite the simple facilities.

School Day is all about demonstrating Indian dancing and explaining powwow traditions to the visiting schoolchildren. When lunch was served to this multiethnic audience, we worked furiously to get the food and drinks out for the hungry children. The tribe charged each teacher a flat fee for the lunch and entrance fee for the children. I noticed that they got large portions and seemed satisfied with their meal. Many teachers thanked me, perhaps thinking that I was somehow responsible for the good lunch. I accepted their thanks but found that if I tried to explain that I was just a volunteer I was greeted with quiet skepticism. Once lunch was over, I had time to search out some of my other old friends and catch up on the news.

Just after lunch around 1:30 P.M. I spotted Mr. Joe,[6] one of my oldest friends and contacts. At eighty-five years old, Mr. Joe always appears neatly dressed in pressed shirt and pants, usually with a bola tie or other item of Indian apparel. Occasionally, during the Saturday powwow activities, men of Mr. Joe's age might appear in a full-length eagle-feathered war bonnet, but I have noticed in the past several years that most now dress more casually. Mr. Joe always makes me feel like family; he greeted me with a big hug and words that reminded me I have not come to visit as often as I should. I asked him how he and his wife were doing. "Fine, I'm fine, but Miss Patty is not. Her brother just had a stroke and is now in a rest home" he explained. "Her sister is also sick." Miss Patty was taking this hard, as she had not been very well either. "She is eighty-five years old," Mr. Joe said. He and Miss Patty have been married for sixty or more years. They live in a very tidy house along the border of the community where until recently in his retirement Mr. Joe had kept a large garden. Miss Patty "put up" all the garden produce, providing for herself and her family. Childless but with a large

---

6. The titles "Mr." and "Ms." are used generally in the Waccamaw community (even I am often called "Ms. Pat"), but they are especially important for the older people. For this reason I have retained use of the titles for Mr. Joe, Miss Patty, and Mr. Paul, who fall into an older generation than the rest of my correspondents.

network of nieces and nephews, they are a beloved couple in the community. As we talked, I learned from Mr. Joe of other deaths in the family. His sister-in-law, nephew, and several others passed away during the year, making it a very sad year for him and his family. Death is always a topic of our conversations now. Years ago, Mr. Joe was my main teacher, explaining his life and role in the struggles for recognition, schools, and rights for Indians.

As we chatted, another old friend stopped by to say hello. Mr. Paul, a former member of the tribal council during the 1980s, greeted me warmly, asking how I'd been. I said fine and then, always keeping in mind my purpose is "research," I asked him whether he ever planned to run again for the tribal board. "No," he laughingly replied, "Not unless they ask me to I'm not planning to." He explained, "When I served before, some from the council asked me to run for election. I told them yes, but I don't think I'll win. Well I did win." Mr. Paul is now retired from a chemical company. Our conversation drifted toward working and retiring. Mr. Joe observed that not many Waccamaw are farm laborers anymore. "There are many Mexican migrant workers now. Big farmers are hiring them because the people in the Waccamaw community won't do that kind of work any more."

As the afternoon passed, I had the opportunity to talk with some of those who were on the powwow committee. This is always a huge responsibility; they plan for months and work long hours throughout the weekend worrying about all the details and wondering whether it will all turn out okay. Mary was officially on the powwow committee in 1999 by virtue of her staff position and noticed how much more responsibility she had to assume. Mary exclaimed, "Working as a volunteer is one thing but as a committee member quite another!" The powwow could not run without volunteer labor but the committee members organize, recruit, and direct that labor so all the powwow projects get done. This is what Mary meant. Women play a major role today, serving on the powwow committee, the staff positions of the WSDA, and the North Carolina Commission of Indian Affairs. As we talked that afternoon, I realized just how vital these women were to the managerial functions of the powwow. Several of the women thought that women make better managers than men, that women are more patient and/or "believe in the effort it takes to be a manager more than men." I wondered whether their comments reflected the fact that they were so busy and stressed by the huge responsibility of the powwow.[7]

Katherine is another old hand at powwows and community work. I had

---

7. Their impression that women take on more managerial responsibility for the powwow seems confirmed by the 1996 breakdown of committee members: 19 percent men and 81 percent women.

previously arranged to sit down later in the afternoon with Katherine to get her perspective on the behind-the-scenes organization of the powwow. Taking advantage of a lull in the afternoon's activities and giving Katherine a chance to rest, we sat together in the community building, where people were coming and going, and talked about the positions at the powwow. "Ray Little Turtle is doing a great job once again," I commented. "Yes," Katherine agreed. "We have had others who have not been so tactful or educational as Ray." The emcee's job is important because it is his (they are usually men) role to educate the non-Indians about the powwow, the dances, and Indian culture. This works best when the emcee has a good personality, as Ray does, and does not offend the people who come to the powwow. I have seen Ray Little Turtle at almost all the Waccamaw Siouan powwows between 1982 and 1999.

Tribal members choose the head dancers. "How is this done?" I asked. "Well, people get together at one of the tribal meetings—an open meeting—and discuss it. Someone is nominated and someone goes and asks him or her if they will serve. It's kind of an honor and the community's way of showing their appreciation for what the person has done for them. The person must have a good track record. If the person agrees to do the job, then the tribal council votes on them." "Can anyone do this job—any age I mean?" I asked. "Well, they must be at least 16 years old or older. The head dancer has to be present at every dance and keeps the dancers in order so they line up right for the Grand Entry on Friday night and again on Saturday night," Katherine explained. "What kind of order do you mean—do they get noisy?" I asked. "Well that too, but the line-up order. First the color guard, then the chiefs and elders, then the royalty, then the traditional dancers (grass and straight), then the fancy dancers, then the jingle dancers, then the Tiny Tots." Keeping order at the powwow is a concern of the powwow organizers. They work to keep the participants authentically Indian by checking the traders' and the dancers' enrollment cards.

The powwow committee selects the people who serve as arena director, head judge, and committee chairs. The arena director keeps order in the arena and works with the head judge. He coordinates with the emcee about what is to happen next. A person with a lot of powwow experience is selected. He does not have to be from the Waccamaw tribe. In 1999, the arena director was a Haliwa-Saponi man. The head judge makes the final decision about the dance competition winners. "This year," Katherine explained, "several men were considered [for head judge]—one Waccamaw, one Lumbee-Cheraw, and one Haliwa-Saponi." Their experience and expertise count more than their tribal affiliation in the selection. The head judge, the arena director, the emcee, and the head male and female dancers

Figure 8.9. Dancers enter the circle (photo by Patricia Barker Lerch)

work as a team to keep the powwow running smoothly. The head singer and the drum group must also be recognized for their central role. The head singer and the drum are the heart of the powwow.[8] There may be two or more drum and singer groups present at the powwow, and they are seated under a shelter behind the emcee and his table. Each drum and singer group may give someone permission to sit with them on the condition that "[a]ny person who sits at the drum must feel in his heart that he is not better than any other person sitting around him."[9]

There are many other committees whose functions provide the structure for the powwow. The princess pageant committee qualifies the candidates, organizes the pageant contest, selects the judges, and confirms the winners of the pageant to the tribal council. The pageant used to be held the same weekend as the powwow; however, recently, it is held a week, or even two weeks, prior to the powwow. School Day is another major committee, responsible for coordinating with all the local schools sending children into

---

8. The 1996 Powwow Booklet described the drum as "the grandmother."
9. Quoted from the 1996 Powwow Booklet. The Powwow Booklet for 1996 was especially complete and elaborate. Booklets are usually published each year; however, depending on the available funds and the participation of the powwow committee, some booklets are less informative than the one in 1996.

Figure 8.10. Drummers and singers at 1992 Waccamaw powwow (photo by Patricia Barker Lerch)

the community. This involves providing a lunch, parking for buses, ample seating, the program, and security. The other important committees are parking, food booth, parade, traders/venders, dancers, and registration.

Dancer registration began on Friday evening, the official start of the weekend powwow. I volunteered for this committee in 1999, hoping to learn more about this aspect of the powwow. I sat in the registration booth alongside the other committee members, one of whom was a current member of the tribal council. Each dancer was registered in one of the dance competition age-graded categories. These are Tiny Tot (1–6 years), Girls and Boys in Fancy or Traditional (7–11 years), Junior Women and Men in Fancy or Traditional (12–16 years), and Senior Men and Women in Fancy or Traditional (17 years and over). Table 8.1 shows the distribution of dancers by gender and tribe. Each dancer was charged $5.00, including their $2.00 entrance fee paid at the gate. Most of the dancers were well known to those sitting in the registration booth, so their tribal enrollment cards were rarely checked. However, those not known had to show a current tribal enrollment card. I wondered whether anyone was ever turned away. Just as I thought this, a young man approached the desk, holding out his money. The tribal council member looked up, saying, "Are you an enrolled tribal member? If so, please show your tribal enrollment card." The young man, flushed, replied, "I have to go an' get it." As he left, the people sitting in the booth discussed this person and the council member said, "I only did what I was told to do. And I was polite about it, too." A little later, the young man returned without an enrollment card but brought someone who could vouch for his registration in a tribe other than Waccamaw. I noticed that the young man look annoyed, but he said nothing about it. When it was time for Grand Entry, we took our clipboards with our dancer registration numbers and went to check off those who participated in this event. Each dancer got fifty points for participating on Friday and Saturday in Grand Entry. Points accumulated over the weekend events for participation in the Parade, Grand Entry, and the age-graded competition levels until the winners were announced on Saturday evening.

The Waccamaw powwows attract dancers primarily from North Carolina. Table 8.1 compiles data on the tribal identity of Indian dancers in 1999. The Waccamaw, who serve as volunteers on all the committees necessary to make it run smoothly for the audience and community, are the hosts of the powwow. The most visible participants like the emcee, the head singer and drummers, the arena director, and the head dancers can be Waccamaw, Haliwa-Saponi, Lumbee-Cheraw, or Coharie. The dancers come from different tribal backgrounds, too. The people who come to watch the dancing and enjoy the food and fellowship come from the Indian communities and from the neighboring African American, white, and Hispanic communities. University students, professors, and international visitors—many people from many different backgrounds—find their way to the powwow grounds for the weekend. Powwows change from year to year. They have introduced customs and patterns of music and dance that do not have a local origin. Yet, after more than thirty years of powwows, these customs have become part of the traditional way of being Indian in the Waccamaw community.

9
Waccamaw Siouan Indians

Since 1950, the Waccamaw Siouan Indians have enjoyed a much wider recognition of their Indian identity. The Pan-Indian activism of the 1970s and the introduction of the powwow as an annual event gave them a sense of place in the American Indian world. Their presence within the state and the country is routinely noted in the federal census. They are a small part of the 80,000 or so people who identified themselves as Indian in North Carolina on the 2000 federal census. They are one of the state-recognized Indian tribes, they participate in the annual Indian Unity Conference, and they contribute to Indian policy through the North Carolina Commission of Indian Affairs. In 1986, North Carolina officially honored its Indian people by designating that year as the Year of the Native American.

The Waccamaw Siouan have made tremendous economic progress in the past fifty years. When the Waccamaw Bill of 1950 was introduced, the Waccamaw people were mired in poverty and struggling to survive. Today, despite the loss of many jobs in the textile, chemical, and construction industries, the Waccamaw have a higher standard of living than their ancestors of 1950. Federal housing programs have helped replace the trailers and old-style houses with new homes of modern construction and layout. Subsistence farming and tobacco allotments have almost entirely disappeared; small kitchen gardens remain tended by an older generation of women who continue to freeze or can vegetables to share with the family. Driving into the community, one is impressed with a certain air of prosperity that is often lacking in the neighboring communities.

Besides the powwow and the Pan-Indian activities of the 1970s, Waccamaw leaders shifted their attention to economic development. A group of young men led by Chief Clifton Freeman organized the Waccamaw Indian Improvement Club and successfully negotiated the start of a small electronics factory at the site of the former Waccamaw Indian School. They tried to attract investment into their community in order to bring jobs closer to home. Club leaders went out into the nearby communities to lobby businesses to hire Indian people. It was then that Chief Freeman and his associates negotiated a gift of five acres of land from a paper company. Today, the Waccamaw Siouan Development Association (WSDA) office building, tribal meeting rooms, day care, baseball park, and annual powwow are located on this land.

The forces of modernism such as government policy, programs, and opportunities for Indian people have energized many Southeastern Indian communities (Paredes 1995). The 1960s and 1970s offered opportunities to apply for federal funds for Indians that never existed in previous decades. The Waccamaw leaders became skilled at writing grants to support local projects. The federal government supported "self-determination" for American Indians by providing funds for economic development projects. Programs like the War on Poverty, the Great Society, and the New Frontier made funds available to all poor people, not just federal-status tribes. The Waccamaw took full advantage of these opportunities, opening their successful day care under a grant from the state.

The incorporation of the WSDA in 1972 offered the tribe a new leadership style. The tribal corporation acts as a business organization whose purpose is to promote economic development and self-sufficiency. Tribal council members are elected to serve for two years; their job is to assist the chief, who serves for life. The staff of the WSDA writes grants to support community activities and further the long-term goal of self-sufficiency for the tribe. Recently, federal housing authority grants have assisted the tribe to upgrade and repair the homes of Indians within the community. The staff people at the WSDA and day care are active in the general life of the tribe. They belong to the churches, support the youth programs, and help people do their taxes, find educational scholarships, and get their GEDs.

Community organizations support the WSDA and tribal board. Tribal churches continue to play a vibrant role in community life. They mark important life events such as birth, confirmation, high school graduation, marriage, and death. Through their deacons, boards of directors, choir members, pastors, youth-group organizers, and congregations, they uphold the Indian values of family, community, and spirituality. The volunteer fire department responds rapidly to community tragedy and offers senior citizens a place to gather for lunch. Powwow social dances have been held in the fire department great room, too.

Staking a claim to Indian identity and a tribal identity offers unique challenges. Federal tribal status, although long desired, is not a panacea for the troubles of the Indians. Even the Eastern Band of Cherokee, the only tribe within the state with a reservation and full federal tribal status, continues to be plagued by controversy over how to define its membership and its Indian identity (Finger 1991). A "working consensus" must be forged within the Indian communities, between them and the federal government, and with other Indians and non-Indians.

The Waccamaw Siouan story is one of a struggle for recognition. What tribe do you belong to? They have answered this question even though their voices have faded in the face of intense opposition or criticism from those with more power. First, it was the local county government officials demanding to know "what tribe?" Next, it was the state of North Carolina. Then, the Waccamaw had to answer to the Indians of Robeson County if they wanted to attend the Indian schools of the state. The federal government almost accepted the Waccamaw into the ranks of federal-status tribes in 1950 but the era of termination had begun and the government hoped to get "clean out" of the Indian business.

"We know who we are but we want others to know," said Sylvester Jacobs in 1950 as he spoke before the congressional committee at the hearing for the Waccamaw Bill (U.S. House of Representatives 1950:3). His comment reflects the central thesis of this book: we define ourselves in relation to others. American Indians, as Nancy O. Lurie (1971) has often pointed out, follow a common strategy for survival that demands recognition as Indian as a starting point for making an articulatory relationship with other people. Based on this recognition, contractual relationships can be forged that will prevent the full assimilation of Indians into the larger social system. For American Indians in the Southeast, the larger social system for a long time denied the very existence of Indians. Systems of racism, prejudice, and discrimination powerfully mold and influence people. Being Indian in the Southeastern United States in the first half of the twentieth century was a most difficult path. At times, it seemed as though all of the power holders and voices of authority were aligned against the Indians. However, as the story of the Waccamaw Bill clearly demonstrates, there have always been people in power who supported the Indians. Without these people, there could not have been bills introduced nor hearings held. The Indian leaders themselves deserve credit for carrying on their fight for so many years. Without them, the struggles of dissent recorded in county board minutes, the newspaper articles describing the "self-styled Indians," the stories grandparents told their children—none of these things would be found in the record to document and comment about. The Waccamaw achieved a considerable measure of success in articulating to others their goals and self-identity as Indian.

On February 14, 2003, Senator Elizabeth Dole of North Carolina introduced S. 420, entitled the Lumbee Acknowledgement Act of 2003. This bill represents a major breakthrough in a battle for federal recognition that has been going on for over a century in North Carolina. The Lumbee-Cheraw have laid claim to Siouan ancestry so their fate is also of central importance to the Siouan story. Whether or not they gain the full federal recognition and status that they desire, they no doubt will continue the struggle into the future.

The Waccamaw Siouan and the other small state-recognized Indian tribes of North Carolina eye their future warily as Congress deliberates on the fate of the Lumbee-Cheraw tribe. In the past, they have often followed the example of this larger tribe, adopting their strategies, political advice, and counsel. The relational nature of Indian identity is at the heart of the recognition battles of these tribes. Today, North Carolina's senators support the Lumbee Bill; locals debate the pros and cons of Indian gaming in Robeson County and the supposed economic benefits that will come to the region if the Lumbee become federally recognized and choose to open a casino. The state's suffering economy provides the current climate for debate over recognition of the largest of the Siouan tribes in the region.

The Lumbee Bill of 2003 will bring up questions of Indian identity, tribal name, and history, and it will repeat themes of past struggles. The Waccamaw do not oppose Lumbee recognition because they have been down the same path. They went to Washington in 1950 to make their case and felt the sting of rejection. If the Lumbee are successful, it may open the door again for the Waccamaw Siouan people.

References

Alexander, James Evans
    1949a   Letters (to Frank G. Speck, October 19, November 2; to Julius C. Krug, November 7; to Robert Ward, November 11, November 29; to John Provinse, November 26, December 2). National Archives, Bureau of Indian Affairs, GEN SERV 57 × 185, Record Group 75, 1948-061 to 1950-061, Box 13, File 22930-1969-061 to 1950-061. Washington, D.C.
    1949b   Letters (to Alexander Lesser, December 12, Box 78:6, Association on American Indian Affairs; to Felix S. Cohen, December 19, Box 78:5, Association on American Indian Affairs). Princeton University Library, Princeton, New Jersey.
    1950a   Letter to Alexander Lesser, January 16. Box 78, Association on American Indian Affairs. Princeton University Library, Princeton, New Jersey.
    1950b   Waccamaw—The Fallen Star. *The American Indian* 3(30):30–39.

Allen, A. T.
    1931   Letter to Supt. C. C. Russ, Department of Public Instruction. General Correspondence of the Superintendent, County Files, Box 11, North Carolina Division of Archives and History, Raleigh.

Ashe, Samuel A.
    1908   *History of North Carolina*. 2 vols. C. L. Van Noppen, Greensboro, North Carolina.

Barnwell, Joseph W.
    1908   The Tuscarora Expedition Letters of Colonel John Barnwell. *South Carolina Historical and Genealogical Magazine* 9(January):28–54.
    1909   The Second Tuscarora Expedition. *South Carolina Historical and Genealogical Magazine* 10(January):33–48.

Barth, Fredrik
    1998   *Ethnic Groups and Boundaries: The Social Organization of Cultural Difference*. Originally published 1969. Waveland Press, Prospect Heights, Illinois.

Beale, Calvin L.
- 1957 American Tri-Racial Isolates. Their Status and Pertinence to Genetic Research. *Eugenics Quarterly* 4(4):187–196.

Bellamy, John Dillard
- 1900 Remarks of Hon. John D. Bellamy, of North Carolina, in the House of Representatives, Thursday, February 1, 1900. Washington, D.C.

Berry, Brewton
- 1945 The Mestizos of South Carolina. *American Journal of Sociology* LI:34.
- 1963 *Almost White.* Macmillan, New York.
- 1978 Marginal Groups. In *Northeast,* edited by B. Trigger, pp. 290–295. Handbook of North American Indians, vol. 15. Smithsonian Institution, Washington, D.C.

Biolsi, Thomas
- 1997 The Anthropological Construction of "Indians": Haviland Scudder Mekell and the Search for the Primitive in Lakota Country. In *Indians and Anthropologists,* edited by Thomas Biolsi and L. J. Zimmerman, pp. 133–159. University of Arizona Press, Tucson.

Bladen County, North Carolina
- 1931–1954 Minute Books, Board of Education. Elizabethtown, North Carolina.

Blu, Karen L.
- 1980 *The Lumbee Problem: The Making of an American Indian People.* Cambridge University Press, Cambridge, United Kingdom.
- 2001 Region and Recognition: Southern Indians, Anthropologists, and Presumed Biology. In *Anthropologists and Indians in the New South,* edited by R. A. Bonney and J. A. Paredes, pp. 143–155. University of Alabama Press, Tuscaloosa.

Boston News-Letter
- 1715 Boston. From Monday, August 29, to Monday, September 5, 1715. No. 194.

Braroe, Niels Winther
- 1975 Reciprocal Exploitation in an Indian-White Community. In *The Nacirema. Readings on American Culture,* edited by James P. Spradley and Michael A. Rynkiewich, pp. 185–194. Little, Brown and Company, Boston.

Brooks, E. C.
- 1921 Letter to D. McRackan, Raleigh, Department of Public Instruction. General Correspondence of the Superintendent, County Files, Box 2, North Carolina Division of Archives and History, Raleigh.

Brown, Douglas Summers
- 1966 *The Catawba Indians, the People of the River.* University of South Carolina Press, Columbia.

Browner, Tara
- 2000 Making and Singing Pow-wow Songs: Text, Form, and the Significance of Culture-Based Analysis. *Ethnomusicology* 44(2):214–233.

Campisi, Jack
- 1975 Powwow: A Study of Ethnic Boundary Maintenance. *Man in the Northeast* 9:33–46.

Churchill, Ward
- 2004 A Question of Identity. In *A Will to Survive. Indigenous Essays on the Politics of Culture, Language, and Identity,* edited by Stephen Greymorning, pp. 59–94. McGraw Hill, Boston.

Clifton, James A.
- 1989 *Being and Becoming Indian: Biographical Studies of North American Frontiers.* Dorsey Press, Chicago.

Cohen, Felix S.
- 1950 Letter to James E. Alexander, January 3, 1950. Box 78:7, Association on American Indian Affairs. Princeton University Library, Princeton, New Jersey.

Columbus County, North Carolina
- 1885–1964 Minute Books, Board of Education, Vols. I (1885–1921), II (1921–1926), III (1926–1935), and IV (1936–1964). Whiteville, North Carolina.
- 1908–1909 *A Pamphlet of Information.* North Carolina Collection, University of North Carolina, Chapel Hill.
- 1926–1933 Minutes, Board of County Commissioners, Vols. 8 and 9. Microfilm, North Carolina State Archives, Raleigh.

Conklin, Abe
- 1994 Origin of the Powwow. The Ponca He-Thus-Ka Society Dance. *Akwe:kon Journal/NMAI* 11(3/4):17–21.

Conner, R. D. W., ed.
- 1915 North Carolina, Members of the General Assembly, Sessions 1915. Edwards and Broughton Printing Co., Raleigh.
- 1917 North Carolina, Members of the General Assembly, Sessions 1917. Edwards and Broughton Printing Co., Raleigh.

Corrigan, Samuel W.
- 1970 The Plains Indian Powwow: Cultural Integration in Prairie Canada. *Anthropologica* XII(2):253–277.

Cowger, Thomas W.
- 1999 *The National Congress of American Indians: The Founding Years.* University of Nebraska Press, Lincoln.

Credle, W. F., J. Henry Highsmith, and James E. Hillman
- 1941 *Report on Chapter 370, Public Laws of North Carolina, 1941.* Department of Public Instruction, Office of the Superintendent. North Carolina Division of Archives and History, Raleigh.

Crosby, Alfred W.
- 1972 *The Columbian Exchange: Biological and Cultural Consequences of 1492.* Greenwood, Westport, Connecticut.

Cypress, Billy L.
- 2001 Comments. In *Anthropologists and Indians in the New South,* edited by R. A. Bonney and J. A. Paredes, pp. 225–228. University of Alabama Press, Tuscaloosa.

Dahl, Kathleen A.
- 1994 On the Pow Wow Circuit in the Interior Northwest. *Northwest Anthropological Research Notes* 28(2):115–134.

Dane, J. K., and B. Eugene Griessman
- 1972 The Collective Identity of Marginal Peoples: The North Carolina Experience. *American Anthropologist* 74:695–704.

Deloria, Vine, Jr., and Clifford M. Lytle
- 1983 *American Indians, American Justice.* University of Texas Press, Austin.

Dial, Adolph L., and David K. Eliades
- 1975 *The Only Land I Know: A History of the Lumbee Indians.* Indian Historian Press, San Francisco.

Dobyns, Henry F.
- 1983 *Their Number Become Thinned. Native American Population Dynamics in Eastern North America.* University of Tennessee Press, Knoxville.

Doty, Dale E.
- 1950 Letter to Jon H. Peterson, August 7, 1950. National Archives, GEN SERV 57 × 185, Record Group 75, 1948-061 to 1950-061, Box 13; File 22930-1969-061 to 1950-061. Washington, D.C.
- 1951 Letter to J. R. Murdock, March 21, 1951. National Archives, GEN SERV 57 × 185, Record Group 75, 1948-061 to 1950-061, Box 13; File 22930-1969-061 to 1950-061. Washington, D.C.

Driver, Harold E.
- 1969 *Indians of North America.* 2nd ed., rev. University of Chicago Press, Chicago.

Dyck, Noel
- 1979 Powwow and the Expression of Community in Western Canada. *Ethnos* 44(1–2):78–98.

Eakin, Paul John
- 1999 *How Our Lives Become Stories.* Cornell University Press, Ithaca.

Easterby, J. H., R. Nicholas Olsberg, and Terry W. Lipscomb
- 1951–1953 *The Journal of the Commons House of Assembly,* 1st ed. Historical Commission of South Carolina, Columbia.

Eddy, Henry Howard, and Frances Harmon, comp.
- 1949 *The Eric Norden Collection.* North Carolina State Department of Archives and History, Raleigh.

Ellis, Clyde
- 1990 "Truly Dancing Their Own Way": Modern Revival and Diffusion of the Gourd Dance. *American Indian Quarterly* XIV(1):19–33.

Erwin, Clyde A.
- 1937 Letter to J. Browning, H.D., October 21, 1937. Department of Pub-

Evans, W. McKee
    1971   *To Die Game: The Story of the Lowry Band, Indian Guerillas of Reconstruction.* Louisiana State University Press, Baton Rouge.

Finger, John R.
    1991   *Cherokee America. The Eastern Band of Cherokees in the Twentieth Century.* University of Nebraska Press, Lincoln.

Fogelson, Raymond D.
    1961   Change, Persistence, and Accommodation in Cherokee Medico-Magical Belief. In *Symposium on Cherokee and Iroquois Culture,* edited by W. N. Fenten and J. Gulick, pp. 213–225. Bureau of American Ethnology, Bulletin 180. Government Printing Office, Washington, D.C.
    1998   Perspectives on Native American Identity. In *Studying Native America. Problems and Prospects,* edited by R. Thornton, pp. 40–59. University of Wisconsin Press, Madison.

Franklin, John Hope
    1943   *The Free Negro in North Carolina, 1790–1860.* Norton, New York.

Frazier, E. Franklin
    1966   *The Negro Family in the United States.* University of Chicago Press, Chicago.

Freeman, Rev. R. T., Hezzie Patrick, Ossie Jacobs, Clifton Freeman, and Jesse Jacobs
    1949   Letter to Secretary of the Interior and Office of Indian Affairs, November 14, 1949. National Archives, GEN SERV 57 × 185 Record Group 75, 1948-061 to 1950-061, Box 13; File 22930-1969-061 to 1950-061. Washington, D.C.

Freeman, W. J.
    1931   Letter to S. A. T. Allen, February 24, 1931. Department of Public Instruction, Office of the Superintendent, General Correspondence. North Carolina Division of Archives and History, Raleigh.

Gelo, Daniel J.
    1999   Powwow Patter: Indian Emcee Discourse on Power and Identity. *Journal of American Folklore* 112(443):40–57.

Gilbert, William Harlen, Jr.
    1945   The Wesorts of Southern Maryland, an Outcasted Group. *Journal of the Washington Academy of Sciences* XXXV:237–246.
    1946a   Memorandum Concerning the Characteristics of the Larger Mixed-Blood Racial Islands of the Eastern United States. *Social Forces* 24(4):438–447.
    1946a   Mixed Bloods of the Upper Monogahela Valley, West Virginia. *Journal of the Washington Academy of Sciences* XXXVI:1–13.
    1948   Surviving Indian Groups of the Eastern United States. In *Annual*

Report of the Smithsonian Institution, pp. 407–438. Government Printing Office, Washington, D.C.

Goertzen, Chris
   2001   Powwows and Identity on the Piedmont and Coastal Plains of North Carolina. *Ethnomusicology* 45(1):58–88.

Gregg, Alexander
   1967   *History of the Old Cheraws.* Reprint of a 1925 edition; originally published 1867. Genealogical Publishing Company, Baltimore.

Gregory, Hiram F.
   1992   The Louisiana Tribes: Entering Hard Times. In *Indians of the Southeastern United States in the Late Twentieth Century,* edited by J. A. Paredes, pp. 162–182. University of Alabama Press, Tuscaloosa.

Griessman, B. Eugene
   1972   The American Isolates. *American Anthropologist* 74:693–694.

Gulick, John
   1960   *Cherokee at the Crossroads.* Institute for Research in Social Science, Chapel Hill, North Carolina.

Hastings, Lucile Ahnawake
   1950   Letter to G. A. R. Mead, November 28, 1950. National Archives, GEN SERV 57 × 185, Record Group 75, 1948-061 to 1950-061, Box 13; File 22930-1969-061 to 1950-061. Washington, D.C.

Hatton, Orin T.
   1986   In the Tradition: Grass Dance Musical Style and Female Pow-wow Singers. *Ethnomusicology* 30(2):197–222.

Hawks, Francis L.
   1857   History of North Carolina: with Maps and Illustrations. E. J. Hale & Son, Fayetteville, North Carolina.

Herle, Anita
   1994   Dancing Community: Powwow and Pan-Indianism in North America. *Cambridge Anthropology* 17(2):57–83.

Heth, Charlotte
   1992   *Native American Dance: Ceremonies and Social Traditions.* National Museum of the American Indian, Smithsonian Institution, with Starwood Pub., Washington, D.C.

Highsmith, J. Henry
   1940   Letter to C. Gordon Hunt, September 12, 1940. National Archives, GEN SERV 57 × 185, Record Group 75, 1948-061 to 1950-061, Box 13; File 22930-1969-061 to 1950-061. Washington, D.C.

Hodge, Frederick Webb
   1907   *Handbook of American Indians North of Mexico.* Government Printing Office, Washington, D.C.

Hoefnagels, Anna
   2002   Powwow Songs: Traveling Songs and Changing Protocol. *The World of Music* 44(1):127–136.

Howard, James H.
  1955   Pan-Indian Culture of Oklahoma. *The Scientific Monthly* 18(5): 215–220.
  1983   Pan-Indianism in Native American Music and Dance. *Ethnomusicology* 27(1):71–82.

Hoxie, Frederick E., Peter C. Mancall, and James H. Merrell
  2001   *American Nations. Encounters in Indian Country, 1850 to the Present.* Routledge, New York.

Hrdlicka, Ales
  1927   Letter to S. F. M. Simmons (July 12, 1927). Ales Hrdlicka Papers, Correspondence 1888–1966, National Anthropological Archives. Smithsonian Institution, Washington, D.C.

Hudson, Charles
  1970   *The Catawba Nation.* University of Georgia Press, Athens.
  1976   *The Southeastern Indians.* University of Tennessee Press, Knoxville.
  1985   *Ethnology of the Southeastern Indians: A Source Book.* Edited with an introduction by Charles Hudson. Garland, New York.

Hughes, Barbara A.
  2001   American Indian Dance: Steps to Cultural Preservation. *High Plains Applied Anthropologist* 21(2):176–181.

Jacobs, Ossie, Lewis Jacobs, and Alex Patrick
  1941   Petition to C. A. Erwin. Department of Public Instruction, Office of the Superintendent, County File General Correspondence. North Carolina Division of Archives and History, Raleigh.

Jennings, Joe
  1950   Letters to John H. Provinse, February 16 and February 21. National Archives, GEN SERV 57 × 185, Record Group 75, 1948-061 to 1950-061, Box 13; File 22930-1969-061 to 1950-061. Washington, D.C.

Johnson, T. L.
  1927   Letter to S. F. M. Simmons. Bureau of Ethnology, General Correspondence, 1909–1949. National Anthropological Archives, Smithsonian Institution, Washington, D.C.

Josephy, Alvin M.
  1998   Modern America and the Indian. In *Indians in American History,* edited by F. E. H. a. P. Iverson, pp. 198–217. Harlan Division, Wheeling, Illinois.

Kavanagh, T.
  1982   The Comanche Pow-wow: "Pan-Indianism" or Tribalism. *Haliksa'i* 1:12–27.

Kersey, Harry A.
  1992   Seminoles and Miccosukees: A Century in Retrospective. In *Indians of the Southeastern United States in the Late Twentieth Century,* edited

by J. A. Paredes, pp. 102–119. University of Alabama Press, Tuscaloosa.

Kidwell, Clara Sue
1986   The Choctaw Struggle for Land and Identity in Mississippi, 1830–1918. In *After Removal: The Choctaw in Mississippi,* edited by Samuel J. Wells and Roseanna Tubby, pp. 64–93. University of Mississippi Press, Jackson.

Koch, Frederick Henry
1921   *A Pageant of the Lower Cape Fear.* Printed by Wilmington Printing, Wilmington, North Carolina.

Kracht, Benjamin R.
1994   Kiowa Powwows: Continuity in Ritual Practice. *American Indian Quarterly* 18(3):321–348.

Krouse, Susan Applegate
1991   A Window into the Indian Culture: The Powwow as Performance. Ph.D. dissertation. University of Wisconsin-Milwaukee, Milwaukee.
1999   Kinship and Identity: Mixed Bloods in Urban Indian Communities. *American Indian Culture and Research Journal* 23:2:73–89.

Kupferer, Harriet J.
1968   The Isolated Eastern Cherokee. In *The American Indian Today,* edited by Stuart Levine and Nancy Oestreich Lurie, pp. 87–97. Everett/Edwards, Delano, Florida.

La Farge, Oliver
1950   Letters to C. R. Hoey, January 20; F. Ertel Carlyle, January 20. Box 78, Association on American Indian Affairs. Princeton University Library, Princeton, New Jersey.
1962   Letter to S. Tax, July 27, 1962. Box 172, Association on American Indian Affairs. Princeton University Library, Princeton, New Jersey.

Lassiter, Luke E.
1998   *The Power of Kiowa Song.* University of Arizona Press, Tucson.
2000   Authoritative Texts, Collaborative Ethnography, and Native American Studies. *American Indian Quarterly* 24(3):601–614.

Lawson, John, Hugh Talmage Lefler, and NetLibrary Inc.
1967   *A New Voyage to Carolina.* Originally published 1701. University of North Carolina Press, Chapel Hill.

Lee, Lawrence
1965   *The Lower Cape Fear in Colonial Days.* University of North Carolina, Chapel Hill.

Lerch, Patricia B. (Barker)
1988   Articulatory Relationships: The Waccamaw Struggle against Assimilation. In *Sea and Land: Cultural and Biological Adaptations in the Southern Coastal Plain,* edited by J. L. Peacock and J. C. Sabella, pp. 76–91. Southern Anthropological Society Proceedings No. 21. University of Georgia Press, Athens.

1992a   Pageantry, Parade, and Indian Dancing: The Staging of Identity among the Waccamaw Sioux. *Museum Anthropology* 16(2):27–34.

1992b   State-Recognized Indians of North Carolina, Including a History of the Waccamaw Sioux. In *Indians of the Southeastern United States in the Late Twentieth Century,* edited by J. A. Paredes, pp. 44–71. University of Alabama Press, Tuscaloosa.

1993   Powwows, Parades and Social Drama among the Waccamaw Sioux. In *Celebrations of Identity,* edited by P. R. Frese, pp. 75–92. Bergin & Garvey, Westport, Connecticut.

1999   "A Good Ol' Woman": Relations of Race and Gender in an Indian Community. In *Neither Separate nor Equal: Women, Race, and Class in the South,* edited by B. E. Smith, pp. 57–73. Temple University Press, Philadelphia.

2001   Celebrations and Dress: Sources of Native American Identity. In *Anthropologists and Indians in the New South,* edited by R. A. Bonney and J. A. Paredes, pp. 143–155. University of Alabama Press, Tuscaloosa.

2002   Considerations of Context, Time, and Discourse in Identity Politics for Indians of the Carolinas. In *Southern Indians and Anthropologists,* edited by L. J. Lefler and F. W. Gleach, pp. 31–42. University of Georgia Press, Athens.

Lerch, Patricia Barker, and Susan Bullers
1996   Powwows as Identity Markers: Traditional or Pan-Indian? *Human Organization* 55(4):390–395.

Lesser, Alexander
1949   Letters (to Oliver La Farge, December 16, Box 78:1; to James E. Alexander, December 21, Box 78:2), Association on American Indian Affairs. Princeton University Library, Princeton, N.J.

1950a   Letters (to James E. Alexander, January 4, Box 78:8; to Dillon Myer, May 26, Box 78:23), Association on American Indian Affairs. Princeton University Library, Princeton, N.J.

1950b   Letters to Dillon Myer, May 16; H. Rex Lee, June 16. National Archives, GEN SERV 57 × 185, Record Group 75, 1948-061 to 1950-061, Box 13; File 22930-1969-061 to 1950-061. Washington, D.C.

Levine, Stuart
1972   The Survival of Indian Identity. In *The American Indian Today,* edited by Stuart Levine and Nancy Oestreich Lurie, pp. 9–45. Penguin Books, Baltimore.

Lipscomb, Terry W., and R. Nicholas Olsberg
1977   *The Colonial Records of South Carolina. The Journal of the Commons House of Assembly. November 14, 1751–October 7, 1752.* University of South Carolina Press, Columbia.

Lurie, Nancy Oestreich
- 1971   The Contemporary American Indian Scene. In *North American Indians in Historical Perspective,* edited by Eleanor Burke Leacock and Nancy Oestreich Lurie, pp. 418–480. Random House, New York.
- 1972   An American Indian Renascence? In *The American Indian Today,* edited by Stuart Levine and Nancy Oestreich Lurie, pp. 295–328. Penguin Books, Baltimore.

McCormack, John W.
- 1950   Letter to John R. Nichols, February 14. National Archives, GEN SERV 57 × 185, Record Group 75, 1948-061 to 1950-061, Box 13; File 22930-1969-061 to 1950-061. Washington, D.C.

McDowell, William L., ed.
- 1992a   *Journals of the Commissioners of the Indian Trade: September 20, 1710–August 29, 1718.* South Carolina Department of Archives and History, Columbia.
- 1992b   *Documents Relating to Indian Affairs, May 21, 1750–August 7, 1754.* South Carolina Department of Archives and History, Columbia.
- 1992c   *Documents Relating to Indian Affairs, 1754–1765.* South Carolina Department of Archives and History, Columbia.

McPherson, O. M.
- 1915   *Indians of North Carolina.* Government Printing Office, Washington, D.C.

McRackan, Donald
- 1921   Letter to E. C. Brooks (February 14, 1950). Department of Public Instruction, General Correspondence, Office of the Superintendent. North Carolina Division of Archives and History, Raleigh.

Mattern, Mark
- 1996   Powwow as a Public Arena for Negotiating Unity and Diversity in American Indian Life. *American Indian Culture and Research Journal* 20(4):183–201.

Mereness, Newton Dennison
- 1961   *Travels in the American Colonies.* Antiquarian Press, New York.

Meriwether, Robert L.
- 1974   *The Expansion of South Carolina, 1729–1765.* Porcupine Press, Philadelphia.

Merrell, James
- 1989   *The Indian's New World: Catawba and Their Neighbors from European Contact through the Era of Removal.* University of North Carolina Press, Chapel Hill, for the Institute of Early American History and Culture, Williamsburg, Virginia.

Mihesuah, Devon A.
- 1998   American Indian Identities: Issue of Individual Choice and Development. *American Indian Culture and Research Journal* 22(2):193–226.

References / 157

Milling, Chapman James
    1969   *Red Carolinians.* University of South Carolina Press, Columbia.

Mooney, James
    1894   *The Siouan Tribes of the East.* Government Printing Office, Washington, D.C.

Morning Star (Wilmington, North Carolina)
    1920a   Dr. Koch Coming Here Next Week. May 6, 1920. Bill Reeves Collection. New Hanover County Public Library. Wilmington, North Carolina.
    1920b   Pageant Wins Approval. May 11, 1920. Bill Reeves Collection. New Hanover Public Library. Wilmington, North Carolina.

Murray, Clara
    1920   *The Wide Awake Third Reader.* Originally published 1908. Little, Brown and Company, Boston.

Neely, Sharlotte
    1991   *Snowbird Cherokees. People of Persistence.* University of Georgia Press, Athens.

News and Observer (Raleigh, North Carolina)
    1950   *Aid for Waccamaw Indians Asked.* February 8, 1950.

News Reporter (Whiteville, North Carolina)
    1929   Indian School Bill. February 14, 1929.
    1930   Self Styled Indians Appear with Request. 1930:1.
    1931   Indians Seeking Legislation for Separate Schools. January 15, 1931:1, 8.
    1936a   Self Styled Indians Are Certainly Persistent. March 12, 1936.
    1936b   Columbus Indian Squabble Flares Brightly Again. July 30, 1936:1, 4.
    1937   Old Question of Indians Finds Way to Legislature. March 11, 1937.
    1950   Commissioners Reject Plan for Indian Reservation. February 9, 1950.

Nichols, John R.
    1950   Letters to John W. McCormack, March 13; Frank P. Graham, April 14. National Archives, GEN SERV 57 × 185, Record Group 75, 1948-061 to 1950-061, Box 13; File 22930-1969-061 to 1950-061. Washington, D.C.

North Carolina
    1923   *The Public School Law of North Carolina, Codification 1923.* State Superintendent of Public Instruction, Raleigh.
    1927   *To Provide Separate Schools for the Cherokee Indians in Columbus County.* General Assembly of the State of North Carolina. North Carolina Division of Archives and History, Raleigh.
    1929   *H.B. 500. An Act to Repeal Chapter 213, Public-Local Laws 1927, Relating to Separate Schools for Cherokee Indians of Columbus County.* General Assembly of the State of North Carolina. North Carolina Division of Archives and History, Raleigh.

Oakley, Christopher Arris
   1996   The Indian Slave Trade in Coastal North Carolina and Virginia. Master's thesis. University of North Carolina at Wilmington.

Olsberg, R. Nicholas
   1974   *The Colonial Records of South Carolina. The Journal of the Commons House of Assembly. 23 April 1750–31 August 1751.* University of South Carolina Press, Columbia.

Paredes, J. Anthony
   1965   Community Celebrations in Northern Minnesota. Paper presented to the 64th Annual Meeting of the American Anthropological Association. Mimeograph copy in possession of the author.
   1992   *Indians of the Southeastern United States in the Late Twentieth Century.* University of Alabama Press, Tuscaloosa.
   1995   Paradoxes of Modernism and Indianness in the Southeast. *The American Indian Quarterly* 19(3):341–360.

Perdue, Theda
   1985   *Native Carolinians. The Indians of North Carolina.* North Carolina Division of Archives and History, Raleigh.
   1998   Indians in Southern History. In *Indians in American History,* edited by F. E. Hoxie and P. Iverson, pp. 121–139. Harlan Division, Wheeling, Illinois.

Peterson, John H., Jr.
   1992   Choctaw Self-Determination in the 1980s. In *Indians of the Southeastern United States in the Late Twentieth Century,* edited by J. A. Paredes, pp. 140–161. University of Alabama Press, Tuscaloosa.

Pollitzer, W. S., R. M. Meneqaz-Bock, and J. C. Herion
   1972   The Physical Anthropology and Genetics of Marginal People in the Southeastern United States. *American Anthropology* 74(3):719–734.

Porter, Frank W., III
   1986   Nonrecognized American Indian Tribes in the Eastern United States: An Historical Overview. In *Strategies for Survival: American Indians in the Eastern United States,* edited by Frank W. Porter III, pp. 1–42. Greenwood Press, New York.

Poulson, Norris
   1950   Letters to John R. Nichols, April 14; Dillon Myer, May 26. National Archives, GEN SERV 57 × 185, Record Group 75, 1948-061 to 1950-061, Box 13; File 22930-1969-061 to 1950-061. Washington, D.C.

Powers, William K.
   1990   *War Dance: Plains Indian Musical Performance.* University of Arizona Press, Tucson.
   2000   Echoing the Drum . . . The Place of Women in Lakota Song and Dance. *Whispering Wind* 31(1):29.

Prescott, Butler
    1949   Letter to R. R. T. Freeman, October 21, 1949. National Archives, GEN SERV 57 × 185, Record Group 75, 1948-061 to 1950-061, Box 13; File 22930-1969-061 to 1950-061. Washington, D.C.

Price, Edward T.
    1953   A Geographic Analysis of White-Indian-Negro Racial Mixtures in the Eastern United States. *Annals of the Association of American Geographers* 43(2):256–271.

Provinse, John
    1949   Letters to Frank P. Graham, December 8; Joe Jennings, December 8; Norris Poulson, December 16. National Archives, Bureau of Indian Affairs, GEN SERV 57 × 185, Record Group 75, 1948-061 to 1950-061, Box 13; File 22930-1969-061 to 1950-061. Washington, D.C.

Quattlebaum, Paul
    1956   *The Land Called Chicora.* Reprint Co., Spartanburg, South Carolina.

Ramsay, David
    1959   *History of South Carolina: From Its First Settlement in 1670 to the Year 1808.* Reprint Co., Spartanburg, South Carolina.

Registrar of Deeds
    1920   *District School Census.* Office of the Registrar of Deeds. Whiteville, North Carolina.

Rights, Douglas L.
    1957   *The American Indian in North Carolina.* J. F. Blair, Winston-Salem, North Carolina.

Robesonian (Lumberton, North Carolina)
    1927a   To Report on Status of Indians in Columbus County. June 20, 1927.
    1927b   Mandamus Issued against Columbus Education Board. December 5, 1927:5.
    1928   Voluntary Non-Suit Is Taken in Columbus Co. Indian School Case. February 27, 1928:1.
    1934   Sentiment among Indians Divided in Change of Name. February 12, 1934:1.

Roth, George
    1992   Overview of Southeastern Indian Tribes Today. In *Indians in the Southeastern United States in the Late Twentieth Century,* edited by J. A. Paredes, pp. 183–202. University of Alabama Press, Tuscaloosa.
    2001   Federal Tribal Recognition in the South. In *Anthropologists and Indians in the New South,* edited by R. A. Bonney and J. A. Paredes, pp. 49–70. University of Alabama Press, Tuscaloosa.

Roundtree, Helen C.
    1979   The Indians of Virginia: A Third Race in a Biracial State. In *South-*

eastern Indians since the Removal Era, edited by W. L. Williams, pp. 27–48. University of Georgia Press, Athens.

1990 *Pocahontas' People: The Powhatan Indians of Virginia through Four Centuries.* University of Oklahoma Press, Norman.

1992 Indian Virginians on the Move. In *Indians of the Southeastern United States in the Late Twentieth Century,* edited by J. A. Paredes, pp. 9–28. University of Alabama Press, Tuscaloosa.

Rynkiewich, Michael A.

1980 Chippewa Powwows. In *Anishinabe,* edited by J. A. Paredes, pp. 31–100. University Presses of Florida, Tallahassee.

Salley, A. S.

1911 *Narratives of Early Carolina, 1650–1708.* C. Scribner's Sons, New York.

1936 *Journal of Colonel John Herbert Commissioner of Indian Affairs for the Province of South Carolina October 17, 1727 to March 1727/28.* Printed by the State Company, Columbia, South Carolina.

1945 *Journal of the Commons House of Assembly of South Carolina November 1, 1725–April 30, 1726; Feb. 23, 1724/5 and ending June 1, 1725.* Printed under the direction of the Joint Committee on Printing, General Assembly of South Carolina, Columbia.

1946 *Journal of the Commons House of Assembly of South Carolina November 15, 1726–March 11, 1726–7.* Printed for the Historical Commission of South Carolina by the State Printing Company, Columbia.

Saunders, William Laurence, and Walter Clark

1886 *The Colonial Records of North Carolina.* Published under the supervision of the Trustees of the Public Libraries, by order of the General Assembly. Microform, 26 vols. P. M. Hale, Raleigh, North Carolina.

1887 *The Colonial Records of North Carolina.* P. M. Hale, Raleigh, North Carolina.

Seldon, Samuel

1988 Koch, Frederick Henry. In *Dictionary of North Carolina Biography,* edited by W. S. Powell and NetLibrary Inc., p. 381. University of North Carolina Press, Chapel Hill.

Sider, Gerald M.

1993 *Lumbee Indian Histories: Race, Ethnicity and Indian Identity in the Southern United States.* Cambridge University Press, Cambridge, England.

Simmons, F. M.

1927a Letter to W. J. Fewkes, June 16, 1927. Bureau of American Ethnology, General Correspondence 1909–1949, National Anthropological Archives. Smithsonian Institution, Washington, D.C.

1927b Letter to A. Hrdlicka, July 11, 1927. Ales Hrdlicka Papers, Correspondence 1888–1966, National Anthropological Archives. Smithsonian Institution, Washington, D.C.

Snipp, C. Matthew
- 1997   Some Observations about Racial Boundaries and the Experiences of American Indians. *Ethnic and Racial Studies* 20(4):667–689.

South, Stanley A.
- 1972   *The Unabridged Version of Tribes of the Carolina Lowland: Pedee-Sewee-Winyaw-Waccamaw-Cape Fear-Congaree-Wateree-Santee.* Institute of Archeology and Anthropology, University of South Carolina, Columbia.

Speck, Frank G.
- 1935   Siouan Tribes of the Carolinas as Known from Catawba, Tutelo, and Documentary Sources. *American Anthropologist,* n.s., 37:201–225.
- 1949   Letter to J. E. Alexander, October 27, 1949. National Archives, Bureau of Indian Affairs, GEN SERV 57 × 185, Record Group 75, 1948-061 to 1950-061, Box 13; File 22930-1969-061 to 1950-061. Washington, D.C.

Spencer, Robert F., and Jesse D. Jennings, eds.
- 1977   *The Native Americans.* 2nd ed. Harper & Row, New York.

Sprunt, James
- 1896   *Tales and Traditions of the Lower Cape Fear, 1661–1896.* LeGwin Brothers Printers, Wilmington, North Carolina.
- 1992   *Chronicles of the Cape Fear River 1666–1916.* Originally published 1916. Edwards and Braughton, Raleigh, North Carolina.

Stevens, Alden
- 1949–1950   *Minutes, Executive Committee Meeting, Association on American Indian Affairs.* Princeton University Library, Princeton, New Jersey.

Sturtevant, William C.
- 1954   The Medicine Bundles and Busks of the Florida Seminole. *Florida Anthropologist* 7:31–70.

Swanton, J. R.
- 1923   New Light on the Early History of the Siouan Peoples. *Journal of Washington Academy of Sciences* 13(3):33–43.
- 1934   Probable Identity of the "Croatan" Indians. In *U.S. Senate Reports, Siouan Indians of Lumber River.* Report no. 204, 73rd Congress, 2nd Session, pp. 3–6. U.S. Government Printing Office, Washington, D.C.
- 1946   *The Indians of the Southeastern United States.* U.S. Government Printing Office, Washington.

Taukchiray, Wesley DuRant, and Alice Bee Kasakoff
- 1992   Contemporary Native Americans in South Carolina. In *Indians of the Southeastern United States in the Late Twentieth Century,* edited by J. A. Paredes, pp. 72–101. University of Alabama Press, Tuscaloosa.

Thomas, Robert K.
- 1961   The Redbird Smith Movement. In *Symposium on Cherokee and*

Iroquois Culture, edited by William N. Fenton and John Gulick, pp. 156–166. Smithsonian Institution Bureau of American Ethnology Bulletin 180. U.S. Government Printing Office, Washington, D.C.

1972 Pan-Indianism. In *The American Indian Today,* edited by Stuart Levine and Nancy Oestreich Lurie, pp. 128–140. Penguin Books, Baltimore.

Thompson, Edgar
 1972 The Little Races. *American Anthropologist* 74:1295–1306.

Thornton, Russell
 1998 *Studying Native America. Problems and Prospects.* University of Wisconsin Press, Madison.

Trinkley, Michael, and S. Homes Hogue
 1979 The Wachesaw Landing Site: The Last Gasp of the Coastal Waccamaw Indians. *Southern Indian Studies* XXXI:3–20.

Turner, Victor Witter
 1974 *Dramas, Fields, and Metaphors; Symbolic Action in Human Society.* Cornell University Press, Ithaca, New York.

U.S. Census Bureau
 1930 Fifteenth Census of Population 1930. North Carolina. Microform Rolls 1674 and 1683. National Archives and Records Administration, Washington, D.C.

U.S. Congress
 1950 *Congressional Record—Appendix.* Pp. A886-A888. [Supt. of Docs., U.S.G.P.O., distributor], Washington, D.C.

U.S. House of Representatives
 1950 Hearing on H.R. 7153 and H.R. 7299. Committee on Public Lands, Bureau of Indian Affairs, 81st Congress, pp. 1–82. National Archives, Record Group 233, Bill Files. Washington, D.C.

Wagley, Charles
 1975 On the Concept of Social Race in the Americas. In *The Nacirema. Readings on American Culture,* edited by James P. Spradley and Michael A. Rynkiewich, pp. 173–184. Little, Brown and Company, Boston.

Waselkov, Gregory A.
 1989 Indian Maps of the Colonial Southeast. In *Powhatan's Mantle. Indians in the Colonial Southeast,* edited by P. H. Wood, G. A. Waselkov, and M. T. Hatley. University of Nebraska Press, Lincoln.

Wetmore, A.
 1927 Letter to S. F. M. Simmons. Bureau of American Ethnology, General Correspondence, 1909–1949, National Anthropological Archives. Smithsonian Institution, Washington, D.C.

Williams, Walter L.
  1979 *Southeastern Indians since the Removal Era.* University of Georgia Press, Athens.

Wilmington Dispatch
  1921a Pageant of Cape Fear to be Greatest Historical Event in the History of North Carolina. February 28, 1921. Bill Reeves Collection, New Hanover Public Library. Wilmington, North Carolina.
  1921b Prof. Koch Talks on Pageant Plans. March 12, 1921. Bill Reeves Collection, New Hanover Public Library. Wilmington, North Carolina.
  1921c Rehearsals Start for the Pageant. May 2, 1921. Bill Reeves Collection, New Hanover Public Library. Wilmington, North Carolina.
  1921d Music in the Pageant. May 31, 1921. Bill Reeves Collection, New Hanover Public Library. Wilmington, North Carolina.
  1921e Distinguished Men and Women to be Here for Pageant of the Cape Fear. June 6, 1921. Bill Reeves Collection, New Hanover Public Library. Wilmington, North Carolina.
  1921f Mayor of City and Dr. Koch Witness Pageant from the Air this A. M. June 9, 1921. Bill Reeves Collection, New Hanover Public Library. Wilmington, North Carolina.

Wood, Peter H.
  1989 The Changing Population of the Colonial South: An Overview by Race and Region, 1685–1790. In *Powhatan's Mantle. Indians in the Colonial Southeast,* edited by P. H. Wood, G. A. Waselkov, and M. T. Hatley, pp. 35–103. University of Nebraska, Lincoln.

Wroth, Lawrence C.
  1970 *The Voyages of Giovanni de Verrazzano, 1524–1528.* Yale University Press, New Haven.

Zimmerman, William, Jr.
  1950 Letter to T. Morris, May 2, 1950. National Archives, Bureau of Indian Affairs, GEN SERV 57 × 185, Record Group 75, 1948-061 to 1950-061, Box 13; File 22930-1969-061 to 1950-061. Washington, D.C.

Index

Admixture. *See* blood quantum; mixed ancestry; mixed blood
African Americans, 23, 45, 53, 123, 132, 142. *See* Blacks (Negroes)
Alexander, James Evan, 80–83, 87, 89, 90–91, 96–96, 98–99, 101, 108, 114
Algonkian (Algonquian), 2, 17, 39, 68
Articulation, concept of, xii, 48, 51, 64, 73–74, 78–79, 80, 84, 145
Articulatory movement, 48. *See also* articulation, concept of
Ashe, Samuel A'Court, 36, 39, 42
Assimilation, xii–xiii, 48, 130, 145
Association on American Indian Affairs (AAIA), 89–90, 93, 95, 109, 114

Battle of Sugar Loaf, 21
Bellamy, John D., 43
Black drink, 3, 37
Blacks (Negroes), xii, 43, 45, 51–53, 58, 60–61, 65–66, 72, 123, 110–111. *See also* African Americans
Bladen Indian Colony, 71. *See also* Wide Awake Indian School
Blood quantum, xi, 63, 65
Blue, Samuel Taylor, 91–92
Bosone, Reva, 101, 103, 110
Boundary line dispute, 10–11
Branch of Acknowledgement and Research (BAR), ix

Brooks, E. C., 51–52
Brown v Board of Education (1954), 117
Buckhead–Ricefield community, 85, 119
Bureau of American Ethnology (BAE), 4, 31, 36–37, 58, 60, 68,
Bureau of Indian Affairs (BIA), ix, 93, 102, 104–105, 112
Bushnell, David I., 36–37

Carlyle, E. Ertel, 87
Carolina Playmakers, 32
Catawba Deerskin Map, 22
Censuses, 11, 18, 27, 46–47, 50, 53–54, 56–57, 65
Charles Town, 8
Cherokee Indian School Bill: 1927, 61–62; 1931, 66; 1937, 73–74
Churches, 55, 66, 74, 129, 144
Civil disobedience, 50, 64, 72, 79–80
Civil Rights, xii, 72, 117–118, 121–122
Cohen, Felix S., 89–91, 93
Collier, John, 96, 107–109,
Colored, xii, 34, 36, 49–51, 53–55, 57, 65, 72, 78, 84. *See also* Blacks (Negroes); African Americans
Columbus County Board of Education, 43, 50, 56–57, 60–61, 67
Croatan School Bill of 1885, 52, 57
Croatan Normal School, 54
Culture area, 3

Davis, George, 36
Desegregation, 117, 122, 124
Doty, Dale E., 114–115

East Carolina Indian School, 76–77
Ethnographic present fallacy, xiii

Federal acknowledgement, ix
Federal recognition, x, xii
Fewkes, J. Walter, 58–59

General Allotment Act 1887, 96
Graham, Frank P., 87, 110
Grand Entry, 139, 142. See also Powwows
Gregg, Alexander, 39–41

Half breed. See mestizo; metis; mixed blood; mustee
Hallsboro High School, 120
Hickory Hill School, 65, 67, 70, 72–74
Hoey, Clyde R., 87
Hilton, William, 5–8

Ickes, Harold L., 60–61
Identity, ix, xiii, ix–x, 48, 78, 117–118, 130–131, 143–146
Indian leaders and leadership: general style, 49–50, 144; Blue, Chief Samuel Taylor, 91–92; Cypress, Billy L., xi; eractasswa, 23; Freeman, Chief Clifton, 87, 126, 143–144; Freeman, Reverend R. T., 78–81, 87–88, 90–91, 95, 102–104, 106; Freeman, W. J., 50, 54–58, 61, 66–68, 70–75, 80; Jacobs, Chief Pricilla Freeman, xiv, 125, 128, 131; Jacobs, D. J., 55; Jacobs, Lewis, 95, 104–106; Jacobs, Ossie, 74–75, 80, 87; Jacobs, Robert, 50–51, 54–58, 61, 80, 95; Graham, Sam, 55, 80; Owl, George Allen, 42; powwow committee, 135–137, 139–140, 142; tribal board, 137–138; Wattcoosa (Watcoosa), 7–8, 34–35, 38, 41; Wide Awake Indian Council (WAIC), 49, 51, 55, 74–83, 86–87, 89–90, 93, 95–96, 101, 108; Wide Awake Tribal Council, 75–77
Indian Princess, 140. See also Powwows
Indian Rangers, 20, 25, 28
Indian Reorganization Act (IRA) of 1934, 90, 93, 96, 107
Indian traders, 10–15, 21, 24–25, 28
Indian tribes and communities: Cape Fear, 2, 4–12, 17–18, 20–21, 26–29, 31, 34–37, 39, 41, 44, 47, 68; Catawba, 2, 9, 11, 14–15, 17–20, 22–23, 25–26, 28–31, 40, 80–82, 88–89; Cherokee, xi, xiv, 3, 11, 13, 19, 28–31, 34, 40, 42, 46, 48–49, 53, 74, 80–82, 88–89; Eastern Band of Cherokee, 42, 99, 106, 110, 144, 146; Cherokee of Columbus County, 49, 57–59, 61–63, 67–68, 73; Cherokee of Robeson County, 55, 59, 61, 63, 69–70, 72, 80, 88; Cheraws (Cherraws, Sarraws), 11–15, 18, 20, 22–25, 26, 28, 39–42, 68–69, 72; Chicora, 4, 9; Coharie, 118, 124, 142; Congaree, 2, 22, 36, 39–42, 81; Croatan, xiv, 31, 42–46, 48–55, 59, 63, 66, 68, 81, 83, 94; Eyota Tribes of Red Men, 34; Friendly Indians (Settlement Indians), 17, 19–21, 26, 28–29; Guacaya, 4, 9; Haliwa–Saponi, 118, 124, 139, 142; Hatteras, 43, 45; Iroquoian, 17, 19–20, 26, 40, 68; Lumbee (Lumbee–Cheraw), ix, 118, 124, 126, 132, 139, 142, 145–146; Northern Indians, 10, 19, 24, 29; Occaneechi, 2, 118; Peedee, 2, 9, 11–15, 20, 23–24, 27, 29, 81; Seminole, xi; Seneca, 19, 21–23, 26; Siouan (Eastern Siouans), 1–3, 9, 11, 17, 27, 31, 49, 68, 72, 81, 83, 105, 146; Siouan Indians of the Lumber River, 69; Tuscarora, 9–11, 19, 21–22, 26, 30; Tutelo, 2; Waccamaw, 3–4, 8–14, 17–26, 28; Wacca-

maw Siouan, ix, xiii, xiv, 48–50, 64, 70, 78–146; Waiwee, 12–13; Wateree, 2, 9, 20, 22–23, 25–26, 28, 40; Wide Awake Indians, xiv, 49, 74; Wineau (Winyaw), 9, 11–15, 18, 21; Woccon, 2, 4, 8–10, 37–38; Yamassee, 11–12, 17–18, 23, 39
Indianness. *See* Identity
Integration, 120–121. *See* Desegregation

Jacobs, Shadrack, 85–86
Jennings, Joe, 99, 110–111
Johnson, T. L., 58–59, 61, 63

Koch, Frederick H., 32, 35, 42
Krug, Julius, 84, 108

Land, 49, 85, 97–99, 102–103
Language, 2, 19, 22, 30, 37–38, 41, –42, 47, 82
Lesser, Alexander, 89, 93
Little Turtle, Ray, 132. See *also:* Powwows
Lost Colony Theory, 42–45, 52–53

McRackan, Donald, 51–53, 56–57, 63
Mestizo, 45
Metis, 45
Mixed ancestry, xi, 44
Mixed blood, xi, 24, 42–46, 48, 67, 71, 108
Modernism, xiii, 144
Mooney, James, 1–3, 36–37, 40, 42, 44, 82
Morris, Tobby, 95, 97, 102–105, 114
Mustee, 45
Myer, Dillon, 112–114

National Council of American Indians. *See* Siouan Lodge
National Congress of American Indians (NCAI), 107–109
Norden, Eric, 85–86
Norden Tract, 85

North Carolina Commission on Indian Affairs, 124–125, 138, 143
Nichols, John R., 110

Pageant of the Lower Cape Fear, 31–47
Pan Indianism, xiii, 117, 143
Pembroke Normal School, 66, 74
Poulsen, Norris, 1, 78, 88, 95, 98, 104, 109–110, 114
Powwows, xiii, 117–142
Powwow paradox, 117, 129
Provinse, John, 87–88, 108–109, 111

Race, xi, 43, 45, 49–50, 52, 54, 59–60, 62–64, 66–67, 71–72, 77, 80, 84, 103, 145
Racial purity, xi, 51
Redressive action, 119, 124. *See also* social drama analysis

Schools and schooling, 42–43, 46, 48, 50–52, 55–57, 61–63, 67, 75–76, 79
Saint Mark's Church and school, 99
Simmons, F. M., 58–61
Siouan Lodge, 69–70, 83
Social drama analysis, 119. *See also* redressive action
Social race, xii
Sorosis Club, 32–33, 36
Speck, Frank G., 2, 80–83, 91, 105
Springtime Gathering of Indians 1663, 31, 34, 35, 37, 41
Sprunt, James, 36, 42–43
Southeastern Culture Area, 2–3, 19
Swanton, John R., 1–4, 68, 110

Termination, United States policy of, 94, 96, 102, 106–107, 145
Tri-racial isolates, xi, 43, 48

University of North Carolina, 31–32, 36
U.S. House of Representatives Bill 7153. *See* Waccamaw Bill

U.S. House of Representatives Bill 7299. *See* Waccamaw Bill

Waccamaw Bill, x, 1, 95–116
Waccamaw Indian School, 119–121, 123, 126, 146
Waccamaw Siouan Development Association (WSDA), 125, 137, 144

Ward, Robert, 81–82, 88
Wetmore, A., 60
Wide Awake Indian School, 71–77
Wooten, F. T., 54
Working consensus, ix, xiv, 145. *See also* identity

Zimmerman, William, 106–108, 114